THE

Hidden Parables

ALSO BY TODD MICHAEL

The Twelve Conditions of a Miracle

The Evolution Angel

JEREMY P. TARCHER · PENGUIN

a member of

PENGUIN GROUP (USA) INC.

NEW YORK

THE

Hidden Parables

ACTIVATING THE SECRET POWER
OF THE GOSPELS

TODD MICHAEL

JEREMY P. TARCHER/PENGUIN
Published by the Penguin Group
Penguin Group (USA) Inc., 375 Hudson Street, New York, New York 10014, USA • Penguin
Group (Canada), 90 Eglinton Avenue East, Suite 700, Toronto, Ontario M4P 2Y3, Canada
(a division of Pearson Penguin Canada Inc.) • Penguin Books Ltd, 80 Strand, London
WC2R 0RL, England • Penguin Ireland, 25 St Stephen's Green, Dublin 2, Ireland (a division
of Penguin Books Ltd) • Penguin Group (Australia), 250 Camberwell Road, Camberwell,
Victoria 3124, Australia (a division of Pearson Australia Group Pty Ltd) • Penguin Books
India Pvt Ltd, 11 Community Centre, Panchsheel Park, New Delhi—110 017, India • Penguin
Group (NZ), Cnr Airborne and Rosedale Roads, Albany, Auckland 1310, New Zealand
(a division of Pearson New Zealand Ltd) • Penguin Books (South Africa) (Pty) Ltd,
24 Sturdee Avenue, Rosebank, Johannesburg 2196, South Africa

Penguin Books Ltd, Registered Offices:
80 Strand, London WC2R 0RL, England

Biblical quotations in the book are from the author's own translation of the original Greek.

Most Tarcher/Penguin books are available at special quantity discounts for bulk purchase
for sales promotions, premiums, fund-raising, and educational needs. Special books or book
excerpts also can be created to fit specific needs. For details, write Penguin Group (USA)
Inc. Special Markets, 375 Hudson Street, New York, NY 10014.

Library of Congress Cataloging-in-Publication Data

Michael, Todd.
The hidden parables : activating the secret power of the gospels / Todd Michael.
p. cm.
ISBN 1-58542-490-0
1. Jesus Christ—Parables. 2. Spiritual life. I. Title.
BT375.3.M53   2006   2006041799
226.8'06—dc22

Printed in the United States of America
1   3   5   7   9   10   8   6   4   2

Book design by Stephanie Huntwork

This book is dedicated to

my mother,
Nancy Michael Franzenburg:
charm, intelligence, wit, wisdom,
and deep spiritual conviction.

and to

My beautiful Essene life partner,
Judy Boller:
strength, intuition, emotional intelligence,
grace, healing, and love.

The more we study reality,

the more we run up against a wall of mysteries.

—*What the Bleep Do We Know*, 2004

⸻

The disciples asked him, why do you teach us in parables?

And answering he said to them,

Because it has been given to you

to know the mysteries . . .

—Matthew 13:10-11

Contents

The Parables

---

*Parable number four is dealt with in chapters one and two.

$\mathcal{T}$HE THIRTY PARABLES REPRESENT more than one-third of all the words spoken by the Nazarene and subsequently recorded in the various Gospels. They were obviously of great importance to him. However, the parables are not what they would seem to be—a loosely collected series of teaching stories. An in-depth translation of the original Greek reveals a hidden layer of meaning, a hidden series of parables. This hidden series of parables clearly indicates that the stories are actually a deliberately sequenced and carefully integrated series of lessons, a singular and superb *system* of learning—a system that is unrevealed in ordinary translations.

The potent sequence of lessons contained within the parables is obviously to be studied, practiced, and ultimately mastered by those seeking true spiritual evolution. Learning about the lessons of the parables is a relatively quick and easy task. Reading this book alone

will suffice to inform you of their general nature. But putting the lessons into practice and staying with them for the years necessary to
truly master them is a much larger matter. You could easily spend your
entire life delving into their depths, staying with them for year after
year, observing their spectacularly powerful effects in your life at
every level.

However, daunting as the attainment of "mastery" might be, true
expertise in the parables' lessons guarantees profound rewards. Even
a modest degree of effort will unlock a considerable portion of the
miraculous and *infinite* potential that lies deep within you, dormant,
and waiting to be awakened. Knowledge and practice of the thirty lessons so carefully constructed and arranged within the sequence will
activate your innate and God-given abilities to heal disease, to manifest more abundant spiritual and material circumstances, and even to
know and communicate with divine intelligence. In truth, mastery
of these powerful lessons will awaken your abilities to accomplish
miraculous things you cannot, in your current state, even *begin* to
imagine.

Remember, the great teacher told us in no uncertain terms that we
would do "even greater works than these." The parables are the direc-
tions for *how* you can arrive at a state of personal evolution in which
you can do such works. For the parables are the way the teacher gave
us that would allow us to perceive as he perceived, think as he
thought, and *do* as he did.

As you will learn, the parables are the distillation of all the great
mystical traditions and mystery schools. Although they are predomi-
nantly an extension of Jewish mystical teachings—from the Essenes
and Kabbalah, as we would logically suspect—they also contain the
classic initiations and core "secrets" of all the great traditions, both
Eastern and Western in origin.

But these great secrets are not simply repackaged and rearticulated by the teacher. Rather, these profound truths and powerful secrets are brought to a brilliant and beautifully blended *synthesis* by the Nazarene. They contain many of the elements of their parent influences and are yet as gifted children, completely different and more highly advanced. This brilliantly conceived and beautifully articulated synthesis contains many recognizable concepts, yet is a system of knowledge that is entirely new and different.

A complaint that is often heard regarding Christianity is that it has, realistically speaking, become irrelevant and obsolete in our technologically advanced world, a world with instruments that can see at once to the end of the universe and deep into the subatomic fabric of reality, a world of quantum truths and paradoxes that even the most brilliant of our Newtonian forebearers could never begin to imagine. However, when the true depths of the parable lessons are unlocked and seen for what they really are, it becomes immediately obvious that their truths easily encompass even the most advanced concepts of our modern quantum world, even the so-called "quantum mysteries." The greatest quantum mystery, for example, is how the human mind can actually influence the way matter and energy behave at the subatomic level. Other quantum mysteries involve things like "tunneling," "entanglement," "non-locality," and multiple universes. These peculiar and wondrous phenomena, which we will study within, are all addressed by the complex metaphors the parables articulate. But more than that, the parables reveal the practical import of these quantum mysteries—how they can actually be applied in useful ways to solve real problems in the real world.

THIS BOOK REVEALS the teacher's hidden sequence of parables and shows you exactly how to *use* their incredibly powerful series of lessons—to remodel your life, your self, and your circumstances in dramatic and extraordinarly effective ways. If you follow the path they illuminate before you, you will, in due course, find yourself in a world of beauty, truth, healing, and fascination—the likes of which you have never before imagined.

Preface

IT WAS TIME to review the lessons of the day. I took a deep breath of crisp desert air and scanned the sky. It was clear and cold in the morning's early hours and the great comet Hale-Bopp burned in the desert sky to the north. Its tail stood out from the black, moonless sky like a pale bridal veil blown back into the constellations. To see the other tail, you had to wait in the darkness, letting your eyes adjust, letting the visual purple accumulate in the retinas until night vision eased in. Then it could be perceived—an exquisitely pale, aquamarine blush, shorter and stubbier than the white tail, but even more striking for its color—a neon aura generated by high-energy solar winds blowing across the tail's complex milieu of gases.

I read later there was a third tail, too. Using special cameras and techniques that reveal details beyond the spectrum of human vision, astronomers photographed a gorgeous, etheric, yellow tail nested within the blue one. This newly discovered tail—a lovely allegory for the potential splendor of the unseen—was caused by the ionization of sodium atoms. I remember thinking while admiring its picture in an astronomy magazine, "I wonder how much else remains unseen, unknown. I wonder if it, too, may be so beautiful."

We had come to view the comet from this vantage point at the edge of the Canyon de Chelly in the northeast corner of Arizona because the light pollution was so low and the view so clear. But mostly we had come because we wanted to spend Easter with our Navajo friends, whose ancestors had inhabited the edge of this spectacular natural wonder since the Anasazi had mysteriously disappeared, leaving it vacant four centuries ago. We were sponsoring the eldest daughter of the family through her early education and had been invited to stay in their home at the edge of the canyon. Earlier that afternoon, I had learned an interesting lesson in their company, and it kept playing in my mind.

It had happened on the descent into the canyon itself. The family, led by the venerable mother, wanted to take us to the bottom to explore some of the ancient ruins. The main trail was a moderately rigorous descent. Granted, the Canyon de Chelly is smaller than its massive cousin, the Grand Canyon, but it is quite formidable in its own right with a vertical drop of around eight hundred feet. The trail offers a spectacular view of Spider Rock, a windblown, sandstone monolith projecting from the canyon floor like a large skyscraper.

Navajo creation legend has it that a great being, Spider Woman, lives at the top of the formation. It is said that, in the beginning, there was a deep purple light at the dawn of creation. Spider Woman, also known as "Thought Woman" and "Creation Thinker Woman," spun lines of silk to form the east, west, north, and south. Then, she used the clay of the earth—red, yellow, white, and black—to create people. To each human being she attached a thread of her web, which came from the doorway at the top of her head. This thread was the gift of creative wisdom. This "Creation Thinker Woman," who weaves existence to-gether like the great strands of a web, then formed the Star People, who walk among us to this day, graced with clear crystal for eyes.

The Dine, as the Navajo refer to themselves, came into the canyon when they emerged from another dimension—the third dimension of their creation legend—and into this one, a fourth world, or dimension, formed to accommodate their evolution. Shortly thereafter, Spider Woman, with her miraculous powers, saved the Dine from annihila-tion, and subsequently made her home at the top of Spider Rock. It is this great being that gave the Dine the art of weaving, which they practice so exquisitely to this day.

As we negotiated the rocky trail to the bottom, winding back and forth in sharp switchbacks against the stratified walls, we de-scended through hundreds of millions of years of evolution. Down and down through countless layers of Permian sandstone in infinite shades of ochre and magenta we dropped, descending through 230 million years of biological history, glimpsing myriad bits and pieces of in-creasingly primitive plant and animal species fossilized in the com-pressed sand of ancient ocean floors—brachiopods, ferns, nautiloids, bivalves, corals, and many others.

It was hot and the trail was lengthy. I calculated it would take about an hour to get to the bottom. Suddenly, without a word, the eldest daughter skipped ahead like a fairy, her long black braid bobbing in the sun. Then, just as suddenly, she hopped onto a large flat boulder bal-anced at the end of the switchback. She turned, waved as if to say good-bye, and disappeared over the edge. "She must have cut the trail to get down to a deeper switchback," I thought to myself. "She'll probably beat us down there by a couple of minutes, but that's an awfully dangerous way to save a little time." Walking on, a short time later we reached the boulder where the nimble girl had disappeared. Shading my eyes, I peered cautiously over the edge. What I saw jolted me with disbelief. There at the bottom, eight hundred feet below, our girl stood at the base of a massive cottonwood tree. She was waving up at us slowly.

This was simply not possible. She had completed a journey requiring the better part of an hour in under three minutes. Her mother just smiled her enigmatic Mona Lisa smile and said nothing.

When I arrived at the bottom, I looked back up to see if I could figure out how she had gotten down with such supernatural speed. Carved into the walls here and there were a few handholds that would allow passage down some of the sheer cliff formations. They were faint in most cases and horribly precarious. They offered a few clues, but I couldn't put together anything resembling a continuous route, much less one easy enough for a preteen to negotiate so quickly and easily.

"Look." She laughed lightly, pointing to her entry point near the top. "There and there. See?" Step by step she pieced together about half the intricate route from the top with a pointed finger and her usual economical narrative. A series of carved handholds here, a series of natural ones there, a swing around a precipice, another run of handholds, a terrifying but very doable jump onto a ledge with a five-hundred-foot drop-off—and a practiced individual could make it to the bottom in no time.

Apparently *the way was a secret,* which was why she wouldn't show me all of it. And it was old, so old it predated recorded history. The ancestrals had recognized centuries ago that proficiency with a shortcut could mean the difference between life and death in an emergency. Knowledge of the route had been precious and top secret. A tribal member was initiated informally into the use of the handholds during early adolescence.

I don't believe these modern Dine thought much about this route anymore. It was just another mundane feature of their daily life. But, like the comet, the route seemed another valuable allegory to me, a kind of personal parable. It was a metaphor illustrating simultaneously the power of secret ways, the value of the initiation process, and the ability for a shift in perception to create an apparent miracle.

As THIS BOOK CAME TO BE, it became clear that the thirty parables of Christ are an analogous kind of secret pathway. As you delve into their depths, you will find that, like the young Navajo's precipitous path to the bottom of the canyon, the action steps suggested by the lessons of the parables offer a less circuitous and more efficient route to deeper states of personal evolution. But you will also find that some of the steps to be mastered along your way are, like the steps along the girl's rocky path, "terrifying but very doable." This is because they are all about *you*.

The strata through which the parables would have us descend are not geological layers but layers of the deep self—encrustations of fear, thick laminations of fossilized resentments, compacted deposits of ego. It is always the self that separates us from the source of true abundance, the source of life. This is why the path to true fulfillment—where your dreams will finally merge seamlessly with reality—must inevitably challenge you to confront anxiety-provoking revelations about your deepest character defects. And the path must of necessity demand that you take *action* to correct them. This can be extraordinarily daunting.

If this seems an exaggeration, be forewarned: It is not. You *will* be challenged. I'll give you an example in order to prepare you for the kinds of self-correction that will be demanded of you. The very first parable in the series we will study will have you open up some of your deepest wounds, and will have you *forgive* everyone for whom you hold a resentment or a grudge. This will apply *particularly* to those who have offended you most gravely.

If there is someone who has deeply offended you and for whom you hold a major and "well-justified" resentment—you will have to go through a potentially painful process in which you honestly confront your *own* role in the development of the conflict that led to your perceived offense. This may then logically require that you meet with and seek the forgiveness of that very person who has "hurt you." If this prospect does not, at the moment, seem particularly anxiety-provoking, just wait until the day when you must actually walk up to that person's door with hat in hand to clear your soul of the darkness that is ruining your ability to work miracles. But take heart, for you will have guidance along the way. Remember: It's terrifying, but doable.

If we think about it, we would only expect this kind of largesse to be demanded of us, wouldn't we? We know the character of the man who taught these lessons. We know that he was all about forgiveness, all about turning the other cheek, all about the Golden Rule—treating others as we ourselves would like to be treated. How could we ever reasonably expect to work the same kinds of miracles the teacher worked if we cannot act with the same kind of generosity, sacrifice, consideration, clarity, and *loving intent* that the teacher demonstrated in such profound ways.

So, know now before you begin that the way is not magic. There is no magic path that will take you to the promised land. Miracles are not magic. They involve hard work, which is why those who perform them are called "miracle workers." Mastery of the parable sequence is not a trivial matter, however. It is not likely that any of us will approach anything resembling true mastery anytime soon. The path the parable lessons form is a long path. Mastery will require as much diligence, practice, patience, and persistence as any other path leading to advanced knowledge—the overall process resembling, in length and difficulty, mastering a classical instrument such as violin or piano, acquiring advanced literacy in a complex foreign language, or finishing a formal doctoral program in medicine or law.

But know also that if you proceed in good faith and do the work on your self that the parables outline, you *will* get to the place you want to be in life. And know that even modest knowledge of the way outlined by the parables will begin to bring untold blessings into your life almost immediately. The way is a promise. And it cannot be a false promise, for it comes not from me or any worldly author, but from Spirit, through a wonderful teacher who did everything he could to try to help us understand. The "secret" steps described by the parables will most certainly allow you to make quantum leaps in spiritual and personal development as soon as you begin putting them into practice. And in due course, the route described in this book *will* take you from your current level to a level of security, prosperity, health, and love of which you have previously only dreamed.

EVOLUTION: THE NEW PARADIGM

We say that we want to evolve and we want to know how the parables can help us. But do we really understand what evolution is? Do we really understand just how profound this radical process is? Or can we only guess, like children, until the day comes that we actually arrive at our future states of consciousness? I for one increasingly believe that I do not understand evolution and cannot therefore fully appreciate it. But I can offer some suggestions. And they are highly in-

telligent suggestions as well, for they come from the German philosopher Hegel.

Hegel was the originator of the concept known as a *dialectic,* which
is just a fancy name for a way of developing or evolving. Dialectical
evolution is much different from linear evolution, which occurs step
by incremental step in a straight line. By contrast, dialectic evolution
occurs via a series of triangles.

What Hegel said is that when true evolution occurs, it begins at a
specific starting point that he called the *thesis.* The thesis can be anything from a political or theological system or belief, a scientific theory, a psychological or sociological process, or merely a point of view.
As the evolutionary process proceeds, this thesis gradually but inexorably turns into its opposite. This new, opposite state Hegel called
the *antithesis.*

But it was the next step where things got really interesting. For
according to Hegel, in the next step the thesis and its opposite, the
antithesis, *merge* into something entirely new. This hybrid state is
entirely different from either of its parents yet contains elements of
both parent states. Hegel dubbed this third step in the evolutionary sequence the *synthesis.*

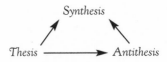

But the process doesn't stop with the synthesis. Now the synthesis is poised to become the starting point for an entirely new triad.
Now the synthesis becomes, in effect, the thesis for the next quantum
step in the evolutionary sequence.

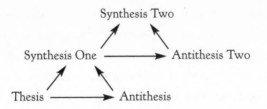

The most effective illustration of this powerful *dialectical* concept of evolution is found in Hermann Hesse's final masterpiece, *The Glass Bead Game.* This book, by the author of such classics as *Siddhartha* and *Steppenwolf,* refines and develops the concept of "evolution" in such masterful and definitive terms that it has never been equaled. Hesse won the Nobel Prize for literature for this unique work that draws together the greatest concepts in human thought.

In *The Glass Bead Game,* Hesse imagined a culture of monks living about three hundred years in the future. The monks, who called themselves Castilians, had devised a sagacious method for reaching higher and higher states of knowledge and evolution, a method that incorporated an intriguing game using glass beads as playing pieces. It is what the glass beads represented that has fascinated readers for so many years. Each glass bead was a two- or three-inch sphere divided into two sides. Each side was painted with detailed symbols, pictures, and formulas. The pictures on each side represented two entirely different forms of art or knowledge—typically something very right-brained, such as math, and something very left-brained, such as music. For example, one side might represent a sequence within a Bach fugue and the other a complex mathematical or astronomical law.

When two such concepts were present on the same bead, it meant that someone had studied the relationship between those two realms of knowledge or achievement for a number of years and had established a relationship between them. This relationship had to be proven logically or scientifically while being at once artistic and intuitively beautiful. Demonstrating such a relationship could be a monk's life work, and having one's work represented on an official game bead was a great honor.

Games would be played with these beads, beginning with one bead being placed on the game board. The opponent—or opposing monastery if entire monasteries were competing—would then study that bead carefully. After a period of meditation, the opponent would carefully select another bead representing the synthesis of two new concepts, a second synthesis that could be related to the synthesis of the first bead.

Now, with two beads on the playing board, each representing the synthesis of two divergent concepts, four entirely different concepts were linked into an altogether new synthesis. In this way, spiritual concepts could be linked to those from physics. These could then be linked to more concepts—from biology, medicine, history, sculpture, mathematics, poetry, linguistics, and so on. The game would continue as more and more beads were added to form patterns and even three-dimensional structures representing increasingly complex and beautiful "cities" of thought. As beads were added, the integrated systems of knowledge created revealed things never before considered, healed things, taught things.

I BELIEVE THAT THE MAN who uttered the thirty parables found in the Gospels was truly enlightened and truly evolved. It seems entirely reasonable to assume he would have understood and used the kind of advanced dialectical evolution Hegel and Hesse so brilliantly described. He would have used this process to develop and attain ever higher states of spiritual consciousness.

This book will attempt to show that this is in fact so. It will show that the lessons locked within the parables are masterpieces of synthe-sis and, like the beads in Hesse's *Glass Bead Game,* merge concepts from different fields to form new concepts. These concepts are so advanced that upon study the question is not *Are these ideas as evolved as those in our modern culture?* but *Are we as evolved as these ideas?* The answer is that in some cases we may not be, that we have much to learn even in contemporary terms from the man known as the Nazarene.

THE MULTIVERSE

In the last century, humanity made enormous advances in its under-standing of the nature of the universe. But what we have learned, via the ideas of quantum physics, relativity, and string theory, has raised more questions than have been answered. What we have learned is so unexpected, so strange, so mysterious, and so counter to our old New-tonian ideas of the universe that we are left in awe and wonder.

For example, we know now that there is no such thing as matter. We have learned that the energy packets we thought were solid are ac-tually pure energy and appear to be composed of tiny vibrating loops or "strings" of energy. We have come to suspect that subatomic "particles" are conscious, that there are not three or four dimensions to our world but perhaps eleven, and that there are vast parts of our universe, so-called "dark matter," that we cannot even find. But the concept that is the most important of all for the student of metaphysics—and the stu-dent of the parables of Christ—is the notion that reality is constantly splitting into multiple realities, multiple dimensions, multiple universes.

As we know, the observations scientists have made at the atomic and subatomic levels of reality are so peculiar that it seems at times that there can be no logical system, no explanation of any kind that can accommodate what we are seeing. Scientists consistently observe events that are simply not possible in this universe, events that cannot possibly take place together in the *same* universe.

However, in 1956, a Princeton doctoral candidate, Hugh Everett III, proposed a theory that suddenly reconciled all such observations and paradoxes at once. The problem was that the theory he proposed was as radical as the observations themselves and upset a lot of scientists. Everett said that the only way to explain what we are seeing is to assume the existence not of mere parallel universes, not of mere multiple universes, but of *infinite* universes. In this theory, which Everett called the Many Worlds Hypothesis, everything that can ever be possible actually happens, actually manifests as reality in some universe at some time.

Although this theory finally succeeded in explaining the strange experimental observations of physics, there seemed to be a fatal flaw in the whole idea: It just *sounded* crazy. The theory was disturbing, weird, and just didn't feel right to some people. Granted, it is almost impossible to refute logically, but it made those contemplating it—both physicists and metaphysicians alike—feel as though they were unscientific and unsound.

But there was another reason scientists rejected the Many Worlds Hypothesis. This reason has to do with a standard concept of analysis called Occam's razor. Occam's razor states that when there are many proposed explanations of an observed phenomenon, the simplest and most elegant of these concepts will always end up being the one that is right when all is said and done. This has turned out to be true so often in the history of science that much credence is given to this notion. Theorists felt that the infinite universes of Everett's theory were far too busy, far too complex to be a viable explanation. The universes were all different, some would contain alternate selves, all would be splitting again and again and interacting in unfathomable ways—it was all very messy, very unelegant, and could not thus end up being true.

But is this theory really so complex, so "messy"? An argument can be made that an infinite number of worlds, where every conceivable possibility is realized, is actually very simple and elegant. We aren't talking about two parallel universes, or even a hundred. We are talking about an *infinite* number. And there is something very elegant about infinity, something very tidy and complete, something very God-like. So, in some people's minds, the Many Worlds Hypothesis holds all the classic characteristics of a great fundamental truth. This is why many scientists no longer use the term "universe," instead calling this vast collection of infinite worlds the "*multiverse*."

Much has changed since Everett's radical proposal was launched in the mid-fifties. In those days, only a handful of brave thinkers dared accept the possibility of infinite universes. A recent poll of contemporary physicists, however, indicates that the vast majority of them now believe that the Many Worlds Hypothesis, or some variation thereof, is the only way to explain the nature of reality. It is humorous to note that the same poll also indicates that most scientists wanted very much to avoid *talking* about the subject. It still makes them very uneasy. But for the metaphysician, and the student of the parables, this theory holds incredible practical significance and is more comfortably embraced.

THE SPLIT POINT

There are many theories of creation. For example, in the Navajo creation legend, the creation of worlds happens as Spider Woman, or "Creation Thinker Woman," weaves together the strands of existence in a grand tapestry. In Christianity, the universe is created from the

Word. In the Kabbalah of the Jewish mystical tradition, worlds are formed when one gives rise to another via the process of "emanation." According to the Greek philosopher Heraclitis, as well as the Taoists, creation occurs as the result of the interaction of the great opposites. There are countless other variations in the world's spiritual traditions.

In the Many Worlds Hypothesis, new universes are created when one *splits* from another. And what triggers such a monumental event? The trigger is not something mechanical. *The trigger is thought.* In the Many Worlds Hypothesis of the quantum age—and its variations—a new universe splits from the parent universe every time a conscious being makes a *decision.* Although this sounds very odd, very unscientific, great minds that have pondered the problem for decades have come to the conclusion over and over that the split point occurs *when a conscious being alters personal intent.*

This splitting of universes doesn't simply occur at the subatomic level when particle physics experiments are run. It also occurs in your everyday life, all the time. Here's an example of how this works in your daily life: You could make a decision to pause your reading briefly after the period at the end of this sentence. Although minuscule, this decision will immediately result in this entire universe splitting into two. In one of these universes, there is a you that pauses. In the other universe, there is a you that does not pause. Each of these universes exists independently until you make the next decision, a second or a minute later, at which point the universe splits again. All that you experience as you split into two copies is a "slight randomness." There is an excellent discussion of this extremely peculiar and even disturbing idea in the cover story of the May 2003 edition of *Scientific American,* if you would like to read what mainstream scientists have to say. Again, although all of this sounds terribly strange and counterintuitive, you can readily see in this article that the best minds of science have examined this apparent

splitting of universes over and over and repeatedly come to the conclusion that this, or close variations thereof, is what is actually happening as reality unfolds.

The metaphysical implications are incredibly important, and enormously *practical*. For decisions are a manifestation of personal intent
and it is *intent*—via visualizations, affirmations, and creative, positive
thought forms—that is the lifeblood of metaphysics. It is the management of intention and decisiveness that allows the modern, self-
empowered person to improve personal reality.

Think about it: If everything that can be possible actually becomes
real somewhere in some universe, then that which you now think impossible to correct in your own life may, in fact, be entirely possible.
After all, one of the most important corollaries to the Many Worlds
Hypothesis is that the laws of time and space in a new universe may
be different from the laws in the parent universe. Ergo, that which is
impossible in this universe may therefore be *possible* in one of the new
universes down the line.

Could a fully enlightened soul such as Christ have known all of
this so long ago, two thousand years before we began to work with
these concepts? Of course he could have known. And, as this book
will show, he did. Moreover, he knew something modern scientists
still haven't figured out: Christ knew how to *harness* this phenomenon,
how to consciously control it so as to produce miraculous events of
healing and supply. The parables are, in part, his lessons on how we
can learn this for ourselves.

ACKNOWLEDGMENTS

I OWE A DEBT of gratitude to the following people, who provided extraordinary support and assistance as this somewhat difficult book was written and refined:

My son, Julian, who was a constant companion, inspiration, and confidant—and the person I admire most in all the world. Julian's influence exceeded that of almost all others who were in contact with me as this lengthy manuscript was perfected.

Brad Sykes, counselor, friend, and adviser par excellence.

Ram Dass and Carl Davis, for additional superb spiritual guidance.

Jean Carpenter, CPA, Austin, Texas, for invaluable counsel and advice far beyond the call of duty.

Mentors and colleagues: Rev. Howard Caesar of Unity of Houston; Rev. Dr. Roger Teel of Mile Hi Church of Religious Science; Rev. Dr. Mary Manin Morrissey; Rev. Scott Awebry; Rev. Marj Brit of Unity of Tustin; and Rev. Mary Omwake, Unity of Maui; Wayne

Francis and Rev. David McArthur, Unity of Walnut Creek; Rev. Dr. Joyce Lichenstein, One Spirit Learning Alliance, New York; Rev. Joel Fotinos, The Sacred Center, New York; Quent and Robin Johnson; Kit Hersey; Michael Metzler, M.D., Ph.D.; Les Khan; Brian Geraths, Prints Charming Photography, Portland; Sean and Mickey Houlihan; Dawn Rasmussen; Lori Wall; John Campbell; Ed, Nancy, and Alex Brauer, Maui; Susan Osborn; Marilyn Wetzler; Brigette Mars; Carol, Roger, and Jeremy Krumel; Mary Ann Richards; Matt and Jon Michael; Al Biela; Lora Michael, The Campus Group; the citizens of Boulder; and Lakewood Medical Center.

THE

Hidden Parables

INTRODUCTION

*T*HE THIRTY PARABLES spoken by Christ are some of the most intensely scrutinized spiritual teachings in history. Over the centuries, scholars and theologians have devoted vast amounts of time and effort to the study of these enigmatic and hauntingly beautiful stories. Fully one-third of all the words attributed to this teacher were uttered in parables. Because they are such a large part of his teachings, we can only assume that the messages these deceptively simple stories contain must have been of enormous importance to their bearer.

To begin our own study, let's look at an important introductory proposition. This is that the parables of Christ are not what they are normally considered to be—a more or less random collection of educational stories with important yet largely unrelated moral messages. Instead, the thirty sequential lessons related in these sparse allegories deliver a *unified, fully integrated system of knowledge*. The foremost intention of this book is to describe and clarify this system of knowledge.

Further, the parables were told to us in a specific *sequence*. They emerge from the verses of the Gospels in a specific chronology well established by biblical scholars. Like the collection itself, this sequence was not random. The order was carefully orchestrated by the teacher to enhance the coherency of the parables as a system. In the pages that follow, you will learn about the intricacy and significance of this chronology. You will see that the order of delivery provides a brilliantly logical and artful way to instruct us in the powerful system of knowledge the parables delineate.

As the parables unfold one after another, you will find they weave a well-knit tapestry of powerful lessons, lessons wholly consistent with those found in contemporary self-empowerment, metaphysical, and psychological thought. The parables even contain concepts consistent with cutting-edge developments in quantum physics and multidimensional theory, as well as other advanced scientific disciplines.

And would this not make complete sense? If Jesus, like other great spiritual teachers, was truly enlightened, would it not be logical that he comprehended great truth on all levels? Great truths are beyond time. What is true now about the mechanisms of the mind and the universe was just as true then. It therefore seems entirely reasonable to posit that Christ was perfectly well aware of how things worked, even in his relatively primitive time period long before the advent of science and modern psychology. And it seems equally reasonable to assume that as a dedicated teacher he would have had an intense desire to *communicate* what he knew.

Consider: How wise do you believe this eccentric Jewish teacher really was? How much do you think he really understood about the universe? Was he what you might call highly intelligent or "brilliant"? Or was he even more? Do you think it possible that he was actually a full-blown genius, a man gifted with an intelligence so massive that his brain power rivaled, even exceeded, that of modern geniuses such as Newton, Einstein, or Stephen Hawkings? In addition, do you think it possible that he simultaneously possessed right-brained gifts—intuitive and creative capabilities—exceeding those of contemporary talents?

If you will grant that he almost certainly possessed simultaneous gifts of both raw intelligence and creative/intuitive talent, would you also allow that it is therefore probable that he understood even then the *essence* of those revelations modern science and psychology have only recently brought to light?

In fact, to carry this conjecture to its logical conclusion, can you see that it is entirely possible that Christ may well have contemplated and mastered even those profound truths that lie ahead *yet undiscovered* by the scientific minds of our time? This book will show that, in reality, the parables were the way this very advanced soul tried to communicate what he knew so far ahead of his time, and what he knew that may yet lie ahead for us to discover.

But *how* would such an enlightened being, embedded in such a primitive time period, have communicated what he knew? Words and phrases, especially those available to him in his native Aramaic, were wholly inadequate to embody the thoughts that coursed through this man's mind. It was very much as though this man was a kind of genius from the future who had appeared in an undeveloped culture and society.

From that isolated venue, he tried to construct messages that could somehow communicate the profound and very useful principles that had awakened in his consciousness. Using the simple words, phrases, and concepts available to him in his native Aramaic and his simple agrarian culture, Jesus had to figure out a way to construct teaching stories of sufficient depth and complexity to transmit the essence of the advanced principles he wanted us to know about.

Christ wanted us to know what he knew. But more important, he wanted us to be able to *do* what he could do. *Of course.* How could this be otherwise? He wanted us to be able to heal ourselves and others; he wanted us to be able to manifest abundant supply when we were experiencing lack; he wanted us to know how to cope with unhappiness and tragedy so effectively that we could turn even our greatest tragedies, our greatest darknesses, into worlds of light and love and happiness. He wanted us to be strong, happy, confident, prosperous, and free. And so he told us a series of unusual little stories. Here, the highly evolved scientific, psychological, and metaphysical principles he comprehended are put into words and communicated.

These lessons are not valuable from a merely theoretical standpoint. The lessons lead inexorably to *action.* They show us what we must actually *do* on a day-to-day basis. They show us how to live in order to embody the potent system of knowledge they teach.

This book shows you how to unlock the power of the parables. It shows you exactly how to put their awesome principles to work in your own life on a daily basis starting *today,* so that you can begin immediately to experience their benefits.

AS WE PROCEED, you may be truly startled. For you will see that one of the great secrets of the parables is that that they are really all about *you.* Each of them addresses a process, a dynamic process of evolution that occurs with *you*—as well as every other soul—as we all make our way to a state of perfect light. This should come as no great surprise for an enlightened being such as Christ would have wanted no trace of codependency in his teachings. He knew that we have to work on *ourselves,* not others, as we make our way back home. His lessons challenge us to understand our own thoughts and attitudes and actions.

THE TRANSLATION ISSUE

The book that precedes this, *The Twelve Conditions of a Miracle,* provides a retranslation of the words that describe how a young Jewish mystic fed more than five thousand people with only two fish and five loaves of bread. The Gospels, including all of the parables, were originally written in Greek in the period of time one to three hundred years after the death of Christ. To understand what they are really saying, we therefore need to know something about the Greek language.

As was abundantly stated in *The Twelve Conditions of a Miracle,* Greek is a very ancient language and reflects the thoughts and experiences of a culture thousands of years old. As a result, one word in Greek, even ancient Greek, can have multiple levels of meaning. Furthermore, in Greek there are many different but closely related words that can be used to parse very fine shades of philosophical or theological meaning. Greek was therefore an ideal language for the Gospels' authors to express subtle philosophical, psychological, and metaphysical concepts in a very accurate and precise way.

When the Greek account of the miracle of the loaves and fishes is broken down and all the subtle levels of meaning in all the words are unpacked and uncoiled, it becomes evident that standard translations leave out large amounts of critical information. When this information is recovered and reconstituted, a previously hidden layer of information is thus revealed. Here, the actual *technique* of the miracle is described in perfect clarity and detail.

You will find the same to be true with the parables as well. When the original Greek words that describe the thirty parables are unpacked and all their information reconstituted, it becomes readily apparent that a layer of previously obscured information is revealed. The retranslation process is very much like cleaning an old painting and finding beneath the surface composition yet another—one more beautiful and far more valuable. As the retranslation process takes place, and the deepest messages of the parables are revealed in sequence one by one, an entirely new system of thought emerges with crystalline clarity. Here the great principles governing success and happiness and self-empowerment—as they relate to our thought forms, our *intentions*—are revealed with stunning clarity.

As you proceed through the lessons so revealed, you will be convinced beyond a shadow of a doubt that Christ was a master of the creation of reality, a master of the use of *intention* to create changes in the world around him, thus his miraculous healings and his displays of superabundant supply. These famous acts of reality alteration were possible because Christ understood the quantum nature of the multiverse, its tendency to split when decisions are made, and the incredible power of the subconscious mind to consciously create *within* the quantum milieu.

In addition, as your study proceeds, you will be convinced of an additional fact: *that whenever Christ lapsed into the parable mode, he did so specifically to illustrate one of the great principles governing the mysteries of reality creation.* Whenever this unusual Jewish teacher told us one of his pithy stories, he was really trying to tell us how to use our own minds, our own ideas, our own hearts to generate better states of supply, better states of health, better lives, better *worlds* for ourselves and those we love.

This great teacher wanted you to know
what *he* knew.

He wanted you to know precisely *how*
to do "even greater things."

ONE

THE MASTER KEY

*A*LTHOUGH THE THIRTY PARABLES are delivered in a well-established chronological sequence, the best place to begin their *translation* into modern terms is not at the first parable but at the fourth. As you will see, the fourth parable, known as the *parable of the sower,* is also the "master parable," because this parable gives us the key, or code, necessary to unlock the deepest levels of meaning of *all* the other parables.

The parable of the sower is unusual because it is delivered in three distinct parts. Each part has a distinct purpose. Part one, which is the first nine verses in Chapter 13 of Matthew, relates the parable itself— the story of a man who sows seed, some of which fall on fertile ground, some on infertile ground. In part three, verses 18–23, the story is *interpreted* directly by the teacher. In part three, we are told what the characters and conditions in the story symbolize.

Part two, Matthew 13, verses 10–17, is nested in a most interesting position—*between* the story and its interpretation. This section provides critical introductory comments pertaining to *all* the parables and introduces several key phrases and comments that set the stage for the entire sequence of lessons. In this chapter, we will concentrate on part two, which will be referred to in the remainder of the book as the Key. The information in the Key is deep and quite fascinating. It begins with the disciples asking Jesus point-blank why he teaches via the use of these enigmatic allegorical stories. His answer is as follows:

THE KEY

Because it has been given to you to know the mysteries of the kingdom of heaven, but it has not been given to the rest. For whoever has, to him will be given, and he will have over-abundance. But whoever does not have even what he has will be taken from him.

Because of this, I speak to them in parables, because seeing they do not see, and hearing they do not hear, nor do they understand. And the prophecy of Isaiah is fulfilled on them, which says: In hearing you will hear, and in no way understand; and seeing you will see, yet in no way perceive.

For the heart of this people has grown fat, and they hear sluggishly with their ears; and they have closed their eyes, that they not see with the eyes, or hear with the ears, and understand with the heart, and be converted, and I heal them. But your eyes are blessed, because they see; and your ears, because they hear.

For truly I tell you, that many prophets and righteous ones desired to see what you see, and did not see; and to hear what you hear, and did not hear. Then hear the parable of the sower.

This passage, which rests so auspiciously between the master parable and its interpretation, provides very clear clues as to the true depth and purpose of the entire parable series. The first clue is found in the first sentence, *"Because it has been given to you to know the mysteries of the kingdom of heaven . . ."* It is important to understand what "mysteries" really are. According to the Greek to English dictionary in *Strong's Exhaustive Concordance of the Bible,* the Greek word used here, *musterion,* technically refers to secret knowledge, knowledge that is silent and transmitted by initiation.

Through the ages, great knowledge has often been handed down from teacher to student through the process of "initiation." Typically this means that a student undergoes intense or prolonged preparation well before the secret knowledge is actually given. Preparation may include a waiting period, educational activities and assignments, and in certain cases some type of purification. Once these requirements have been established, a private ceremony takes place in which the initiate receives a particularly important secret about the way life and the universe operate. And what *are* the great secrets thus passed from generation to generation in this classic way? A case can be made that a variety of key truths comprise the bulk of these "secrets." But two or three of these great truths appear and reappear so consistently that they seem clearly to be the greatest and most profound of all.

First among such great secrets of the ages is that our attitudes, visualizations, and intentions have the power to change reality—that mind over matter is a process that can be learned and managed. The second great secret of the ages that arises naturally along with the first is that of all the attitudes and intentions *available* to a human being, the attitude of kindness and generosity, the mind-set of *love,* is the most potent thought form possible. This is the greatest and most profound paradox of abundant living, that love—and *selflessness* in general—is the most powerful way to help the *self*.

THE SOURCES

At this point in our study of the Key, the question arises: If Jesus was engaged in the process of initiating his students, including you, into the "mysteries," what were mysteries into which *he* was likely initiated? The process of initiation subsumes a sequence of events in which knowledge is first *obtained* through initiation *then* passed along through initiation. In other words, if Jesus was going to pass along secret knowledge, he was very likely to have been first initiated into it himself. This has excellent practical import because, if we can know which mystical sects or traditions likely initiated Christ, we can look at those traditions and learn a great deal about the kinds of secret knowledge Christ was likely trying to pass along through his stories.

To answer the question of Jesus' sources, remember first that Jesus was a Jew. As such, many of the secret initiations he was likely to have undergone were likely to have been through one of the Jewish mystical traditions. And what Jewish mystical schools were active during Jesus' time and available to him in his formative years? The two most active Jewish mystical sources available in his day were the Kabbalah and the Essenes.

THE KABBALAH

The Kabbalah is a system of mystical doctrines and techniques more than four thousand years old that is thought to predate all religions.

Creation, in the kabbalistic tradition, is via a process of "emanation," by which a series of "sephirots," or worlds, give rise to one another—father worlds emanating child realms or universes. The genealogy of worlds so created is represented by the Tree of Life, which outlines a path of ascent to the highest levels of spirituality via exercises and meditations with many similarities to Eastern yogic practices. The Kabbalah includes, among other things, the idea of *metempsychosis*, roughly equivalent to reincarnation; *thaumaturgy*, the performance of miracles; and the use of the word *Yahweh*, the name or sound of God, to achieve higher states of consciousness.

Contemporary author Michael Berg presented a fascinating distillation of the Kabbalah in his best-selling book *The Secret*. According to Berg, the entire wisdom of all kabbalistic teachings is reducible to one great secret that he states as follows:

The only way to achieve true joy and fulfillment
is by becoming a "being of sharing."

In other words, the only effective route to the kingdom of heaven—the world of abundance, success, and happiness we seek to generate and inhabit—is by constantly living and breathing generosity, the highest and most practical manifestation of love.

THE ESSENES

The Essenes were a highly unusual, free-thinking, monastic community active in Christ's place and time. Their thinking and their ways were so different from the establishment that they tended to isolate themselves in self-sufficient settlements as far as possible from the rest of civilization. Their most important community was known as Qumran, where the authors of the Dead Sea Scrolls lived.

The Essenes were a very distinctive and intense group of people. They placed a great deal of emphasis on living a natural, healthy lifestyle and particularly on eating only raw, vegetarian, live foods. They believed in fasting to cleanse the body and mind and to attain mystical states of revelation. They were highly disciplined, even strict, in their attention to work, selflessness, cleanliness, purity, and chastity. The Essenes maintained their own economic system, based on natural laws of abundance, and believed that all man's material needs could be attained without struggle, through knowledge of the laws.

It seems only natural that Jesus of Nazareth, himself a very unusual and creative thinker who shunned the conventions of the establishment, would have spent a good deal of time with the Essenes in the rural areas of his small country during the "lost" years of his life between the ages of fourteen and twenty-nine. Many authorities even think Jesus was a fully dedicated Essene who lived and trained with them extensively. It seems likely that he had in fact lived and worked in the Essene communities for a number of years but had branched out on his own. This due to the fact that his ideas were so creative and out of the box that they could not be contained even within the relatively radical Essene ideology.

What do we know of these people? Manuscripts from the ancient Essenes come from two primary sources: manuscripts contained in the Dead Sea Scrolls found in 1945, and manuscripts from the Secret Archives of the Vatican, translated by Edmond Bordeaux Szekely. Szekely derived his translations from a previous translation accomplished by St. Jerome and St. Benedict in the Middle Ages. In the fourth century AD, St. Jerome began to find a specific kind of manuscript fragment, which had come to be in the possession of religious hermits living in small huts in a hidden valley of the desert of Chalcis. As Jerome learned Hebrew and Aramaic, he began to understand the significance of the Essene words on these fragments and translated them into Latin.

In the next century, these translations came into the possession of St. Benedict, who copied and preserved them in the library of his monastery at Monte Cassino. Eventually finding their way into the Secret Archives of the Vatican over the next centuries, they were discovered by the young Szekely, translated into modern English, and published. The most famous of these is *The Essene Gospel of Peace*.

Influences on the mystical order of the Essenes were eclectic and far-reaching. Szekely believes the Essenes existed as a brotherhood for centuries prior to the life of Christ, perhaps under other names in other lands. Although a distinct belief system with its own character, the essence of the Essenes teachings—according to Szekely—derived from sources as diverse as the Zend Avesta of Zarathustra, the Vedas and the Upanishads, the yoga systems of India, Buddhism, Freemasonry, Gnosticism, and the Kabbalah. And, of course, all of these hold at their core the fundamental ideas that (1) intention creates reality, and that (2) the most potent of all intentions is that of love. Consider the following five-part Essene quote from the Lost Gospels of the Essenes.*

Blessed is the Child of Light
Who is wise in Mind,
For he shall create heaven.

The Mind of the wise
Is a well-plowed field

---

*From *The Essene Gospel of Peace*, International Biogenics Society, Box 849, Nelson, BC, Canada, V1L6A5.

Which giveth forth abundance and plenty.
For if thou showest a handful of seed
To a wise man, He will see in his Mind's eye
A field of golden wheat.

And if thou showest a handful of seed
To a fool, He will see only that which is before him,
And call them worthless pebbles.

And as the field of the wise man
Giveth forth grain in abundance,
And the field of the fool
Is a harvest only of stones,
So it is with our thoughts.

As the sheaf of golden wheat
Lieth hidden within the tiny kernel
So it is with our thoughts.

As the sheaf of golden wheat
Lieth hidden within the tiny kernel,
So is the kingdom of heaven
Hidden within our thoughts.

If they be filled with the
Power, Love and Wisdom
Of the Angels of the Heavenly Father,
So they shall carry us
To the Heavenly Sea.

THE SYNTHESIS

As Hegel and Hesse demonstrated with such elegance, true evolution occurs via a dialectical process in which parent influences are merged into a synthesis. The synthesis contains elements of the parent influences yet is entirely new and different. The parables are the synthesis Christ offered. They are the marriage of traditional Jewish ideas, kabbalistic ideas, Essene ideas, and key ideas from other mystical traditions. Thus, the deepest messages of the parables contain elements similar to the parent influences yet far surpassing them. If we consider the Essene and kabbalistic influences on Jesus' personal evolution as a synthesis, we can now understand his words at a much deeper level. Look again at the first two sentences of the Key:

> And answering he said to them, "Because it has been given to you to know the mysteries of the kingdom of heaven, but it has not been given to the rest. For whoever has, to him will be given, and he will have over-abundance. But whoever does not have even what he has will be taken from him. Because of this, I speak to them in parables . . ."

To paraphrase, he tells us that he wants us to know the secret knowledge of the Kingdom of Heaven through the parables, that this is what they are all about. It is therefore critical to translate this phrase with care so as to unlock its true depth. Remember that one of the primary ideas of this book is that Jesus may well have been knowledgeable, in some way, of advanced concepts such as those found in modern physics and modern psychology. If he were in fact attempting to communicate such advanced concepts, this intention should be clearly reflected here, at the very beginning of his ministry with parables, here in the key explanatory passage. Therefore, it would be wise to carefully translate the exact terms that he used in this important passage.

The term traditionally translated as "kingdom" is from the Greek word *basileia*. As traditional translations indicate, this word can be translated as "kingdom." However, according to *Strong's Concordance*, *basileia* can also be translated as "realm." A *realm* . . . what could he mean by that? If he were somehow "trapped in the past" trying to talk to us about advanced concepts of time and space he knew we would be studying now so many years later, why would he use the word "realm"? What would the term "realm" mean to a contemporary scientist? Would it be too big a stretch to think that the modern words "dimension" or "universe" would be a more accurate and meaningful translation? By extension, would it be reasonable to suggest that a metaphysician might use the term "personal reality" when referring to a "realm"?

But the complete phrase, realm, or dimension *of heaven*—what could that mean precisely? The Greek term used here for "heaven" is *ouranos*. *Strong's Concordance* translates *ouranos* as follows:

Ouranos, *oo-ran-os;* from *oros* (through the idea of *elevation*); the *sky;* by extension, heaven (as the abode of God); by implication, *happiness, power, eternity.*

As indicated, in order to translate *ouranos* correctly, we have to first go back to the word *oros,* which means "to lift or to rise." It is as though "heaven," as used in this context, is more a *verb*—something that happens—and less a noun or thing. Heaven is a *process*—of elevation, of rising, of *lifting*—a process characterized by happiness and power, a process that has always been going on and will always go on, in "eternity."

And *where* is this higher dimension or universe found? He was absolutely clear on this point when he told us, "*Heaven is within.*" This dimension of heaven is *a state of mind.* The entire universe is a state of mind. Thus the phrase "kingdom of heaven" becomes, in modern terms:

A universe or dimension, a personal reality, which is a *process* that occurs *within.* The kingdom of heaven is a process of rising, of being lifted up, into a dimension of happiness and power—the ability to change things—a universe that is always present and will always be present, a universe of Mind.

To put it all together, when the teacher says that he is speaking in parables because he wants us to "know the mysteries of the Kingdom of Heaven," he is saying that he wants to initiate us into the great secret— that our thoughts and intentions create and shape our separate universes, our personal realities, and that we can create and enter entirely new dimensions, worlds lifted to higher levels with our very thoughts and visualizations—lifted into universes of happiness and personal power *through the power of love.*

"TO HIM WILL BE GIVEN"

Recall that the second statement in the Key is as follows: *For whoever has, to him will be given, and he will have over-abundance. But whoever does not have even what he has will be taken from him.* What could this mean exactly? It certainly doesn't sound fair—that those who are already lacking would have what little they have taken away. What was he talking about?

He was talking about a principle of propagation that is at the core of all the great mysteries of reality creation, the *principle of expansion.* This can be stated most succinctly as "Whatever you focus on expands." If your thoughts and intentions dwell on what you have, what you have will expand and you will have more, even to the point of overabundance.

The Greek word used for overabundance is *perrisseuo,* which translates as "*To superabound (in quality or quantity), be in excess, be superfluous; also, to cause to superabound or excel . . .*" Your reality will be a direct reflection of the sum total of your thoughts. If you tend to concentrate on what you lack, in any way, however subtle, your lack will expand. If you concentrate, focus, and dwell upon what you already *have,* your reality will morph into a new state, a state that is not merely abundant but goes beyond to a state of *excess or "superabundance."*

And why would that be a good thing? Because excess supply can be *given away.* When you create more than you need for yourself, you have created enough for others as well. Now you have become a miracle worker, a being who has the means to improve the lives of everyone around you in many different ways. We will now turn our attention to the parable of the sower.

TWO

THE PARABLE OF THE SOWER

Jesus sat down by the sea.

And great crowds gathered to him,

so that boarding a boat, he sat down.

And all the crowd stood on the shore.

And he spoke to them many things in parables.

"Behold, the sower went out to sow, and in the sowing of him,

some seeds fell by the wayside, and the fowls came and devoured them up:

Some fell upon stony places, where they had not much earth: and forthwith
    they sprung up, because they had no deepness of earth:

And when the sun was up, they were scorched;

and because they had no root, they withered away.

And some fell among thorns; and the thorns sprung up, and choked them:

But others fell onto good ground, and brought forth fruit, some a hun-
    dredfold, some sixtyfold, and some thirtyfold.

Who hath ears to hear, let him hear."

HAT A BEAUTIFUL little story—an allegory so elegant and versatile that it has actually become an integral part of the Western Zeitgeist, its component metaphors used in a wide variety of applications to illustrate all sorts of ideas. Although different shades of interpretation exist, it is generally thought that the "seeds" that are being sown by the "sower" are the words of the Bible—particularly the Gospels—which bear the words of the teacher, the very teller of the story. These "seed words" are disseminated freely and received by different kinds of people. Some people pay attention and use the lessons to change their attitudes and their lives. Some people pay either little or no attention to the words and do not change their ways for the better. The "seed words" are able to take root and thrive within the first group. They are presumably saved and go on to heaven. Conversely, the word shrivels and dies in people who *don't* pay attention, who don't change their lives. These people will not fare so pleasantly.

And there is little question that this general interpretation is entirely valid and clearly useful in the sense that it provides very clear guidance on how to live. But any reasonable person would wonder at this point—given what we now know about the surprising depth that may be contained within the original Greek words—is there more to this important parable? It would certainly be interesting to know as this is, after all, the parable in which the teacher introduces all the other parables. Up until this point, the parables' mode of teaching has not yet been explained to the disciples. The first three parables came with no explanation as to their mode, per se. At this fourth parable the disciples have noticed a trend: that the teacher has started to use a new, indirect, enigmatic, and very challenging method of communica tion. It is not until this parable that anyone actually speaks up and asks what all the others are surely asking within, "Why, exactly, are you talking to us like this now?" Little did they know at that point that fully one-third of everything that the teacher would teach them would be in the immortal sequence of thirty such stories that would follow.

THE PARABLE OF THE SOWER contains several superb lessons showing how the quality of thought forms, and the quality of their management, *predicts* their success in manifesting as reality. Our new translation and interpretation needs to start with a close examination of the very first phrase, "*Behold, the sower went out to sow, and in the sowing of him . . .*"

The terms normally translated as "the sowing of him" or "his sowing" are the Greek words *speiro* and *autos*. According to *Strong's Concordance, speiro* means to scatter, to sow—literally or figuratively—or to "receive seed." *Autos* is found in many modern words and means "of the self." Therefore, a more accurate translation of this first statement is "Behold, the sower went out to sow, and in the sowing of the self . . ." The "sowing of the self"—what could that mean? How does one "sow the self"? What would be the "seeds" of the self? If it is the self that is being figuratively "sown," what would its metaphorical "seeds" be? To know that, we first have to know what a seed really is in general terms.

A seed is *potential*, potential in the form of unmanifested, unexpressed genetic *information*—information that tells a growing organism *how to manifest*, how to germinate, how to successfully find supply, how to become stronger, and how to reproduce. This potential, this information can unfold and become active if and when a specific set of *conditions* is present. When this set of conditions is in place—moisture, darkness, warmth, etc.—the information coiled in the seed unfurls and expresses itself. Randomly distributed molecules surrounding the seed are *organized* into proteins, the proteins are organized into cellular components, and eventually cells are manifested. As the information continues to express itself, the cells are further organized into an entire organism, a living being that can reproduce itself by bearing more fruit, more seeds—often one hundredfold or more.

So what would the seeds of your self be? What within you qualifies as unexpressed potential? What is it of our selves that is comprised of information that is capable of organizing the raw materials of our environment and turning them into life? Clearly, it is our ideas, our plans, our visualizations, our *intentions,* of what *can* be, what we will make happen. Nothing is ever created or built or accomplished that is not conceived and directed via thought. The seeds of the self are our thought forms.

THE INTERPRETATION

Perhaps the most interesting thing about the parable of the sower, something that makes it unique, is the fact that Jesus actually interprets it for us. Along with its partner parable, the parable of the tares, which immediately follows, the parable of the sower is the only parable to be explained and decoded by the teacher himself. This interpretation is found in Matthew, verses 19–23, where Jesus explains exactly what the characters and conditions in the story represent. This section is of great importance because it provides a key that allows all subsequent parables to be similarly decoded so that the deepest lessons embedded within are revealed for what they are.

In the parable, there are four places in which seed is sown—the roadside, the stony places, the thorny places, and the good ground. As was said, many people believe that the seeds that are being sown by the sower are the words of the Bible, and the Gospels specifically, which bear the words of the teacher. The words are heard by different kinds of people and different situations result. But this interpretation and variations thereof cannot possibly be correct—at least, they cannot be the whole truth. We have already discussed this to some degree in the first section. The wording of Matthew 13:3 is clear and precise: That which is being sown is not the word, it is *the [seeds of] the self.* If there is any uncertainty as to the truth of this, Jesus' first statement when interpreting the parable in verses 19–23 removes all doubt. To paraphrase slightly for clarity: *That which is sown is "everyone hearing the word of the kingdom . . ."*

This phrase is a little tricky to unravel. There are four terms of interest in this important statement: "everyone," "hearing," "word," and "kingdom." Let's take a close look at *Strong's* Greek-to-English dictionary to see precisely how these terms translate.

The Greek term usually translated as "everyone" is *pas.* The dictionary tells us that *pas* can indeed be translated as "everyone," but can just as easily be translated as "the whole." The Greek term traditionally translated as "hearing" is *akouo.* The dictionary states that *akouo* can mean "to hear" but can also mean "to understand." We have already discussed the term *basileia,* which can mean either "kingdom" or "realm." In contemporary terms a "realm" would be a dimension, a universe, a state of being, or a personal reality. And there has been clear information that the specific dimension the teacher wants us to know about is the dimension of happiness and power, the higher reality that is *within* each of us.

But what is the *word* of the kingdom, the *word* of this dimension of happiness and power? The Greek term used for "word" here is *logos,* a concept so large it requires a separate section for discusssion.

THE LOGOS

Logos is one of the deepest and most fascinating terms in the entire Greek language. The term *logos* evolved over many centuries of use by some of the most intelligent people in history. In 600 BC the Greek philosopher Heraclitis used the term *logos* to refer to the entire creative process by which the universe is created and sustained. Heraclitis believed that the energy that powered the creative process, the force that generates and sustains the entire cosmos, came from the interaction of the great opposites—light and dark, heat and cold, large and small, the ordered and the disordered. Although wholly Western in its origin, this is a concept strikingly similar to if not identical to Taoism. Surely the author of Matthew was well aware of this when he selected the term *logos* to express himself.

A study of the term *logos* in Eliade's classic *Encyclopedia of Religion and Philosophy,* a standard twelve-volume reference set found in most libraries, reveals no less than twelve pages of detailed discussion on this term. Certainly, *logos* can mean simply "word" as standard translations of the Bible invariably indicate, but there is so much more to it.

The term *logos* can also refer to the *origin* of words. And what are the origins of words? Where do they come from? From our *thoughts,* obviously. Words are representations of thoughts—all different kinds of thoughts: Concepts, ideas, plans, visualizations, projections, feelings, memories, impressions, *intentions*—these are the things that give rise to words. Words are symbolic representations of these thought forms. Words are created by human beings so that that which resides internally in the mind can be communicated and shared externally, where it can direct action and change things.

The most famous use of the term *logos* is in the first sentence of the book of John, *In the beginning was the logos.* The *logos* is the source of all being, the undifferentiated pure potential through which all creation is activated. As pure unmanifested, undifferentiated potential, the *logos* is the most powerful force known. It is this conscious potential that generates the entire universe with its myriad particles, dimensions, stars, expanding galactic formations, and countless life-forms.

But more important, *logos* refers to the entire causal sequence: Pure potential giving rise to thought forms, the concepts and ideas of thought forms then generating internal words, internal words giving rise to spoken words, spoken words leading eventually to actions, and actions altering the environment.

If we add all this information together, the phrase "everyone hearing the word of the kingdom (of heaven)" means: *the whole understanding—of the process of creation by which thoughts manifest entirely new dimensions of happiness and power.*

In summary, the three sections of the parable of the sower indicate that we will be taught in parables in order to initiate us into the mysteries, the great secrets, the laws that govern the use of thought forms in creating higher dimensions of reality. We are told a story in which a sower sends forth the seeds of his self, sends forth his thought forms into the universe, a story that will teach what happens with these thought forms as they encounter different sets of conditions.

THE WAYSIDE

As the sower sows the seeds of his self, they meet with different sets of conditions. The first group falls by the wayside, and the birds come and eat them. In the explanation section, the teacher explains that with this set of seeds "the evil one comes and plucks that which is sown in his heart."

This is traditionally interpreted to mean that with this group, the word of God is heard, but the "evil one," the devil, intervenes and counteracts any good that has been learned. This is a perfectly valid interpretation and works well for traditional Christians. But there is a deeper interpretation that has equal validity and arguably more practical value in that it offers information that will empower us to change things for the better.

To reveal this deeper layer of meaning, let's examine some of the key terms starting with the very last word. The Greek term used here for "heart," *kardia,* is still used today in medicine—as in "cardiac." *Strong's Concordance* translates this term as follows: "Probably from kar (Latin: cor, "heart."); the heart, i.e. (figuratively) the thoughts or feelings, mind . . ."

Surely there can be no doubt by this point that the teacher is indeed talking about the sowing of thought forms. What he is saying here is that a person can discover the truth, the great secret—that his thoughts are creating and sustaining his personal reality—but if he fails to *comprehend* the truth at a sufficiently deep level, the "evil one" will nullify his thought forms and they will fail to germinate into reality.

Clearly, understanding is a vital element in the manifestation process. The more a person really "gets it" at a deep visceral level, not just in the mind, but in the heart as well, the more likely a thought form can be sustained and focused for sufficient time as to allow manifestation as a new dimension of happiness. One of the most important and obvious conditions of a miracle was demonstrated by the teacher immediately before the manifestation of the loaves and fishes that fed the five thousand in the desert. Taking the five loaves he had on hand, Matthew tells us, he "looked up to heaven." This action of looking up to heaven is described by two Greek words, *ouranos,* which we have already examined in detail and which means to lift or rise, and *anavlep-sos,* which means to see or restore vision. The two terms together most closely resemble our modern term "visualization," the act of seeing something higher in the mind's eye, seeing and intending something better than that which is currently manifesting.

But there is a term used in Christ's explanation that is trouble-some. The thing that is plucking out the thought forms from the heart is referred to as the "evil one." In all mainstream interpretations this is thought to mean the "devil." However, the Greek term used here, *poneros,* can also be translated just as accurately as "diseased" or "ill." As we will learn when we study the third parable, which directly pre-cedes the parable of the sower chronologically, Christ taught us that there is no devil or organized conspiracy of "evil." So, translating this term as "evil" does not seem to make sense in this context. "Diseased" or "ill" sounds much more logical.

But what could the "diseased one" refer to, particularly in the con-text of "sowing the seeds of the self"? Most likely the *lower* self, which "suffers" from the illusion of separation, and all that goes with it. The "diseased one" is the ego. Moreover, if the term "ego" is substituted for the term "evil" *whenever* subsequently mentioned in the series of para-bles, considerable clarity is gained.

In summary, thought forms that go by the wayside are those that are cultivated with insufficient depth of intellectual and visceral conviction and thus fall prey to the doubt and illusion, the dis-ease, of the lower self or ego. Having fallen into this infertile milieu, they never even germi-nate, much less manifest as fully formed changes in personal reality.

THE STONY PLACES

And that sown on the stony places is this; the one hearing the word and immediately receiving it with joy, but has no root in himself, but is temporary—and tribulation, or persecution occurring because of the word, he is at once offended.

The next condition that sown thought forms can meet is to fall on "*stony places*," which, he tells us in his explanation, represents someone who "hath no root in the self." What a fascinating phrase. What precisely could this mean? In the most general terms possible, what would any spiritual teacher say is the "root of the self"? *How* does a person have a root in him- or herself?

A "root," from the Greek word *rhizoo,* is the part of a plant that extends below the ground, beyond sight, and into the earth. It is this invisible part of the organism that enables it to penetrate areas of rich supply, to tap the nutrients necessary for life, and to transport them up into the visible growing point aboveground.

A person who has a "root within the self" is a person who has opened the channels to the source of all good, all supply. These channels are opened through *consciousness*—by being increasingly *aware* of the presence and significance of the source. Thus, a root of the self, which can tap into the rich substrate of divine consciousness, is a channel of consciousness, a channel developed by meditation, by thinking about God, by *focusing* on the source. And whatever we focus on expands. Like the arteries of an athlete that expand as his muscles and lungs are used, our channel, our connection, our root into the wellspring of infinite supply expands as we use our attention to focus upon it. The lesson:

Conscious contact with the Source,
with divine energy and presence,
is critical for the germination of thought forms.

THE THORNY PLACES

And that sown into the thorns is this: the one hearing the word—and the anxiety of this age, and the deceit of riches choke the word, and it becomes unfruitful.

Translation of this passage does not reveal anything too surprising. *Merimnao* translated as "anxiety" can be translated as such, but can also mean "to take thought." *Aion,* the word traditionally translated as "age," can also mean eternity or perpetuity, and by implication, the world. The word for deceit, *apate,* can mean deceit, but can also mean delusion. Riches is represented by the Greek word *ploutos,* and means riches, wealth, or abundance.

Therefore the traditional translation is reasonably accurate here. But a slight improvement would be:

That which is sown on the thorny places are those, the people hearing the word of the kingdom, who are being distracted by the external world, including the delusions caused by external forms of wealth. The thoughts of people so distracted will not bear fruit.

This seems to convey a dual message. The first part of the message is that if we want to have success in creating a more beneficial dimension of reality, we have to be able to concentrate. This in turn will require that we are able to focus on our intention regardless of what is going on in the world around us. If it is true that a large part of our purpose here on earth is to learn about the power of our intentions, and in particular the power of love, we are going to be confronted with vast amounts of sensory stimuli telling us that reality is something different from what we are trying to create.

Perhaps the most difficult task we have as miracle workers, as creators, is to learn the ability to see something better with the mind's eye than what the world shows us through our physical eyes, as the teacher did immediately before the loaves and fishes expanded to feed the masses. This is profoundly challenging, especially when we are confronted by highly convincing and reliable sensory and intellectual data indicating there is something dangerous, painful, or disastrous happening. If we receive a letter notifying us of a potential tax audit, learn from a licensed physician that we have a potentially lethal disease, or watch an entire country fall into chaos and starvation through a reputable news source, it will be extraordinarily difficult to sustain a visualization of something higher, something better. But it is precisely during such periods that we most need to be able to shift to our creative, spiritual eyes in order to see something better. If we cannot *see* something better than the problems that are apparently developing in our lives, we cannot competently *redirect* the universe to correct the situation.

But the process of visualization is not a momentary one, rather an ongoing one. It is not effective to merely see a situation as improved for a few seconds or even a few days, while the preponderance of our thoughts continue to be pulled away from the focal point by contradictory sights and sounds, news, scientific data, and the opinions of others. Those who will best succeed in learning to manifest better worlds, better dimensions, are those who will stay with their "elevated" vision, no matter what information is presented indicating that the vision is not already a reality. The most successful thought form artists are the ones who remain steadfast to the vision, no matter how grim the external "reality" before them. Obviously this can be so difficult as to be virtually impossible for the average person, but it is nonetheless a goal worthy of striving for.

The second part of the message concerns the delusions of worldly riches. Those who fall into the illusion that worldly riches are true riches will eventually devolve to a state in which they are no longer able to manifest realms of heaven—personal realities of happiness and power. In other words, if we employ the correct spiritual techniques of thought forms, we can achieve a state of superabundance, an excess of supply that can certainly qualify as wealth. But the minute we turn our attention from our inner vision, our inner reality, to the false reality of the externally manifested riches, we will falter and fall back into a state of unfruitfulness wherein our manifestation efforts begin to fail. The teacher is warning us of a paradox, a stumbling block. The techniques of thought forms can manifest riches, but as soon as we begin to *rely* on those riches and not upon our inner vision, and our connection to the One, we will become spiritually impotent. This is a situation so common among younger souls as to be proverbial:

The man is born who grows to become proficient in thought forms. A man of vision and conviction, he grows in stature and wealth. But as he accumulates more money and more power over others, more superabundance, he finds his personal life slowly deteriorating in disturbing but superficially unrelated ways. The changes are at first subtle and creep in unrecognized. Gradually, he finds he no longer has love or intimacy in his life. He is unable to sustain loving relationships or a loving family and experiences the anxiety of the world. He can no longer experience fun or pleasure without the aid of alcohol or other vices and spends hours obsessing that he does not have enough. On the surface he is confident but inside he is worried that he will lose everything. The riches have distracted him from the Source within, which is infinite and cannot be exhausted as long as he follows the law. Even though he believes he still understands this, he has in truth forgotten.

Such a person no longer relies on spirit but upon his retirement account to save him from the perils of reality. He begins to tighten his grip, doing anything and everything to increase his riches even more. Although he becomes lonelier and lonelier, he continues to take from others, paring their salaries, increasing his prices, reducing his contributions to charitable and spiritual causes in order to pad his assets just a little more. He gives lip service to the law but all around him people suffer in many subtle ways because of his greed, his reliance on money to provide him with a better life.

In the end, he finds that he loses even the ability to generate money with his intentions and, in some cases, loses even his worldly wealth. Such a person can ultimately grow old and die with many people in attendance, but none who truly love him. He is feared but not truly respected. For he lost the "root" within himself. It is not until he hits bottom and experiences a true rebirth that he realizes his error and is able to proceed successfully as a truly generous, giving human being.

None of this is to say that wealth or riches *automatically* lead to devolved states of consciousness. There are many fine examples of people who grow wealthy in a worldly sense yet maintain an excellent sense of generosity and selflessness. But the lesson is a stern warning. It is a reminder to remember the vision, a reminder to maintain your connection to the Source even when the manifestation of abundance occurs.

THE GOOD GROUND

*But that sown on the good ground is this: the one hearing the word,
and understanding it; who indeed brings forth and produces fruit; one
truly a hundredfold; and one sixty, and one thirty.*

Remember, the word of the kingdom is the *logos* of the new dimension, the cause-and-effect relationship between thoughts and the generation of reality. The person who truly comprehends the truth of this
process, the great secret—that our thoughts are what is actually responsible for the manifestations of matter and energy and circumstances we see unfolding in our personal realities—this is a person who
will experience tremendous increase. This is a person who understands
the law at a deep visceral level, a person who has a root himself—an
open channel of consciousness to the source, a person who is not distracted by conflicting external information or the delusions of false
wealth. This person will be able to harness the laws of increase and receive huge returns on the energy expended on positive, loving thought
forms and generous actions.

The Parables

———— ✦ ————

THE TWO DEBTORS

The Law of Forgiveness

LUKE 7:40—43

. . . and the Teacher said, "Two debtors owed a certain creditor. One owed him five hundred denarii and the other owed him fifty. Neither had anything to repay him and so he forgave both of them freely. Which of the debtors will then love him more?"

And answering, Simon said, "I suppose the one who was freely forgiven the most."

And he said, "You have rightly judged."

As NOTED, fully one-third of all the words spoken by Christ, and subsequently recorded in the Gospels, are in the form of parables. It would thus be reasonable to believe that the parable with the auspicious position of number one in the delivery sequence might have a very special importance in the teacher's mind. As any good teacher will tell you, the first lesson, the introductory lesson, is always a matter of profound importance, a matter requiring deep and lengthy contemplation. For example, it is traditionally said about

the *Tao Te Ching* that a student who can grasp the first verse alone understands all eighty-one verses. In the first lesson, it is necessary to at
once interest students and challenge them. That combination, *interest
and challenge,* serves to simultaneously "hook" the promising students
and to winnow away students with insufficient personal evolution to
successfully negotiate the challenging series of learning events that
will ultimately follow.

As you will see, the first of all the parables, the parable of the two
debtors, is certainly capable of squeezing out any insincere supplicants.
It provides a narrow isthmus, a kind of exclusive metaphysical bottleneck through which all who seek to be admitted to the mysteries—and
their realms of knowledge and personal power—must pass.

You may make it through this narrow strait, and then again, you
may not. If you do, you will find that in passing through this spiritual
bottleneck you will undergo one of the most classical spiritual rites of
passage known, an initiation universally required of highly evolved
seekers over the centuries—monks, adepts, ascetics, masters, nuns, hermits, and avatars alike. The passageway is invariably required along all
true paths to God. In fact, if you find a path that does *not* require the
quantum leap in evolution this parable outlines, you may well be on a
false path, a path that probably isn't taking you to the vibrant personal
reality you so longingly seek.

It is no way an idle exaggeration to suggest that it is entirely possible that you, or any of us for that matter, may not make it through this
perilous passage. For to make yourself sufficiently lean and spiritually fit
to negotiate the narrow gateway of this channel, you will have to identify and dismantle the most portly and distended aspects of your soul—
the deeply rooted and ferociously guarded games and indulgences of
your very ego. And nothing could be trickier, or more necessary.

Not everyone will be able to complete the action steps outlined at the end of this chapter. It is my own belief that the parable of the two debtors has been placed directly at the forefront of the parable sequence specifically to *winnow out* those who are not yet ready to actually do all that must be done to receive the enormous power conferred by mastery of the remaining parables, those not yet ready to assume the profound *responsibility* of that power, those not ready to commit to a long and very challenging program.

The most important quality that the parable of the two debtors selects as it winnows out initial applicants is *humility*. Because humility and the ability to forgive are really but two faces of the same coin. Basically the teacher is saying this: "If you cannot be under sufficient control of your ego, if you cannot be modest, respectful, and *humble* enough, I won't be able to work with you on learning this system quite yet. If you are still arrogant and egocentric you are going to have to keep repeating the lessons this parable demands until you can pare your self-importance down far enough to pass through this bottleneck, this strait of humility."

It is interesting: As it turns out, it is not impressive intelligence, it is not great metaphysical knowledge and verbal proficiency that is the doorway to the realm of the mysteries. It is not one's stature in the spiritual community. It is not a person's visible and impressive works. As it turns out, the bottleneck is *humility,* plain and simple. What a fitting primary rite of passage for you, for anyone—a rite of passage we must all master. Over and over. For the duration.

Remarks about the difficulty of the universal rite of passage of forgiveness are not made to discourage you or to keep you from going forth. They are only to forewarn you to have your guard up and be firmly braced for an intense and tricky battle. It is important that you be realistic regarding the challenges ahead. Make no mistake about it: The ego is an incredibly cunning and resilient opponent. It has a variety of extraordinarily potent and baffling mechanisms designed to foil all but the most intelligent and persistent of efforts to tame it. The good news is that you won't be up against an *external* opponent. In the final analysis, you will be found to be your own worst impediment. It will only be your own ego, your own denial, your own pride, your own selfishness that will have the power to stop you. For these are the things that are necessary and nonnegotiable—to attain a state of true forgiveness.

All of the ego's defense mechanisms are manifestations of *fear. That is common knowledge.* This matters because the techniques required to effectively confront and conquer the ego's excessive pride and selfishness can bring you into contact with that fear. This is nothing unusual. Virtually all of the classic initiatory bottlenecks—rites of passage—include difficult, painful, and anxiety-provoking experiences. Confronting your self in such a way that you have to humble yourself to other people, *real* people in your life and your past, can be extraordinarily threatening to the imperious paper dragon of the ego. The sheer *unpleasantness* of dealing with the Medusa of fear that underlies the ego has the distinct potential to overcome your higher intent and sentence you to failure. This will be particularly true if you try to take a shortcut through the process detailed at the end of this chapter. And it will be especially true if you have an especially large and pathological ego. But fear not. Everything along the path is doable. And it all leads to a series of rewarding and cleansing experiences that will clear your life and all of your relationships. This in turn will lead to the clearing of your *mind, and even your body and spirit.*

The parable of the two debtors is normally thought to be about God forgiving sinners. The traditional, conservative interpretation of the parable is that if you have sinned very greatly and are subsequently forgiven by God, you will have more gratitude to God than someone who is relatively virtuous and has to be forgiven little. It seems a way of welcoming people who are, or perceive themselves to be, too guilty or un-worthy.

But this is only the most superficial level of meaning. In order to perceive the deeper level, the level through which you will access the limitless ocean of grace and abundance, you have to begin by remem-bering that the parables are all about *you*. All great masters through history have known that the only thing we can really change is our-selves. One of the great secrets of the parables is that, in many cases, when the characters and elements in the stories are interpreted as be-ing parts of the soul, parts of the self, the meaning becomes much clearer, and much deeper. Applied to this parable indicates that the real message is about *you* forgiving *others*. Specifically, the parable di-rects you to *particularly* forgive those who have committed serious or multiple offenses, those who have hurt you in some way that you see as important.

The mechanism of the first and most important of all preparatory steps for admission to the mysteries is the process of forgiveness. In fact, forgiveness is so important, so critical that the teacher tells us in Matthew 5:23–24 that

> *there isn't any point in tithing to the church*
> *if you have not forgiven your brother.*

In other words, there is no point in even bothering to try using the laws of increase, the laws delineated in the mystery teachings, if you have not taken the most basic and preliminary step of clearing your soul of negative, energy-sapping baggage by forgiving those you hold resentments against. If you attempt to proceed with learning the mys-teries *without* this critical step, nothing will work right and you will fail. Your subconscious will still be filled with malignant thought forms that pollute your spiritual environs and sap its energies. If the soul is not sufficiently cleared of this negative energy, tithing or visualizing or using *any other spiritual techniques to correct lack and bring about happiness will certainly fail.* This is a profound idea and one that is often glossed over in other self-help systems.

Put first things first. Before you begin any act of abundance, any use of the mysteries, you will have to first make peace with your brothers and sisters. This will be in your best interest. Making peace with your neighbors, your family, and your world will bring *you* peace. Only when you are clear and in a state of internal harmony can you return to tithe and do the other kinds of things necessary to set the laws of increase into motion successfully. And this will never go away. This is something that is just part of being a spiritual adult, something that we might as well master and soon.

We know from the Lord's Prayer that we will be forgiven our debts "as we forgive our debtors." And it is no accident that the other half of the sentence in which we remind ourselves of this is "Give us this day our daily bread." That supply and foregiveness go hand in hand is a point of such massive importance to the teacher that they are prominently mentioned in his final master prayer.

A debt of any kind, material or otherwise, is a reflection of thought, like everything else in your external reality. If your thoughts are permeated at a subconscious level with anger and resentment, your external world will reflect this and you will find yourself intermittently or even continually in a state of energetic, monetary, and emotional debt. Clearing this subconscious debris is a logical launching point for the entire parable sequence.

But *how* are we to undertake this? Do we just *say* that we have forgiven everyone, *think* that we have forgiven everyone and everything? Surely that alone will not suffice. It certainly hasn't worked up until this point, has it? The resentments you must release are often wired into the deepest parts of your nervous system and body. These are the kinds of thought forms that can make you have vivid dreams, make you nervous and flushed, make your heart pound, even create or heal disease. We can *talk* about forgiving all day long but easily be left with the same deeply embedded feelings of ill will that we had to begin with. Forgiveness is so difficult, so tricky, so easily foiled by the cunning tricks of the ego that we will have to have some help, a methodical *system* that will allow us to clear the powerful grudges and resentments that have resulted from a lifetime of taking umbrage at all sorts of real and imaginary offenses.

Fortunately such a system exists, and in keeping with the eclectic spirit of this book, seeking to draw upon the best that humanity has to offer, this system must be included for it is undeniably the most specific and effective system of forgiveness that has been developed. It is a system born of the powerful spiritual exercises of monks, ascetics, Kabbalists, and mystics through the centuries, manifested by the Oxford Group in the 1800s, and finally refined into one of the most significant spiritual developments of the entire twentieth century. This system, known as the Twelve Steps, is found in one form or another in all of the sixty-plus varieties of so-called "Twelve Step groups." All of these groups are designed to help people who need a miracle, people who either need to *solve an unsolvable problem*—such as depression, overeating, overspending, codependency, sex addiction, alcoholism, drug addiction, gambling, rage, or any number of "incurable" personality defects and obsessive-compulsive behavior patterns—or risk destruction, disease, or even death.

These groups have become incredibly popular around the world and there is a good reason for this: They actually *work*. They are really capable of solving "impossible" problems and thus qualify as *miraculous* in their own right. Anyone who has known a person with an apparently hopeless problem who has actually worked through these steps correctly will testify to their power. The transformation that can result is truly spectacular. So, it is precisely because this simple system of steps works better than any other in dealing with the process of forgiveness that it has been chosen here to guide you through a successful and genuine process of personal forgiveness.

We are going to take a close look at six of the classic twelve steps, the six that deal specifically with the issue of resentments—the powerful, stubborn, and highly destructive thought forms that lurk just beneath the surface of our minds. You will learn exactly how to *apply* these six steps that have such ancient monastic and mystical roots to your own stubborn set of life experiences and related resentments. In the process you will clear your soul, free your whole being of the weighty baggage that keeps you from flying.

Undoubtedly some of you will be wishing at this point that this step was more "mystical," more magical, more glamorous, more complex. Perhaps you were hoping for a special ritual with crystals, a magical mantra, or a secret prayer. Some of you will think that this step is too mundane, too boring, too stodgy to be of significant interest and value to you. But nothing could be further from the truth. For the process of forgiveness, *real* forgiveness, is arguably *the single most powerful thing that you can do to free yourself.*

For many of you, a lack of effective forgiveness is the single most significant snag that is holding up your entire spiritual progress, your success, your abundance, your happiness, the stumbling block that lies between you and your dream. You may be performing all kinds of other spiritual techniques and performing them correctly yet finding yourself in the same lackluster life of mediocrity and ill-defined angst. Resentment is that powerful. It can hold back *everything.* So, dealing with resentment is *real* spirituality. *This is what it is like.* Throw yourself into this step and you cannot fail to be lifted to a new quantum level of energy and happiness.

ACTIVATING PARABLE LESSON 1

1. The activation of parable lesson one is considerably more involved than any other parable due to its obvious importance. The first step that will be required of you to begin a thorough and effective process of forgiveness may surprise you. Yet the rationale for this unexpected exercise will become increasingly clear as you make your way through the entire sequence necessary to clear the subconscious and prepare it for the mysteries that await you in the parable.

The first step is to make a *list* of every resentment you hold within your mind. This is only logical. If you are going to forgive everything, clear everything, you will have to bring to *conscious awareness* everything that has become a focal point of ill will within you. A carefully composed list will provide the perfect lattice to guide your growth as you proceed through the process.

The list should be created in a very specific way. Each resentment should be written at the top of a separate page in a notebook. A good spiral notebook will do nicely. Leave the back of each page blank. The pages of your list will include all significant *people, events, institutions, and even ideas* that have caused you to react with pain during your life. You will use about half the pages in your notebook for this part of your resentment list and leave the last half of the notebook blank for now.

Begin with your childhood. Childhood resentments can be the deepest of all. In some cases, when they are the result of particularly intense or long-lived abuse—real or perceived—they can actually shape your very personality, and your *reality*. Accordingly, they deserve particularly close scrutiny.

Move carefully and chronologically through your entire life until you reach the present. Obviously, this may take some time. But not *that* much time. If you work steadily you can accomplish most of your list in an hour or two. Don't let any feeling of anxiety, boredom, or fatigue keep you from getting started immediately. All of these things are but the ego's defense system and are to be expected. Don't be fooled. Keep your guard up against the ego's tricks. *And don't procrastinate.* One of the ego's most effective defense mechanisms will be to simply put the task off again and again. Don't fall prey to this simple trick. *Get moving and keep moving until you have completed the task.*

2. Now, beginning with the resentment at the top of page one, meditate on what happened as the resentment was formed. Look within, and then look even deeper. Virtually every resentment, by the definition we will use, has at its core *fear*. Make certain you understand precisely how the person, the institution, the idea or principle *threatened* you in some way.

   The five primary ways that you can experience fear are through real or perceived threats to:

   1. your ego or self-esteem
   2. your physical body
   3. your relations with the opposite sex
   4. your security
   5. your finances

   Look deeply at each listed resentment and do not move to the next until you can clearly see the fear that festers at the core of each. Make sure that you can unequivocally see how the other person threatened something about you, something within you. When you are finally clear about the basic mechanism, you will be able to briefly list in writing which of the five basic fears catalyzed the formation of each listed resentment.

To show you how this works at a practical level, we are going to use a very mundane example of a man who has formed a resentment about another man who snubbed and offended him. He lists the resentment—"I resent John Smith because he offended me by snubbing me and flirting with my wife." He then notes that the man's comments and actions threatened his *self-esteem,* his *security* because his job could be affected, his *sex relations,* and his *finances*— because he feels there could be an adverse effect on his reputation and standing at work.

3. Now, beginning with the first resentment on the first page of your notebook, turn the page over to the back side. You will call this portion of the inventory you are undertaking, this back side of each page, "My Part." Along the left-hand column of the back side write the following five words: (1) Selfish, (2) Dishonest, (3) Inconsiderate, (4) Self-seeking, and (5) Frightened. Leave enough lines between each word to accommodate a brief paragraph that will follow each.

This is real spirituality. Here is where the real work, the real *transformation,* the real *evolution* begins. This is where you will actually begin to dissect your resentments, begin to crack them open so that you will be able to conquer them. Here, you will look at each resentment to see how *you* contributed to the situation surrounding its formation. As the situation developed that led to the resentment, did you think or act selfishly in any way? If so, *how* were you selfish? Be courageous and be *brutally honest.* There are two sides to every story. And it usually takes two to have a disagreement or fight of some kind. There are exceptions to this for sure. In certain special instances a person might be a pure victim of, say, a random crime. But such purely one-sided events are relatively rare. In the vast majority of resentments, you have contributed in some way to the situation. Analyze each situation honestly to see if you were in any way dishonest, inconsiderate, self-seeking, or frightened. But don't be afraid to list anything you did within the situation that was admirable, selfless, and mature. Be balanced and give yourself credit where credit is due.

Knowledge is power. And the parables are designed to empower you by giving you knowledge about yourself. This is the most important and most powerful kind of knowledge you can have as a human being. As Socrates said, "*Above all, know thyself.*" Bring *your* contributions, *your* reactions that enabled the situation to develop to the surface. Only then can you begin to work with them.

Be intrepid and ruthlessly penetrating in your self-examination.

Pay no attention whatsoever to what the other person did even if the problem was 90 percent their "fault." You have no power over the other person, so there is no point in focusing upon them. That is what you have been doing up until this point, and it hasn't helped clear you at all. Every time you recognize another way in which *you* contributed to the problem, you *empower* yourself. As your inventory proceeds, you will learn more and more about what you have thought and done along the way; you will learn about the part of the problem that is under your control—your part. The power you receive is the power to *improve* the situation, or at least your reaction to it.

The power you will receive is a power that will energize your life and confer grace and prosperity in many subtle ways. And it will, of course, prepare you to receive the awesome knowledge in the remaining parable sequence.

4. Next, at the bottom of each back page, write a concise paragraph about how your resentment has affected your thinking, your actions. Summarize *how* the resentment has restricted your growth, *how* it has engendered or contributed to the persistence of external conflict, and in *what ways your reactions and feelings have kept you from enjoying life.* Write down every way you can think of that the resentment has been destructive to you and others.

5. When the first four stages are completed, continue on in your notebook to a series of new pages that will follow the ones devoted to resentments. At the top of each of these new pages, write down all the important things you have done or said to *cause harm* to others. Again, start with your childhood and work forward carefully and chronologically. If there is something particularly shameful, embarrassing, or disgusting that you have done—something that you have never or rarely discussed with another human being—be *particularly* thorough and diligent. These are often things that have *especially powerful contributions* to diseased states of self-image and self-esteem.

6. Now, find a person with whom you will *share* the list. It has been recognized for millennia that it is imperative to *externalize* the contents of your mind, the contents of your troubled subconscious with another human being if you are to reduce the bloated and destructive baggage you carry deep within. This is the only way. *How* is this person selected? Begin by looking for someone who has

three vital qualifications: They feel safe to you, they have conquered codependency, and they have a great reluctance to judge
others.

Codependency is the primary pathology of our society, a kind
of spiritual cancer that can metastasize throughout your entire
emotional substructure. It is pure poison for a miracle worker.
What is it exactly? Codependency is the excessive preoccupation
about what other people are thinking and doing. It expresses itself
as a tendency to want to obsess over others, to change others, or
to conform to others.

In its fully expressed stages, codependency causes a person to
be overly concerned, even upset about what others are thinking or
doing. A person with strong codependency is anxious to give un-
solicited advice and is certain he or she knows "what is *really* going
on with you." Such a person is typically very controlling, although
the control behavior may be disguised and subtle.

How can you recognize a person who has a very *low* degree of
codependency and is thus spiritually and psychologically fit to help
you conquer your resentments by listening to your inventory? Stren-
uously avoid anyone who is *eager* to dwell on your faults, to change
you, or to give you advice. Find a friend who has a neutral stance on
the subject, perhaps someone who works in the service professions
as a therapist or physician or minister. Find a person who never
seems to be critical of others and is quick to admit how *they* have
contributed to the problems in their *own* lives, a person who naturally tends to take full responsibility for their own problems.

You will know the right person because they are willing to listen
to you, have a kindly and helpful attitude, but will display no eager-
ness to be in the position of listener and advice giver. Such a person
has an attitude of live and let live and rarely, if ever, expresses a

strong negative judgment about another person, an institution, or a principle. They seem at peace with what everyone else is doing and are likely to focus naturally and effortlessly on their own problems. This person can help you rise to their level of freedom.

7. When you have found the right person, *set up an appointment* that will allow you enough time to discuss all the items in your inventory with *special attention to your own contributions* to the formation of each resentment. *Meet* with the selected person in a quiet, private place free from any potential interruptions. *Share* each item listed in the pages of your notebook. *Don't omit anything.* If there is something especially embarrassing or shameful that you have done, make certain you disclose your contribution fully and frankly. If you are to be free of the painful and destructive effects of the resentments embedded in your psyche you must *externalize them fully* at this stage.

What may amaze you is how accepting the other person will be as you reveal these diseased layers of your self. A person free from codependency, a person who has taken full responsibility for their own lives will typically reciprocate with stories of their own. Very often people report that as they proceed, they become increasingly aware that the deeply seated negative thought formations they thought were so unusual and shameful are really not that unusual, nor are they nearly as big a deal as they thought.

8. Once you have externalized your negative thought forms with someone else, it is time to take action. Now you will have to do something about the problems within yourself that you have disclosed. This is done by going back through your list one more time. This is where things can get very difficult. For in most cases the

people you have harmed have also done things to hurt you. *That is not the point.* You can't do anything about their contributions. You only have the power to change *yourself.* So, in this step your job is to clean up your side of the problem, your side of the street, as it were. In this critical step you will write down exactly how your re-action in each related situation, your resultant resentments, have harmed *the other person,* or *anyone* for that matter.

Pray about the process. Invite God into the process at every step and you will have help. Spirit will always go out of its way to help you if you are sincerely attempting to clear your resentments in a mature and appropriately humble manner.

9. Paying no attention whatsoever to their contribution, now *contact* the people on your list, each of the people who are involved in each of your resentments unless, of course, contacting them would do more harm or be otherwise entirely inappropriate. Some of these people will need to be contacted in person, some on the phone, and some perhaps in writing.

What do you say to these people? First of all, know what *not* to say. *Under no circumstances regress to your old self and say a single thing about what you think they have done to contribute to the problem.* Stay completely on your own contributions, your own *side* of the street. And don't apologize. Apologies are for the less spiritually evolved and parables are designed to take you to a higher level. Instead, ask the person what you can *do* to make peace and make amends.

How are they likely to react? Some will be very magnanimous, very evolved, and will immediately forgive you with a wave of their hand and quickly point out their own contributions. But such mature and advanced reactions will not always occur. Be forewarned that some people are still in a stage of spiritual immaturity and will seem to have no clue whatsoever that they have contributed in any way, shape, or form to the problem, even when their thoughts and actions are glaringly selfish, petty, or malicious. Particularly immature souls will even use the opportunity to belittle you. *Expect this, and do not let it throw you.*

Remember that this process, or some variation, is a very classic spiritual initiation that is required in many highly advanced spiritual programs. And this is what the initiation feels like. It is a process of *humbling* the self, *deflating* the massively bloated ego, getting into the *lean fit spiritual condition* that will allow you to pass through the narrow straits of the first parable and into the realm of higher knowledge that awaits you. Don't expect this to be easy or to be fun. It's hard spiritual work.

But it is also enormously rewarding. For after you have completed this monumental undertaking, you will be an entirely new and different person. You will have undergone a true spiritual transformation and cleansing. *You can rest easily inside now knowing that you have done everything that you can from your side.* And everyone you have spoken with will know it deep inside, too, regardless of what they may say externally. Now you will be *clear,* at peace with everyone in your life, and you will be freed from the awful torment of submerged and repressed conflict that your previously embedded resentments were generating. Now you are ready to receive and *use* the powerful knowledge that awaits you in the remaining parables.

The parable of the two debtors illustrates the Law of Forgiveness. Simply stated it is this: Forgiveness is the first and most powerful spiritual necessity, and the more someone owes you, the more you need to forgive them.

THE STRONG MAN ARMED

The Law of Good

MATTHEW 12:29

He knew what they were thinking and said to them, "Every kingdom divided against itself is laid waste, and no city or house divided against itself will stand.

If Satan casts out Satan, he is divided against himself; how then will his kingdom stand?

If I cast out demons by Beelzebub, by whom do your own exorcists cast them out? Therefore they will be your judges.

But if it is by the Spirit of God that I cast out demons, then the kingdom of God has come to you.

Or how can one enter a strong man's house and plunder his property, without first tying up the strong man? Then indeed the house can be plundered."

ONE OF THE MOST CENTRAL of all the ideas in the New Metaphysic is that there is only one consciousness, one good in this universe—and that is God. There is no room anywhere within this all-pervading good for any notion of "evil," any organized conspiracy of malicious intent, no "devil." Although that may sound simple and benign, even naive, anyone who has tried to explain this idea to a person who *does* believe in the concept of evil will tell you that there is almost no other concept that will generate more resistance and dismay.

The concept of evil, the concept of the devil for some ideologies is a central theme and core belief. And it should be respected. There are many paths to God. A belief system with a devil can create a very useful universe for individuals on certain paths and certain levels of evolution. Avoidance of an eternal afterlife of torment with the "Prince of Darkness" and his ilk can be a powerful motivator to straighten up certain kinds of souls in a very efficient manner. It is therefore disrespectful to belittle the concept of Satan and does little to bring peace with our more conservative spiritual brothers and sisters. Let us not fall into a judgmental or superior state of mind. That is codependent and dysfunctional. Live and let live.

Many would argue that the idea that Jesus of Nazareth himself taught that there is no devil is absurd. Did the teacher not speak of this malignant ruler many times? Without a doubt, scripture may be interpreted, at one level, as supporting the view that Christ fully endorsed the prevailing, conservative idea of a vast and well-organized army of evil led by a highly intelligent and invincible leader, Satan.

But did he really? And, if he did not, where is the *evidence* of this position? The answer is that although he had to give the *appearance* of working with such established concepts for political reasons, deep down Jesus of Nazareth actually did *not* endorse the concept of evil. He showed this clearly in the parable of the strong man armed. To see how this is, we need to look much closer at the original text recounting the story.

Remember, the parables were delivered in a known chronological sequence. In the first parable, you learned how to drop a sizable portion of your personal, internal negativity by completing a systematic inventory and externalization of your resentments. So prepared with a cleaner slate and a humble mind, you are now led to the second initiation. This second lesson is designed to convey you further along your path by allowing you to release even more of your internal negativity.

In this second metaphysical rite of passage, you will be freed of a great and entirely unnecessary burden—another massive and destructive burden of *fear*. The type of fear addressed in the second parable is automatically generated day by day when a person lives within a belief system that endorses the concept of evil. And this fear silently and steadily accumulates. As this fear accumulates, it becomes so powerful within the psyche that inevitably a large part of a person's very *personality* is sculpted by it, either directly or indirectly.

In many religious traditions, vivid images and stories of Satan's insidious methods are inculcated in children at an early age. They are taught as toddlers to fear, taught as adolescents to fear, and taught as adults to fear. Moreover, they are taught that this fear is a *good* thing, a necessary thing, a protective thing. They are taught that fear of organized evil is normal. It can be a truly monumental task to free a mind so thoroughly indoctrinated at a deep, subconscious level. The problem of deprogramming such a fear-impregnated mind is compounded by the notion that one of Satan's oldest and most reliable "tricks" is to entice you to let your guard down by convincing you that he does not, in fact, exist and thus presents no threat. So, for some people, the very idea of getting rid of evil is evil itself.

It is no wonder that a teacher like Christ, who was considerably more enlightened than the culture moving around him, would want to let us know in a very subtle manner that there really is no such thing as evil. He couldn't come right out and say this. That would mark him as an agent of Satan immediately. But he had to tell us the truth nonetheless. He knew that for a soul to advance it *had* to conquer the grip of fear sinewed by the concept of evil.

Eventually every advancing soul needs to grow out of evil, out of fear. There is no other way. It was as true then as it is now. To explain this, the teacher resorted to his favorite mechanism to deliver controversial lessons, the parable. Let's take another look. As we will see, this parable explains that there actually is no devil, no evil. What it says is that a conspiracy of evil, an organized army of evil would, of necessity, be "divided against itself" and automatically self-destruct. This is why all the great evils have extinguished themselves over time.

Evil is thought to be a well-organized destructive force, a kind of massive *conspiracy* of "darkness" that systematically works to sabotage and degrade processes of goodness and light. The problem is, this is a pure oxymoron. It is like saying there is an ordered-disorder, a designed-chaos, a purpose behind that which destroys the purposeful.

The idea of evil is wholly obsolete in the New Metaphysic. In cutting-edge metaphysics, God is pure love, and God is *everything*— period. But this is not to say in any way that there are not unpleasant things to experience, destructive people to deal with, chaotic forces to overcome. What the New Metaphysic says is that something that *appears* evil is simply "disordered." That's all. There is no attitude, no *agenda* to the disorder. It has no personality and nothing organizes it into a coordinated army or force. The disorder is simply *entropy*—plain old impersonal, mechanical chaos.

What is entropy exactly? According to *The American Heritage Dictionary,* entropy is ". . . a tendency for all matter and energy in the universe to evolve toward a state of inert uniformity," or "The inevitable and steady deterioration of a system or society." For the scientist, entropy is the universal tendency of organized systems of energy and matter to automatically fall apart, erode, and disintegrate. We know from Newton's Laws of Thermodynamics that within a closed energy system, if more energy, more order is not continually added, things will automatically tend to become less and less ordered until they are perfectly and uniformly disordered.

For the metaphysician, entropy is similarly defined. But the force of entropy in the New Metaphysic is not seen as something "bad" or "evil," rather as a necessary and *useful* force intentionally built into the universe to keep it from becoming *stagnant*. This force is an important part of God's creative toolbox—something like an eraser. Without an eraser, an artist cannot reshape, improve, or redo any aspect of a design or composition. Each of us is a son or daughter of this creator and possesses his characteristics. As lesser but nonetheless powerful creators, entropy is an important tool in our creative armamentarium as well.

Think about it: Without some kind of force to stimulate disorganization, everything would swing too far to one end of the spectrum. Without entropy, everything would become more and more ordered until the universe and various worlds in it would steadily reach a state of *perfect* order. It would become like a crystal in which the component atoms are perfectly linked, each and every one, in a lattice of exquisite symmetry with no deviation anywhere.

What would a world, a universe of such perfect order be like? Not too exciting really. A world without entropy would inexorably reach a crystalline state—a frozen, motionless, lifeless state of affairs in which nothing new could ever again move, nothing ever again be created. A universe without entropy would be a stagnant, dead-end universe.

At this stage of your evolution, you have begun to suspect that you choose everything that you experience and that you have done so, in many or most cases, for good reasons—even though it can be difficult to see those reasons here in the material world with the veil drawn behind us. Some believe we even choose the very worlds we incarnate within and that we have complete free will in this choosing. If this is true it follows that all sentient creatures in our world chose to be here knowing full well in advance that they would encounter a variety of entropic processes during their stay here, including aging of the body, disease, financial difficulties, war, confused and malignant people, and so on.

That we will experience entropy in our lives is not a question. But the *ways* in which we will interact with entropy, the ways that we will choose to have it affect us, the ways that we will choose to *use* it to grow and evolve, are highly variable. We choose our relationships with entropy consciously, knowing full well what lessons we will learn and what evolutionary transformations we will accomplish as a result. There is no external devil or even a god to "blame." It's all our own choice. One of the greatest evolutionary leaps we can make as conscious beings is to accept this and take responsibility for it.

It would be naive, however, to believe that growing out of the need for evil is easy, and it would be wise to carefully examine some of the most prevalent and convincing arguments for the existence of evil. To begin with, one of the most articulate and reasonable objections to the idea of no evil centers variously on processes that occur within the very mind, and since the parables are presumably all about what happens within the self, we can use this example to study the objection in a particularly relevant manner

The objection centers around the fact that not only do certain people have very organized malignant personalities, everyone has at least part of their mind seemingly organized into malignant and destructive structures. Some people refer to this as their "dark side," which seems to qualify, in one sense, as a form of "evil." To deny that this part of one's self exists would seem to many to be just that, simple denial, a kind of Pollyanna naiveté. How are we to understand that these negative parts of ourselves are not conscious, not *organized,* and thus unworthy to be qualified as a type of "evil"?

To understand the answer to this very cogent line of questioning, we can use a simple analogy. Consider a plant. The seed of a plant contains exquisitely ordered information. When the seed germinates, this information begins to order the chaotically and randomly arranged molecules surrounding it. As this ordering process progresses, tissues are formed and a viable, living, reproducing organism creates itself. Molecules that are incorporated into the structure of the plant's cells become a part of the order. Molecules that remain outside the organism in the air or soil remain disordered. There is no personality or agenda within the disordered, external molecules that have not, as yet, been incorporated into the organism's ordered whole.

So it is with our personal selves. The parts of us that are in a higher state of love and light and goodness are the parts that have been incorporated into our higher, ordered, *real* selves. Everything else just remains a part of the entropy-disordered universe around us, the part that has not yet been incorporated into higher consciousness, not yet fully ordered. There is no "darkness" to the still disordered parts of ourselves and thus no "dark side"—just parts of our illusory personality that have not as yet been sufficiently integrated into our *real* Divine Selves. Instead of being "evil," these aspects of our personality are simply works in progress.

We choose to be here in this place, this world, this universe with its entropic processes. Moreover we *wanted* entropy, asked *specifically* for entropy to be here with us. Entropy, as it takes the form of challenge and hardship, makes us struggle. And struggle, like the energy required to work an exercise machine at the gym, makes us stronger—in many highly desirable ways.

We want our exercise; we want our entropy very badly. Just as we go to a lot of trouble to go to the gym and exercise so that we will have strong, beautiful, healthy bodies, we go to a lot of trouble to set up course work in the "gymnasium" of life that will strengthen, deepen, beautify, and *heal* our souls. We are, all in all, a very highly motivated group of souls that have congregated here. It is truly amazing, truly impressive that we contract to experience and overcome such difficult experiences through the lifetimes of our souls in order to strengthen ourselves and so contribute to the higher good, the larger plan.

Of course, we experience—as *apparent* parts of our self—confusion, depression, anxiety, aggression, and all sorts of other undesirable thought patterns. But these kinds of entropic processes do not work together to make up an organized "dark side." They are internal situations that allow us the opportunity to work the muscles of the soul. The pain we have within is the burr beneath the saddle that spurs us forward, stimulates us to think about things in new ways, stimulates us to create, encourages us to seek the light, and eventually makes us strong and whole. The pain can be used as an eraser that helps us delete and re-create the disordered parts of the self so that new and better ideas and attitudes may ultimately enter into our lives and integrate with our higher selves. This is the very process that produces saints and great teachers, such as the teller of the parables.

This is not to say that the *concept* of a dark side or evil can't be useful. There is no such thing as a zero, either, but the *concept* of a symbol for nothing is quite practical and enables mathematicians to do many useful and constructive things. Likewise, therapists can use the concept of a dark side to accomplish very practical therapeutic goals. And some souls can use the concept of evil, the concept of the devil to execute helpful and moral actions and avoid destructive courses of action. But like a zero, the dark side, the evil, doesn't really exist. The Law of Good is true, "It's all good. You are all good."

Ironically, one of the best things about the Law of Good is that even if it isn't true, it is still a great way to think about things. For even if there were a devil or "evil one," thinking about him, giving him any sort of mental energy, would only make him expand within your life. Almost every modern school of self-improvement and self-empowerment teaches that the only profitable and effective thought forms are positive thought forms. So, clearing yourself once and for all of any trace, any vestige of "evil" will go a long way toward the advancement of your spirituality and your overall effectiveness as a human being.

The parable concludes with the metaphor:

Or how can one enter a strong man's house and plunder his property, without first tying up the strong man? Then indeed the house can be plundered.

The ego is a powerful opponent, the "strong man" of the story. When it is "tied up" by understanding, by flooding it with the light of knowledge that it doesn't really exist, the house—the belief system within which it resides, from which it emanates—can also be conquered.

ACTIVATING PARABLE LESSON 2

1. To activate this evolutionary step it will be necessary to *change all of your attitudes about evil.* For some of you, this will be a difficult and lengthy task. Vestiges of this cancerous concept may have metasta-

sized and infiltrated your subconscious so deeply that it will take a lot of care and diligence to clear yourself. But this is a step that is absolutely essential if you are to be admitted to the knowledge of the mysteries that await you in subsequent parable lessons.

To begin clearing yourself of the subtle, subliminal ideas of evil that likely pollute your conscious and subconscious minds, start by making another inventory. Write out on paper every way in which the concept of evil was inculcated within you, beginning with your childhood. Like resentments, evil is conquered by first becoming fully *conscious* of the kinds of input that have gone into your mind. This inventory should be done in the same way as the resentment inventory. Use a separate page in your notebook to list each way that your mind was programmed to accept evil or one of its subtle subprograms. For example, you might have pages that include things like "My Sunday school program taught extensive lessons that included the 'devil' as a character. I watched movies X, Y, and Z about the devil or evil. I knew a person who thought they were possessed. I have had a convincing dream or vision in which I thought I perceived some type of dark or evil entity."

Next, on each page write out a brief answer to each of the following questions:

1. How has each input affected the way you *think* about the universe in general?
2. How does each input tend to affect the way you process new *information*?
3. How does each input tend to affect the way you analyze *events* both good and bad?
4. How does each input sometimes affect your moods and your emotional well-being?

5. How does each input affect your relationships with others?

6. How does each input affect the way you see God and the way you relate to God?

Write a paragraph or two about the ways the concept of evil has prevented you from *recognizing and taking responsibility for your contributions* to the difficult situations that have arisen in your life. Be sure to include how the concept of evil may have, in any way however subtle, kept you from reaching higher, from *believing* in yourself, from *trusting* in God, and from *accepting your own power to create a better world.*

The Unclean Spirit

Using Breath

MATTHEW 12:43—45

When an unclean spirit leaves a person, it wanders through waterless places in search of a resting place. When it doesn't find one, it then says, "I will return to the home I left." It then returns and finds it empty, swept, and refurbished. Next, it goes out and brings back with it seven other spirits more vile than itself, who enter and settle in there. So that person ends up worse off than when he or she started. That's how it will be for this perverse generation.

I THINK YOU WOULD agree that this parable is either very frightening or most curious and enigmatic. What precisely can the teacher be saying? The traditional *literal* interpretation of the parable is that the teacher was speaking historically and most likely referring to Israel. At that potential split point in the story of Judaism, Israel had a "decision" to make. It had a good chance to be God's holy people, if it was willing to make the extra effort to choose the high road—the more disciplined and more difficult road. On the surface, the parable seems to be saying that if the nation of Israel makes a decision to take the lower and easier fork in the road and turn away from God, it will end up in even worse shape than it was to begin with.

Traditionalists also have a *metaphorical* interpretation of the parable: that it is not enough for a person to be merely freed from the influence of Satan. Even *more* will be required of the newly freed soul, or matters will have the potential to regress and become worse than they were to begin with. Some conservative interpretations would even have it that the parable is referring literally to "possession" by "demons," that if a demon is "exorcised" it may return in certain cases and bring with it seven additional and more malignant entities.

But is this what the parable *really* says? To find out, let us look closely at the precise wording of the parable, beginning with one of the first terms used, "unclean spirit." The actual Greek word traditionally translated as "unclean" is *akatharios,* which is arguably best translated as "not-cleansed" or "impure." The word invariably translated as "spirit" is the Greek *pneuma,* which is found in scores of modern words, such as *pneumatic* and *pneumonia.* This important root, used widely throughout the natural sciences, is almost invariably translated as "*of or having to do with air or the breath.*" Which is the best translation? Let's look at what the dictionary in *Strong's Exhaustive Concordance* says exactly, and you can make up your own mind.

> *Pneuma.* From the root *pneu*—to *breathe* or to *blow*: a *current* of air, i.e. *breath (blast)* or a *breeze*; by analogy, or figuratively a *spirit,* i.e. (human) the rational *soul,* (by implication) *vital principle,* mental *disposition,* etc. or (superhuman) an angel, demon, or (divine) God, Christ's *spirit,* the Holy *Spirit;*—ghost, life, spirit (-ual, -ually), mind.

In a spirit of gentle teasing, it would be entirely fair to say that con-servatives and fundamentalists aren't the only ones who can use the lit-eral meaning of a word as its primary meaning in parable interpretation. We can do that just as well and with equal validity. The fact is that, in all the rest of our language, words with the root *pneuma* refer to breath, air, or a current of air. Of the twenty-nine words listed in the *American Heritage Dictionary* beginning with the root *pneuma*, not a single one has a meaning that refers to the spirit or soul. Therefore, it hardly seems un-reasonable to believe the teacher may well have been referring to *breath* as well—specifically *breath that has not yet been cleansed.*

This has profound implications. For by extension, he is also saying that breath that *has* been cleansed *is* Spirit—and carries with it all the power of Spirit. In other words, he is alluding to the fact that cleans-ing the breath is a way of magnifying Spirit, connecting to Spirit—a way of hooking up to the power station of Spirit and recharging one's entire bioenergetic body, one's entire life.

In effect, you are offered your own split point at this step—lesson number three in our sequence: At this point, you can choose to make a *decision* to believe that this third lesson will concern demons and the sequela of exorcism from them, or you can choose the other fork in the road. To take the other fork in the road you can make a conscious decision to believe that this lesson will concern the breath and its re-lation to spirit.

In making this decision, you are given some help via parable num-ber two, the previous lesson that tells us that there can be no evil be-cause "a kingdom divided against itself cannot stand." Therefore, you should already be leaning to the other side of the split point—toward an interpretation that rejects a focus on evil. For if there is no evil and no devil, it is highly unlikely that "unclean spirits" or demons exist, either. This discussion will therefore concentrates on a discussion of the spiritual significance of breath—specifically the *cleansing* of the breath.

This is a novel approach to the parable's interpretation and requires a bit of research to determine whether it is in any way reasonable. To begin with, we need to know if there is any evidence to believe that the teacher had some kind of training with breath and its "cleansing."

Jesus of Nazareth was the epitomy of a "mystic." We know this because a mystic is defined as "one who believes in or practices the religious mysteries" and because he told the disciples very directly that the entire parable sequence was all about the "mysteries." Because the Essenes and Kabbalists were the mystical arms of Judaism at the time, it therefore seems very difficult to imagine that he was not associated with these influences, as discussed in the introduction. And recall Edmond Bordeaux Szekely's statement:

> The essence of the Essenes teachings derived from sources as diverse as the Zend Avesta of Zarathustra, the Vedas and the Upanishads, the yoga systems of India, Buddhism, Freemasonry, Gnosticism, and the Kabbalah.

So, if Szekely is correct, and he was the single greatest authority on the Essenes, the Essenes had definite influences from the sciences of yoga and other Eastern belief systems. And yoga, via the practice of pranayam, obviously makes an entire science of the cleansing of the breath. The same is true of many other systems of meditation and certainly Buddhist meditation: The breath and its cleansing and regulation are critical tools for spiritual evolution in these venerable traditions. William James was even prompted to note in the first pages of his classic *The Varieties of Religious Experience* that in many such systems, outside the traditional Judeo-Christian realm, "*the foundation of all religious discipline consists in regulation of the inspiration and expiration.*"

So much for the Essenes and their Eastern influences. But what of Kabbalah? Without a doubt, Kabbalah is a school of spiritual evolution that has always advocated breathing exercises and meditation techniques that incorporate breath control as a tool for spiritual growth. Clearly, it is entirely reasonable to believe that the term "unclean spirit" may, in truth, refer to "breath which has not been purified." With that in mind, let us continue our examination of the parable.

What does the term "dry places" mean in the context of the parable? The term normally translated as "places" actually comes from the Greek work *topon*. The dictionary in *Strong's Exhaustive Concordance* tells us that *topon* can refer to more than a simple "place." Most interestingly, *topon* can also refer to a "condition or opportunity."

So, the term "dry places" could also refer to a "condition" that is dry or waterless, an "opportunity without sustenance, supply, or energy." A "dry place" is *potential* that has no energy, no fire, no conviction to actualize, grow, or sustain it. We are thus offered here a kind of "split point" in which a decision can be made to take a road of opportunity and potential that *has* sufficient spiritual energy, sufficient conviction to feed and sustain it, or a decision can be made to take the fork that leads to an opportunity that has *insufficient* conviction behind it.

The parable seems to indicate that if the decision—and it *is* a decision—is made to take the fork in the road that leads to a mind-set of opportunity *without* spiritual power, the person making the decision will find that the personal reality that then manifests will provide no "rest." Here the word usually translated as "rest" is the Greek *anapuasis,* which comes from the root word *anapauo,* which translates as "*to repose, refresh, or recreate.*" Ergo, the entire passage may reasonably be translated like this:

When a person is working with the cleansing of breath and the impure breath leaves the body, that person will become pure. This state of purity is a very powerful place, for it is a condition or place of great opportunity, a place of great potential. At this place of great potential— this great energy that is as yet unmanifest—a split point emerges. If one is not careful in this state of potential, there will be a tendency to choose the easy or lower path once again. And for many people this easier path will be the default mode. If we are not aware of this split point, we will be automatically inclined to take the path in which we lack conviction. If we do, we will not find the recreation and refreshment we are looking for.

But the wrong decision need not be made *if* there is sufficient vigilance and awareness. If a person has been thus *forewarned* of the impending pitfall, he will be led to another decision point. Here a person so cleansed by the breath must work deliberately at cultivating the belief, the conviction to create the new universe, the new personal reality. This will lead to a world, a personal reality, that offers "refreshment," a universe of recreation, satisfaction, relaxation, play, and *fun*. And is that not what you were looking for?

The parable continues by telling us that as we become purified and powerfully energized by the cleansing of the mind and body by using the breath correctly, we must be careful. If we fail to make a conscious decision to take the higher path, the path of strong conviction and belief, the negativity that has been removed will return. When this split point is chosen, it will lead first to a universe that is unsettling and very unrestful. But this progression of universes or personal realities will not stop here. Rather, the splitting of realities will continue such that there will be an amplification of the original level of negativity, and we will end up in a universe, a personal reality, that is much worse than the one in which we began.

And what is this negativity? What does it really look like in our lives? The negativity as always will manifest as ego, selfishness, pride, and greed. If these qualities of the self are removed through the use of breathing techniques and associated meditative processes, the universe that will result is one with a lot of play and recreation and energizing refreshment. But these qualities may easily return if the person now gloats over his purity, becomes selfish in the use of the powerful energies that are generated.

But does any of this make any sense? Do techniques designed to cleanse the breath, loosely categorized in Hinduism as pranayam, really generate powerful energies, energies that could actually lead to a dangerous devolution if handled incorrectly? Most certainly so. Any expert on yoga will tell you that the practice of pranayam is one of the most reliable ways known to develop powers or "siddhis," as such powers are technically referred to. "Kriyas," which are a combination of meditation techniques, posture, and pranayam—along with other elements—have been used for millennia by adepts to develop extraordinary powers. These can include intuitive or psychic powers, the power to heal disease, and the power to manifest material supply. And experts agree that developing such powers without maintaining a sense of humility and connectedness to spirit can lead to irresponsible use of the powers. This, in turn, can easily lead to various states of distress and confusion, or even more serious sequela. If a practitioner of pranayam fails to remain highly conscious of where her powers are coming from, which is God and not the efforts of the self, the powers that are generated lead to powerfully damaging consequences, the "seven other spirits more vile than itself" the parable references.

ACTIVATING PARABLE LESSON 3

1. There are many forms of pranayam, breath control, and breathing exercises. It is beyond the scope of this book to recommend any particular form. What is important is that you *take the responsibility to do what you can to learn an exercise that will cleanse the breath* in an effective way, in a way that works for you.

   With that said, beginners may want to start with the following classic breath-cleansing exercise. To begin, sit comfortably. If you are familiar with cross-legged yoga-style sitting poses, by all means use one of these. If you are uncomfortable with this kind of pose or have health problems that make it difficult to sit in this manner, sit in a comfortable chair.

   Take a deep breath and completely expel it. The emphasis is on the word "completely." Push all the breath out of the lungs, and then, a little extra until *all* the breath is exhaled. Next, take four breaths in. It will take a little bit of practice, but you will quickly be able to divide your inhalations so that *four approximately equal breaths* take you from a state of completely empty exhalation to a state of completely full inhalation.

   After you have completed the final, fourth inhalation and your lungs are 100 percent full, hold your breath for a count of four. All of this is done rhythmically. The four inhalations are equal and like the four equal beats of a measure of music. The four counts of inhalation continue the same rhythm, except that the four inhaled "beats" are silent.

   Finally, after the fourth count of the "hold," exhale in four equal counts. These four equal counts will take you from a state of complete inhalation back to a state of complete, 100 percent exhalation. When the fourth exhalation is completed and the lungs are completely empty, begin the cycle again by inhaling four equal breaths.

When you first begin, each of the four "counts" or "beats" will be about half a second. As the minutes go by, gradually lengthen the counts until they are about a second each in length, then two seconds, three, and so on. You will be surprised to find how far you can gradually lengthen each cycle. As you lengthen the breath cycles, you will gradually calm the mind, your blood will become less acidic, and you will achieve a state of peacefulness and well-being.

2. By all means, if possible, go to a class that is specifically designed to teach pranayam. Simple yoga, such as hatha yoga, which concentrates on postures, is an excellent practice, but it alone will not suffice if you want to truly activate this parable lesson. Look for a teacher who is knowledgeable and experienced specifically in breath control. Kundalini yoga is arguably the best of all breath-cleansing systems.

3. Continue your practice, doing at least a little breath cleansing every day. Expand your practice, learning more techniques and staying with the ones that really work for you. Add this to your daily practice of meditation by performing the breathing exercise prior to meditating. The depth and clarity of your meditation will improve noticeably.

4. Follow the advice of the parable. As you are practicing your breath-cleansing exercises, negative and irrelevant thought forms will continually arise. Don't worry. This happens for all practition-

ers at all levels and is entirely normal. But it is very important to know precisely what to do with these thought forms. Under no circumstances should you try to deliberately suppress them, become irritated or disturbed by them, or in any way give them any energy at all. Attempting to intentionally "remove" a negative thought form is a way of focusing upon it. Therefore, this will only cause the thought form to multiply in consciousness due to the law "*What you focus on expands.*"

If you give undesirable thought forms any attention at all, you will encourage seven others, even more disruptive, to enter back in. The best thing to do is to simply note that a thought form has arisen and then immediately turn your attention back to your breathing. The breathing is a physical process and, as such, is an excellent and effective target for your mind to focus upon.

Note: Parable number four is dealt with in chapters one and two.

THE TARES AND THE WHEAT

Managing the Subconscious Mind

MATTHEW 13:24–30, SHORE OF GALILEE

Another parable put he forth unto them, saying, The Kingdom of Heaven is likened unto a man which sowed good seed in his field:

But while men slept, his enemy came and sowed tares among the wheat, and went his way.

But when the blade was sprung up, and brought forth fruit, then appeared the tares also.

So the servants of the householder came and said unto him, Sir, didst not thou sow good seed in thy field? from whence then hath it tares?

He said unto them, An enemy hath done this. The servants said unto him,

Wilt thou then that we go and gather them up?

But he said, Nay; lest while ye gather up the tares, ye root up also the wheat with them.

Let both grow together until the harvest: and in the time of harvest I will say to the reapers, Gather ye together first the tares, and bind them in bundles to burn them: but gather the wheat into my barn.

Chaos: The disordered state of unformed matter and infinite space supposed in some cosmogonic views to have existed before the ordered universe. *Physics.* The aperiodic, unpredictable behavior arising in a system extremely sensitive to variations in initial conditions and exhibited by phenomena such as turbulent flow. (THE AMERICAN HERITAGE DICTIONARY)

SOMETIMES PEOPLE using the New Metaphysic to guide and quicken their personal evolution develop a Pollyanna or "pink cloud" mind-set with regard to their belief in the theory of self-created reality. It can be tempting to blindly accept the idea that our positive intentions shape the fabric of reality in a direct and infallible manner. How easy it is to conveniently forget the fact that, in reality, this belief system contains a number of tricky problems and paradoxes. Many authorities gloss over these thorny issues and present a convincing case that self-created reality is an absolute—something that should never be questioned by a faithful believer. But we have evolved in our understanding to the point where we face these paradoxes and problems head-on like adults and actually solve them. The parable of the tares does just that.

A question often asked by people working with the use of thought forms to create better personal realities, better universes, is this: Why is it that I can generate and sustain very organized, positive thoughts and feelings about all kinds of things only to find that most of my life remains the same? Try as I might, some complain, many of my days unfold as a random soup of unremarkable events, a bland slurry of coincidences and happenstance. Often it seems that we sow very specific and constructive thought forms, yet continue to reap a world of insipid chaos.

To make matters worse, the chaos in our lives is often muddied to the extent that it is next to impossible to work *backward* and link a specific element of the chaos with a specific thought form that led to its creation. Because we can't seem to work backward reliably, we can't even pin down the thought forms that produced the chaos. The parable of the tares explains how this happens and what to do about it. Let's take a closer look.

The first sentence of the parable says that the Kingdom of Heaven is likened unto a man who sows seed, as was the case of the parable of the sower. In this parable, the man sows wheat seeds. The sower represents a person who has implanted into the fabric of the universe positive thought forms in an organized and disciplined manner. In the parable, this man goes to sleep, and while he is asleep, his "enemy" comes. Unbeknownst to the sower, this enemy goes over the freshly sown field and sows "tares," or weed seeds, into the soil. When the crop appears and begins to grow into recognizable plants, the wheat seedlings are choked by a mass of weeds that spring up around them everywhere.

The man's servants wonder what has gone wrong. They go to the man and ask him if he in fact sowed good wheat seeds. They want to know why there are so many unexpected weeds growing up. The man tells them that it would appear that his enemy came and sowed weed seeds in the field, and that this must be the cause of the problem. The servants then ask the man if he would like them to go out into the fields and gather up the weeds. But he tells them not to handle the problem in this manner, that if they gather up the weeds, they will also pull out the wheat seedlings and terminate their growth. He has a better idea. He tells the servants to let both wheat and tares grow to maturity.

Then, only when the plants are harvested, will the winnowing process occur. Only then will the wheat be separated from the tares, the tares bundled together and then burned.

The traditional interpretation of this parable is very straightforward. The sower is God. The wheat seeds and wheat plants are good souls, those who have done what has been prescribed to enter heaven at the end of the world. The tares are evil souls. The field is the world. Here in this world we will see many good people, but we will also see many "evil" people, people who have not taken the prescribed steps to make one eligible for heaven in the afterlife. These undesirable people, or "weeds," make it difficult for good people to live and function, and the fact that they are present and apparently prospering confuses the good people. God allows both good and bad to coexist here in the material life of this world. However, at the day of reckoning, the good souls are carefully and efficiently separated from the evil souls. The good souls go on to heaven—the barn in the story—and the evil souls are burned in hell.

However, after studying the third and fourth parables, we know this interpretation cannot be correct because we have already been told that there is no devil in parable three. We also know that the parables are all about things that happen within the self, they are all about *you*. Therefore, we know from the parable of the sower that the sower is *you,* and the seeds that are sown are your thought forms, your dreams, your aspirations, your fears, your ambitions, your loves, and your hatreds fed into the fertile "field" of a universe that responds inexorably to thought, to consciousness. Let's take a close look at what happens in the parable of the tares when we shift to this deeper level of interpretation.

We find a man who is sowing good seeds, the seeds of a very useful and sustaining crop of wheat. The wheat seeds represent your very best and most magnanimous thought forms, thought forms that are programmed to manifest love, beauty, fun, joy, pleasure, and peace. You sow these thought forms consciously and deliberately during your waking hours.

But at night you go to sleep. And what happens during sleep? As sleep overcomes you, control over your consciousness weakens and weakens and finally dissolves as you descend into light, and then heavy, slumber. In slumber, there is no overriding conscious observer who can monitor and control thought forms. Consequently, the vast libraries of thought forms, both ancient and new, that fill the massive memory banks of your subconscious spew out images and sequences in an uncontrolled and relatively chaotic manner. This is how dreams are formed.

This is a problem. For if we are interpreting the parable correctly, the teacher is telling us that these dream thought forms, and the unmonitored and unfiltered thought forms of the subconscious in general, are also viable seeds. He is telling us that these unmonitored seeds germinate within our personal realities just as well as our high, intentional thought forms. This will be especially true if the preparatory *clearing* processes directed by parables one and two have not been properly completed.

Now, anyone who has ever tried to circumvent this problem by controlling the content of their dreams knows that it is a very nearly impossible task. Additionally, anyone who has ever attempted, either alone or in therapy, to completely rid their subconscious of undesirable thought forms knows that this is an impossible task as well. Like a field with millions of seedlings, our subconscious is packed with millions upon millions of memories and impressions and ideas. Trying to go through this field of the subconscious in an attempt to identify and destroy only the undesirable thought forms is futile.

This is why the teacher told the servants not to attempt to weed out the tare seedlings from the desirable wheat seedlings. In the first place, it can't be done. And in the second place, it would waste a lot of time and effort and cause unnecessary disruption to desirable thought forms germinating in the subconscious. If we try to weed out the negative thought forms we are only focusing upon them. And what we focus on expands. We talked about this in parable lesson number three.

Here is what the teacher is suggesting we do about the situation: He tells us not to make any attempt to tamper with the germinating undesirable thoughts. He tells us to work with our "servants," which are our innate powers of creation, our genetically ingrained abilities of discrimination that "serve" us. These innate powers, with which we have all been generously gifted, will spring to work automatically and with flawless precision *if we will only turn the task completely over to them.*

We are told to "wait until the harvest." This is somewhat surprising but does, in fact, appear to be the message the teacher is trying to convey. He is telling us to go ahead and let the undesirable thought forms, which are springing up constantly around us, germinate and manifest as reality. He tells us *not to fight them.* He is telling us this not because he thinks it is a good thing that our "weed" seeds germinate but because, like the sower in the story, we have no choice. We cannot in any effective way separate desirable from undesirable thought forms, at least while they are germinating and growing within the subconscious mind. Apparently, according to the teacher, things just don't work that way. Once undesirable thought forms have been sown by the subconscious it is too late. They are going to germinate, they are going to manifest within our realities, and we might as well get used to the fact. Giving the situation more energy by trying in vain to separate the desirable thought forms from the undesirable will disrupt the entire process and adversely affect the germination of positive thought forms.

However, he tells us that we can do *something.* Once the thought forms have finally manifested, we can now clearly identify them as undesirable and are now in a position to deal with them. Only now are we to gather them up and separate them. And what are we to do when this has been completed? According to the teacher, we are to turn them over to Divine Intelligence. He states that at this point, God will help us personally. *If we let go and turn the undesirable manifestations over to God, he will help us neutralize them so that they cease to be a problem.*

ACTIVATING PARABLE LESSON 5

1. Begin now to take a completely different attitude about the negative thought forms that arise within your mind. Doubts, fears, distrust, suspicion, misgivings, apprehensions—all of these will be arising from your subconscious mind in a regular and reliable way. Don't waste any time or energy fretting over these inevitable thought seeds. That will only give them more fertilizer, more energy to grow. And don't waste time trying to suppress them or separate them from desirable thought seeds deeply embedded within the subconscious.

2. Follow the parable's advice and just let them go; don't try to do anything to "fight" them. Instead, as the farmer turned the task of burning the tares over to his servants, turn your own undesirable thoughts completely over to God, to your higher consciousness, to your angels or spiritual guides if you are in contact with them, and know, *trust,* that they will be neutralized effectively by Divine Intelligence.

   Your attitude of trust, your conviction that God and his angels can and will help you, will make it so and you will be able to manage your subconscious mind effectively in this way.

3. The beauty of the mind is that it can be "programmed" to do amazing and surprising things. To further activate this parable, try the following thought exercise. Realize that your mind is very much like a computer. Using you positive personal intent, imagine that you are setting up a kind of "program" within yourself. Design this program such that it will automatically neutralize any undesirable thought form. You might even imagine that you have a kind of "recycle bin" within the computer of your mind. As soon as you become conscious of a negative thought, simply "place" this thought into the recycle bin and know that God will dispose of it properly. Then, just forget about it and go on about your business of generating positive intentions. A negative "seed" handled in this manner will now be deactivated. Knowing, *trusting* that the thought will be taken care of in this way will *automatically activate* this helpful program and it will be so.

———— ✧ ————

THE MUSTARD SEED

The Law of Organic Growth

MATTHEW 13:31,32, SHORE OF GALILEE

Another parable put he forth unto them, saying, The Kingdom of Heaven is like to a grain of mustard seed, which a man took, and sowed in his field:

Which indeed is the least of all seeds: but when it is grown, it is the greatest among herbs, and becometh a tree, so that the birds of the air come and lodge in the branches thereof.

The great principle or beginning, heaven,
is infused into man the microcosm,
who reflects the star-like natures and thus,
as the smallest part and end of the work of Creation,
contains the whole. (C. J. JUNG)

———

HAT A SIMPLE and straightforward analogy: The kingdom is like a seed growing into a tree. On the surface, the parable seems to be talking about the small and humble origins of what will become a great church, a great society of human beings growing out of the teachings of this great man. In this sense, Jesus is the mustard seed.

But going deeper, we find some interesting adjuncts to this idea. If Jesus, as the son of God, is a kind of seed, this suggests that God, as the Father, is the sower of the seed. And with God's infinite knowledge and infinite wisdom, he can compute precisely, far in advance, the effects of any change he makes in the cause-and-effect milieu that defined humanity at that point in time. Within his son, this "seed" of good, he has genetically imbued, if you will, powerful organizational properties such that the "tree" growing from this seed becomes an organizational force imparting order to the entire world. This is a seed that will grow and grow for many centuries, gaining momentum, blossoming again and again even to this day.

Traditionally thought to represent Jesus, and his body as the Church, the growing mustard seed actually represents something even larger. The seed represents the highest and most powerful of thought forms—love, the *logos* or original thought form, God, from which Christ and the world itself sprang forth. In this sense, Christianity, which grows from this seed, becomes the "largest tree."

But there is so much more to the parable.

In the parable of the mustard seed, the Kingdom of Heaven, the conscious universe, God, is likened to a seed, a seed that germinates and grows into a massive tree. This is a deceptively simple analogy. For although the simile is direct, it contains a much greater amount of information than we might expect. This information has enormous practical value. It can tell us something about how to live, and it can tell us something about the nature of the quantum universe.

To see how this is so, we first have to remember what a seed really is. This was discussed when we talked about the seeds in the parable of the sower. For if Jesus Christ really was the man we believe he was, he surely would have known a great deal about the nature of life and living things—not with the rudimentary detail we would normally attribute to a simple carpenter living in ancient times, but with insight similar to that of a modern scientist. In fact, there is no convincing reason to believe the knowledge of *any* truly enlightened person with *full access* to Divine Intelligence—which includes complete knowledge of the processes of life or biology and cosmology or astrophysics—could not in truth *exceed* that of our contemporary systems of knowledge. Let us not sell the great teacher short, but rather elevate him to his deserved position as a man of profound intelligence.

A seed is a package of *information*. This information is contained in genetic nucleotide sequences of spectacular complexity. This information is capable of directing the construction of enormous and highly complex organic molecules like proteins and enzymes. Such genetic information can further coordinate the intricate and convoluted series of chemical reactions that bind trillions of atoms and molecules into the large biochemical structures that form cell walls, cellular organelles, cells, tissues, organs, and finally entire organisms.

In essence, a seed is a package of intelligence that can organize randomly distributed atomic and molecular structures in the soil and the air into living organisms. This is not only a form of intelligence but an intelligence so profound and precise that it boggles the mind. Even the intelligence and precision of the most highly trained scientists, using the most sophisticated and advanced laboratory equipment known, are *crude* in comparison to the stunning sophistication and complexity of the processes that occur at the biomolecular levels of a germinating seed.

As the plant continues to grow and to organize and integrate the raw materials around it, a pattern of development begins to emerge. This pattern of systematic organization and integration is known as "organic" growth. All living organisms share the basic characteristics of this pattern. And it is apparent from the direct analogy made within the parable that the growth of the *universe,* the "kingdom," follows this pattern as well.

Surely there can be no doubt at this point in our study that the teacher was a believer in the venerable axiom "*As above, so below.*" This parable is such a direct and unambiguous expression of this principle that there seems little if any equivocation remaining to confuse the issue: The Kingdom, *above,* operates like a tree, *below.* Because this parable is, in essence, an authoritative and definitive expression of the Hermetic Axiom, it is essential for the student of the parables to be very clear on the basic characteristics of organic growth, the characteristics of life itself. What the teacher is saying in this parable is that the processes that characterize a living and growing organism such as a tree also apply to the universe, with all its quantum complexity and mystery, and to our day-to-day lives as well.

THE CHARACTERISTICS OF LIFE

What exactly are the characteristics of life, of organic growth? There is a certain degree of disagreement on this matter among scientists, but most would probably concur on the following basic points:

1. *Cells.* All living things are comprised of one or more cells. Different types of cells have different "jobs" within the organism. Each life form begins from one cell, which then splits. These child cells split again, and their progeny split again.

2. *Organization.* Complex organizational patterns are found in all living organisms. Cells arrange themselves on very small levels, grouping like cells together into microstructures and tissues.

3. *Energy Use.* All organisms use energy. The sum of the chemical energy they use is called "metabolism." This energy is used to carry out everything organisms do during their life span.

4. *Homeostasis.* All organisms have stable internal conditions that must be maintained in order to remain alive. These include temperature, water content, heartbeat, and other such things. For example, if the organism becomes too cold, it has to take measures to heat itself up either by going somewhere where there is more external heat or by increasing metabolic processes that generate more internal heat.

5. *Response.* All living organisms respond in some way to stimuli in their environments.

6. *Heredity.* All living organisms inherit traits from the parent organisms that created them.

7. *Growth.* All living organisms grow, at least in their developmental stages. We have already discussed the basics of how this occurs. Genetic information tells the developing organism how to assimilate

or take in external molecules and materials, and how to integrate them into the existing structures such that the organism becomes larger and more complex.

As this process transpires, each individual cell within the organism splits into two new cells in a process known as *cell division*. Over and over the splitting occurs until there are millions, billions, and even trillions of cells composing the tissues of the organism. After the splitting process has been completed, a human body at maturity has approximately 100 trillion cells.

In the case of a tree such as a mustard tree, "parent" cells split into new "child" cells over and over until growing points at the tips of roots below the ground and growing points at the tips of branches aboveground branch or split at the macroscopic level. In other words, we see the Hermetic Axiom at work even within the plant itself. Cells split into two new cells at the microscopic level, and growing points at the macroscopic level, called "meristems," split into two new growing points.

8. *Reproduction.* At the microscopic level, individual cells split into two new cells as development occurs, but this process of splitting takes place at an even higher level in reproduction. Here the entire parent organism may, in effect, "split" such that an entirely new "child" organism is formed.

As above, so below, and as below, so above. The characteristics of life demonstrated by a growing mustard tree are all present in one way or another in the universe itself. The universe is comprised of many kinds of cells. Subatomic particles, atoms, molecules, organisms, stars, and galaxies are all types of "cells," and they all exhibit various kinds of *organization*. The universe *generates and uses energy* at all levels and has elaborate processes of *homeostasis* that keep things in balance.

For example, *entropy* is one of these homeostatic forces. When things become too ordered, entropy brings things back into balance by stimulating disorder. Gravity, electromagnetism, and other forces also contribute to states of stability and balance in the big picture. Every-thing in the universe *responds* to everything else. For example, a star "responds" to an adjacent star when their gravity fields *pull* each star slightly closer together. Subatomic particles "respond" to one another by attracting and repelling each other and by forming and breaking chemical bonds.

As for *heredity, growth, and reproduction,* these are most elegantly il-lustrated by the splitting of universes as described in astrophysics and quantum physics. Our universe is expanding in every direction and clearly exhibits *growth.* When a universe splits off, a child universe is in effect *reproducing* and the child universe demonstrates the charac-teristic of *heredity* in that it shares many identical features with its par-ent. In fact, everything in the child universe may be identical with the parent universe except, say, the position of a pencil on your desk—if you have made a decision to move it slightly.

THE RADIAL UNIVERSE

We know now that there are an infinite number of universes and that everything that can be possible *becomes* possible somewhere in some universe. We also know that each of these infinite possible universes splits into two additional "child" universes every time a conscious be-ing in one of those universes makes a conscious decision.

We also know now that after a universe splits, each of its "child" universes also reproduces or splits into four "grandchild" universes. As it so proceeds, the progression of universes looks exactly like a family tree, which in turn looks just like the branches of a real tree. In fact, in physics books that discuss the branching of universes, diagrams of the sequential splitting process usually look just like a small tree. The tree begins with a thick trunk, which splits into two main branches and then splits again and again until tiny twigs remain at the tops of the branches.

When Jesus told us that the kingdom was like a seed growing into a mustard tree, he was trying to tell us about this progression of universes. But he did not have the kind of words or mathematics that would allow him to tell us directly what he was perceiving. Besides, the knowledge of how universes were created through decisive thought forms was a deep secret—and very controversial within his traditional religious society. It was one of the true "mysteries" then, just as it is now. Even today, cutting-edge scientists refer to the splitting of universes as one of the great "quantum mysteries." And so, the teacher resorted to his favorite method for teaching secret or controversial lessons, the parable.

Now, however convenient the image of the mustard tree is to showing the lineage, the progression of universes, it is not exactly accurate. Actually a tree would only show us *part* of the progression process as it grows from the ground upward. The progression of universes is actually not quite as linear as the *upward* growth of a tree. Instead, the progression is *radial*. What this means is that there is a kind of blossoming explosion of universes that grows outward in *every* conceivable direction.

To visualize this, it would be best to use the image of an exploding firework. Imagine a rocket exploding in the night sky. From a central point, colored balls of fire should propel outward in every direction. As they shoot away from the center, each of the colored balls may split into two different colored balls, and those into yet more of yet different colors. This is how the progression of universes would best be visualized by three-dimensional beings in a three-dimensional world such as ours. Thus, every single universe that exists now could be traced backward through its branchings to a single unified point. This would be referred to as the *logos* by Western theologians: *John 1:1*—And in the beginning was the *logos* (word).

But the truth is that the sum total of all the universes that exist does not have their existence within a three-dimensional world like a tree. There are actually an *infinite* number of dimensions that enclose the sum total of all universes. We do not have the neural hardwiring to imagine such a state, at least in normal states of consciousness. However, mystics of all persuasions over the millennia have reported visions of this great universe of universes, or "multiverse," to use modern physics terminology. Granted, they invariably describe these visions as ineffable or beyond words and cannot communicate the substance of the vision, but they do nonetheless have common elements in their descriptions. The teacher was doing the best he could considering the relatively primitive time and culture of those he was addressing and the linguistic elements he had to work with.

THE NEUROANATOMY OF GOD

The above image of a firework exploding—splitting sequentially outward in a radial pattern—is neat and tidy and easily visualized. However, to be truly accurate we have to add yet another element to the picture in order to understand the true complexity of the sum total of all universes—the so-called "multiverse." This image is similar to a human brain and is an enhancement to the mustard tree analogy that will bring us more up to date.

In a human brain, there are ten billion brain cells. Each of these brain cells has a main cell body. Extending from this cell body is a network of arms, arms that branch like a tree again and again and again. A single brain cell or neuron may have several hundred final branch points.

Every individual brain cell in a brain communicates with other brain cells. A single brain cell and its two hundred branches may have connections or synapses with hundreds of branches from hundreds of other brain cells. The brain cells are *not* alone and isolated. And that is what the image of a radially expanding firework explosion implies— that the universes at the ends of each branching sequence are isolated and independent. But the infinite universes of the mulitverse are not independent. They are thought to communicate with each other via complex connections—black holes, "wormholes," and certain kinds of atomic and subatomic interactions. A single universe may thus "communicate" with many other universes, influencing the others and being influenced by them, just as neurons within a brain. Quantum physicists, particle physicists, and astrophysicists are working out the details of how universes communicate with one another and affect one another, but the subject is in its infancy. Some think that vast numbers of parallel universes exist directly around us, overlapping one another in fantastically complex ways, and thus sharing many features.

The resulting network of universes is like a human brain in another respect: It is *conscious.* So conscious that we cannot conceive of it. For the consciousness that lives in the "brain" formed by the radial multiverse and all of its complex inter-universal connections is Divine Intelligence. Now we can get a somewhat better grasp of what the teacher meant when he said that the mature tree that had started with a single seed was the "greatest of all."

ACTIVATING PARABLE LESSON 6

1. As is the case with many of the parables, this lesson is about cultivating a state of consciousness, a "mind-set" that will lead to higher states of awareness—and ultimately to more refined and effective decisions and actions.

   Find a particularly large and healthy tree, one that is mature and very well developed. Then set aside some high-quality time when you are well rested and in good spirits. Sit near the tree and really look at it. Study the way it grows, noting carefully how the roots descend into the ground around the base. Contemplate the massive trunk and how hundreds of thousands of "pipelines" within the trunk are delivering water and nutrients upward into the branches. Note how the trunk splits, then splits again and again and again, following the splits one by one until they terminate in tiny twigs and leaves at the very ends. Think about how even these twigs are in the process of splitting and how they, too, will in time become larger branches. *Know* that even within the tinest leaves at the tree's growing tips, microstructures and cells, even subcellular structures, are dividing and splitting and growing—massive, complex, organic molecules bonding and unbonding thousands of times in a matter of nanoseconds in the cells of the growing tips. You will use the images you are storing away later when you meditate on the parable's real lessons.

2. Now you are ready to meditate on the parable's lessons. Again, when you are rested and able to concentrate, sit down in a quiet

place where you will not be disturbed and use the images of the growing, living, branching tree to understand your life. See in your mind's eye how your own life is like the tree, how it grows and expands in the same way. *Know that every one of your decisions is a split point, a branch point that births an entirely new world, a world of your own choosing.*

Realize at a deep conscious level that your own life is every bit as magnificent, every bit as big as the tree you studied. *Claim your part in the creation process* and resolve to take full responsibility for the decisions you are making as your life and the universes it grows within continue to expand and develop in miraculous ways.

Above all, realize that you are a cell in the whole, and that every thought you think, every decision you make, every choice and intention you exercise, will ultimately manifest and take form as an integrated and *important* contribution to the living, organic tree of life that is God.

———— ⟋⟍ ————

THE SEED GROWING SECRETLY

The Subconscious Mind

MARK 4:26—29

And he said unto them, Take heed what ye hear: with what measure ye mete, it shall be measured to you: and unto you that hear shall more be given.

From him shall be taken even that which he hath.

And he said, So is the kingdom of God, as if a man should cast seed into the ground;

And should sleep, and rise night and day, and the seed should spring and grow up, he knoweth not how.

For the earth bringeth forth fruit of herself; first the blade, then the ear, after that the full corn in the ear.

But when the fruit is brought forth, immediately he putteth in the sickle, because the harvest is come.

One of the most poetic of the parables in its traditional translation, the parable of the seed growing secretly is fascinating to decipher. The process begins with the first lines.

And he said unto them, Take heed what ye hear: with what measure
ye mete, it shall be measured to you: and unto you that hear shall more
be given.

From him shall be taken even that which he hath.

The first statement, "Take heed what you hear," is normally thought
to be a statement that prefaces the parable, a way of saying, "Listen
carefully." However, the deeper level of meaning takes a wider view of
the word "hear." The Greek word is *akouo.* Here is what *Strong's Ex-*
haustive Concordance has to say about it:

> *Akouo,* a primary verb; to *hear* (in various senses) . . . come (to the
> ears), be noised, be reported, understand.

At the deeper level of interpretation, he is telling us to be very
careful what we hear internally, what we *understand—*in *various senses.*
It is common knowledge in the New Metaphysic that real visualization employs all senses. The first sentence of the parable advises us to
exercise extreme care in what we are seeing, hearing, touching, tasting,
and smelling as we create our new world, our new personal reality.
For if all other conditions for conscious creation are met, the new
world *will* manifest. The responsibility is thus rather awesome, even,
perhaps, foreboding. For as flawed individuals we will be sure to create flawed worlds. It's just the way things are. In many ways we don't
really know what we are doing. We have so little knowledge of and
control over the thought forms in our conscious and subconscious
minds. And in spite of this, our subsconcious minds are nonetheless
sowing viable, sprouting seeds—as we know from the parable of the
tares—and these seeds are germinating and bearing fruit, constantly all

around us, weaving through the loom of creation the web of circumstances we find ourselves living within.

The parable of the seed growing secretly illustrates the power of the subconscious mind to germinate, manifest thought "seeds"— automatically and unfailingly. The seed cast into the ground is cast into a place where it can no longer be seen, where its processes can no longer be observed, where it will appear—from the surface—as though nothing is happening. The ground obviously symbolizes the part of the mind that is below consciousness, in the subconscious mind where the germination of thought forms begins. It is where both your good seeds and your weed seeds take on life and sprout into manifestation. The subconscious mind can imbue your thought forms with living energy because it ultimately merges in its murky depths with the Collective Unconscious of mankind and finally with the Infinite Intelligence, the Infinite Energy and Supply, of God.

When the man in the parable sleeps, he is immersed completely in the subconscious mind. It is here in this vast sea of consciousness that includes his deepest and most ancient memories, the consciousness of humanity *and* the consciousness of God, that the seed springs up and grows "*he knoweth not how.*"

This is a statement of enormous significance and is perfectly in alignment with what all modern experts on the subconscious mind teach. What this last statement means is that we cannot *understand* the mechanism by which thoughts manifest through the subconscious. Furthermore, we don't *need* to understand the mechanism. We just need to be aware of the fact that they *do* manifest and that this automatic germination and growth of thought forms is a property of the universe, part of the personality of God, as it were. This multiverse that exists all around us, that is the embodiment of God conscious ness, automatically germinates thoughts. We can use this property to our advantage if we are fully aware of it and honor the accuracy of its reflections.

UNDERSTANDING THE SUBCONSCIOUS MIND

In the later part of the nineteenth century a man by the name of Sigmund Freud, who was aspiring to be a medical doctor, published his first scientific paper in Vienna—a study of the most ancient and most primitive aspect of the nervous system, the spinal cord. He became a professor of neuropathology and began studying with the famous neurologist J. M. Charcot in Paris. He quickly developed a special interest in the study and treatment of illnesses that appeared to have no physical causes, illnesses now referred to as psychosomatic disorders or somatization disorders. He became convinced that these were the result of experiences, often of a sexual nature, that occurred as far back as childhood and even infancy, when the roots of memory take form in the empty libraries of the nervous system. These memories were not directly accessible, according to Freud, but had, nonetheless, enormous influence on personality and behavior. He called the unconscious reservoir of deeply embedded memories and primitive instincts the "id."

Freud's most famous protégé, Carl Jung, further developed the idea of an unconscious mind through his study of myths, legends, and fairy tales, which he believed illustrated unconscious mental processes common to entire cultures or societies. Jung believed that not only did human beings have individual unconscious minds, but that a larger unconscious mind exisited that held these larger societal memories, dreams, and stories, a mind he called the "collective unconscious." According to Jung, individual subconscious minds had an intricate and ongoing relationship with the collective unconscious and merged seamlessly with it in certain instances.

This is an absolutely fascinating and critical idea for the student of the parables as we will see, in due course. What it means is that the mind of an individual does not end with its own nervous system. Our mind, our *whole* mind, does not end with our brain. This idea is wholly obsolete in the New Metaphysic. Certainly neurotransmitters within our own brain allow our neurons to communicate with one another and hold our personal physical memories of this life. But we have additional external "neurotransmitters," or "messengers," if you will, that allow us to communicate in fabulously intricate ways with the collective unconscious around us. These messengers are the words we speak, the stories we tell that implant powerful hopes and fears and beliefs deep within us, the traditions that shape our behaviors and the thoughts that surround them. They are the viruses that pass between us, the telephone signals that deliver information to our ears, the electronic waves that carry radio and TV signals, the optical impulses that deliver our high-speed Internet. The list goes on and on.

The subconscious mind is like the hard drive on your computer. It contains a vast quantity of information, so vast that for even the most simple of personalities the amount of data contained might be likened to the contents of the Library of Congress. It contains all the experience and information you need to breathe, to regulate incredibly complex adjustments to the array of hormones and neurotransmitters coursing through the nervous system at every level, to operate biochemical elements of metabolism, to store information on all the millions of reflex pathways that protect our most basic behaviors. And it contains memories at some level of every experience we have ever had, every conversation, every interaction, every sensory impression, every touch, every smell, every taste, everything that we have ever said or done or thought. Plus, it contains vast amounts of information from the collective unconscious.

But this incredibly enormous sea of information is unlike the hard drive on your computer in another respect. For while the data on your hard drive is static and unchanging when you are not operating the computer, the reservoir of information deep beneath your conscious mind is constantly active in many intricate ways. The information held within moves and breathes and thinks. It processes things, analyzes things, and even tries to amuse itself with dreams, tries to cope with conflicts through neuroses and even physical illness—does all sorts of intelligent and amazing things.

Your conscious mind, to carry this computer analogy one step further, is very much like the monitor. It can display *one screen* of this sea of information at a time. When it does display something within, we call this a conscious thought.

The collective unconscious, in the computer analogy, is like the World Wide Web to which your computer is connected. Through it, the subconscious mind of the world moves and exchanges and processes information, sensory impressions, fears, dreams, and creative thought forms of every kind.

But your nervous system, your personal subconscious, does not connect to the collective subconscious with a cable or any obvious definitive physical connection. And so it is difficult for some people to grasp the connection because they are erroneously convinced that such a connection must be physical. Nothing could be further from the truth. The connection we have with the Collective Unconsious and Infinite Intelligence is far, far better than any physical cable could ever be. The words we speak, the media we watch, the viruses and genes, glances and whispers we pass from one to another are more than sufficient to connect us to the world subsconsious, more effective than any existing physical cable or nerve, like a million wireless network transmitters all around us.

THE SUBCONSCIOUS AND THE
MYSTERY TRADITIONS

We have looked at the modern, Western story of the subconscious. But this is not, by far, the *whole* story. For the study or science of the subconscious mind in truth began millennia ago. In fact, allusions to the subconscious by one name or another permeate the history of all the great mystical traditions from the Kabbalah, to the Alchemists, to the Freemasons, the Gnostics, the Taoists, the Buddhists, the Rosicrucians, the Theosophists, the Transcendentalists, the twentieth-century positive thinkers like Napoleon Hill and Norman Vincent Peale, to viritually all contemporary self-empowerment gurus.

Why all the fuss? For some people the idea of a subconscious mind is an interesting albeit impractical concept. It is fascinating, but there seems little about the concept that we can *use* on a day-to-day basis to improve our lives and the lives of others. But nothing could be further from the truth. For the subconscious mind, which stretches from the confines of our own vast subterranean libraries to the infinite reaches of our entire society, our entire culture—and even the entire universe— has some built-in properties that have profound *practical* importance.

Think of the subconscious mind as a kind of entity, an entity with a *personality*—which predisposes it to certain kinds of habitual, instinctual, and reflexive behavior. You should be able to grasp with little difficulty how tremendously important it is to understand this personality and the habitual tendencies that go along with it. For obvious reasons, you will want to work *with* these tendencies and not *against* them. This parable and the four that follow are specifically designed by the teacher to educate us in the laws that rule the automatic behaviors—and define the personality—of the subconscious mind.

ACTIVATING PARABLE LESSON 7

1. If you are not already well versed in the basics of the subconscious mind and how it works to germinate thought forms, make an effort to *learn now as much as you can.* You will have to be proactive, have to search out knowledge of the subconscious mind and immerse yourself in it for a week or so. If you had lived two thousand years ago and could talk to the teacher for a few days about the subject, that would, of course, be greatly preferred. But, in his absence, you need to make at least a respectable effort on your own, to brush up on a few of the classics in the field. Three tiny but golden classics that are *highly recommended* at this point in your systematic "initiation into the mysteries" are *The Power of the Subconscious Mind,* by Dr. Joseph Murphy, the compact Rosicrucian classic *Consciously Creating Circumstances,* and *As a Man Thinketh,* by James Allen.

   There are many other books that specifically address the importance of the subconscious mind and explain its quirks and characteristics beautifully. If you find, as many do along the path, that you become fascinated by what you read, that you gain hope and *motivation from what you read,* by all means seek out and study the best literature you can find until you have a very deep and clear understanding of the way your larger mind really works. "Above all, know thyself." It is critical that you become convinced, at a very deep level, of the power and importance of the subconscious mind in order to proceed with the remaining parable lessons.

2. One of the most important things to remember about the subconscious mind—something that is now common knowledge—is that it is very similar to a three-year-old child. The subconscious mind is different from the logical, learned part of your mind. There are many things that it does not understand. For example, it does not understand negatives. If you plant within it "Have no fear," all it hears is "Have fear." Consequently, it is very important to plant basic, simple, positive, happy terms in the subconscious: e.g., "I feel secure."

If you speak *to* it, and it is certainly a recommended prerogative to do so internally on occasion, speak calmly, happily, with simple explanations and commands. Explain what must be done and gently insist that it cooperate. One of the most important personality quirks of the subconscious mind is that it is obedient, it wishes to comply and please. Not only does it not mind having you tell it what to do, it prefers it, craves direction, guidance, and strength. Speak to it truthfully, respectfully, happily, fairly, and maturely and it will be there to help you every minute of every hour of your life.

3. Set aside thirty to sixty minutes today or very soon—before you proceed to the next parable lesson—to meditate specifically on the subconscious mind. Sit yourself comfortably and do about ten minutes of the breathing exercise you learned in parable lesson number three. When your system has been lightly cleansed and cleared, begin to meditate silently, going down as deep as you can.

4. If you are successful, you will gradually descend into a state that is known as hypnogogy, the state that immediately precedes light sleep. In this state, you will notice dreamlike images emerging into consciousness and then fading away as you attempt to focus upon them. At this point, you are actually "watching" the surface of the subconscious mind. This is the interface where your conscious mind merges with all that lies below.

As you continue to relax the conscious mind with your meditation techniques, *watch* these dream images take form and bubble to the surface, where they become conscious thoughts. *Note* the complexity, the playfulness, the whimsy and creativity this marvelous device exhibits as it generates and releases thoughts and images up into your consciousness. *Know* that this is the part of your deep personality that ultimately connects at an even deeper level with the Divine Mind, with the sea of infinite intelligence that knows everything—including everything you need to know to make your own life better.

5. *Invite God into the learning process.* Don't take this for granted. Ask him specifically at this time to help you perceive and better understand the deep reaches of your being that ultimately merge with him. Because its *all* him. *Ask* him to help you understand how he is always there deep inside you to help you, to guide you, as *you* help *him* with the beautiful process of creation.

THE LEAVEN

The Law of Expansion

MATTHEW 13:33

Another parable spake he unto them; The Kingdom of Heaven is like unto leaven, which a woman took, and hid in three measures of meal, till the whole was leavened.

IN THE PREVIOUS PARABLES we learned about some of the major personality characteristics of the universe, which are sometimes referred to by scientists as "universal laws." We learned, for example, that within a closed energy system, things naturally fall apart—a tendency known as *entropy.* The law expressing this tendency is called Newton's Second Law of Thermodynamics.

It is important to briefly review this concept in order to proceed with an intelligent interpretation of the parable of the leaven. In essence, entropy is the automatic tendency for *imbalances* in this universe to "even out." If something is very highly ordered, it will automatically tend to steadily fall apart until it is no more ordered than all the randomly distributed environments surrounding it. If there is a condition of emptiness, a *vacuum,* nature will automatically and invariably mobilize to fill that emptiness so that it is as "full" as its surroundings. This tendency for things to automatically even out is so pervasive, so perfectly consistent throughout the universe, that it can be found to be working at all times and at every level of reality from the subatomic to the astronomical. This law perfectly illustrates the Hermetic Axiom "As above, so below."

In the parable of the leaven, we will learn about another important personality characteristic of our universe. This characteristic—this tendency for things to behave in a certain way—is exactly like entropy in the sense that it permeates everything. It operates at every level of reality from the subatomic to the astronomical and from the mental and emotional realms to the purely material. Furthermore, like entropy, this new characteristic successfully explains and predicts many important phenomena in our world. But most important, this new characteristic is something that you can actually *use, a characteristic that can be written as one of the most important of all the laws governing the use of creative intention.*

What the parable of the leaven tells us is that the creator of this universe placed within it some kind of "substance" or energy that, although relatively infinitesimal and undetectable—like yeast mixed into bread dough—is nonetheless a powerful and effective *catalyst* that enables automatic expansion and growth in response to intention. This mysterious and powerful "substance" is so thoroughly mixed into the milieu of atomic and subatomic particles that compose the building blocks of all material circumstances that, like leaven, it becomes an integral and *undetectable* part of the fabric of reality. This would explain why physicists have not as yet been able to directly measure or confirm the presence of this substance, even though there is ample evidence of its existence—and even though mystics have known of its presence for millennia.

The primary message of the parable is that this mysterious sub-stance, or energy, causes things to automatically expand, and, like the rising of the bread in response to the plans and intentions of the woman baking it, the tendency of things to expand in response to our thoughts can be *useful, controllable, and can produce creations with real, practical value.*

The parable of the leaven is related to the parable of the mustard seed. The parable of the mustard seed tells us *how* expansion, or growth, will occur. It tells us that as things expand and grow in re-sponse to thought, the proliferation will occur in an organic manner. To review this in succinct terms, this means that throughout the uni-verse, growth will proceed in the same way living things on Earth can be observed to grow. This will include the way the ever splitting uni-verses predicted by the Many Worlds Hypothesis will grow and di-vide by *branching.* The living organism used to illustrate this in the parable is a large, vigorous tree.

As you will learn, the parable of the leaven confirms this notion of "organic growth" *and* ties it to a new and extremely important law. To understand the parable, we first need to understand what leaven is. The teacher was not your average man. With his brilliance, he chose the components of his metaphors with great care and precision. Leaven is comprised of yeast. And yeast is comprised of cells, cells that are capable of rapid growth and reproduction. When a yeast cell grows, it soon splits into two new "child" cells.

As this splitting process occurs, the yeast cells metabolize the raw materials around them. In the chemical reactions of metabolism, mole-cules like sugar, which contain chemical energy, are broken down and the energy extracted. The extracted energy feeds the complex processes that enable the cell to grow and the splitting to occur. The processes of *mitosis* and *meiosis* duplicate and delicately separate the ge-

netic information, or chromosomes, within the cell's nuclei that regulate every process of growth and metabolism in order to prepare the
cell to split.

The by-products of the energy-using reactions occurring within
the cell as it prepares to divide include gases. Yeast cells split into child
cells again and again and again, each time releasing gases that cause the
bubbles to expand. These bubbles collect within the matrix of the
bread dough and cause it to expand like a sponge.

Could the constant splitting of universes and the splitting of our
personal realities take place in the same manner? And could the
teacher have been alluding to this in his parable? At first this seems an
almost outlandish and peculiar question. But upon further reflection
there seems no compelling argument to *exclude* the possibility that the
teacher did, in fact, know about these extraordinarily important aspects of reality. It is entirely possible that he perceived in his own time
what quantum physicists have only recently ascertained—that universes, personal realities, *split* again and again, just like yeast cells. And
that the fabric of reality may in some way resemble rising bread dough.
Is that reading too much into the simple metaphor? That depends on
how insightful you think this Jewish mystic really was.

We can gain perspective on the likelihood of the master's understanding of physics, metaphysics, and biology by looking back at the
parable of the mustard seed. There he told us that the kingdom was
like a seed growing into a tree. He didn't say the kingdom was like a
seed or like a tree, he said that it was like a *tree in the process of growing*.
And how does a tree grow? Its roots penetrate the earth, bifurcating
repeatedly and extending yet more deeply. Above, its branches also
develop along sequentially splitting lines as the growing tips, or meristems, divide again and again into branches and the branches of
branches. This would certainly jibe with the current Many Universes

theories of reality and the infinitely branching universes these con-structs postulate.

At this point it would be most interesting to ask whether current astronomical data actually supports the hypothesis that, according to the parable of the leaven, the "kingdom," or universe, has expanded like bread dough. For if the notion is true, scientific observation should confirm it in certain ways. Here's what we know.

The astronomer Margaret Geller wanted to know exactly how the galaxies were strewn through the cosmos. Up until her study we didn't really have a clear idea how all the galaxies that we can see are *distributed* through space. Geller became so fascinated with the prob-lem that she spent many years painstakingly determining the position of each of tens of thousands of visible galaxies, finally having their po-sitions drawn out in an exquisitely detailed, three-dimensional illus-tration. The resulting image of the known universe is most remarkable for one thing: The resulting galaxies are not strewn *randomly* through space, as we would certainly expect if they had simply been blown apart by an impersonal big bang. Instead, the structure of the visible universe appears very much as a vast reach of galaxies arranged in the vast reaches of space as if they were expanded outward in *formations—* formations resembling organic bubbles and clumps—that look exactly like foamy bread dough. Astronomers now often describe the macro-texture of our universe as "foamy."

But there is yet another scientific observation that supports the Law of Expansion as expressed in this parable. For many years now, scientists have known that the universe is expanding, that the trillions of galaxies strewn through the cosmos are flying away *from one another* and away *from some central point* of origin where the big bang is thought to have occurred. But there is more. Reletively recently, scientists dis-covered something else: The expansion of the universe is actually *speeding up*. This makes absolutely no sense whatever, if you think about it. For if a gigantic explosion blew all the galaxies apart, we would think, using common sense, that this expansion ought to be slowing down after fourteen billion years. But it is not. Everything is flying away from everything at an *increasing* rate of expansion. And no one knows why. This is one of the greatest mysteries of the modern, quantum world.

The problem is that if the expansion is speeding up, energy must somehow be *added* to the expansion. But no one can find any source of energy that could be responsible for the expansion. This is expecially mysterious because the *amount* of energy that would be required to cause the *entire universe to expand* with ever greater speed and force would have to be spectacularly enormous. So enormous, in fact, that it would be about ten times greater than all the observed *known* energy present in the universe. Because scientists cannot find this massive energy, they call it "dark energy." For our purposes, as students of the mysteries, this dark energy is part and parcel of the "leaven" the teacher spoke of, the "substance" hidden within the multiverse that causes it to expand.

Metaphysical Expansion

Fascinating as it is to explore how the parable of the leaven may explain the structure of the physical universe, this line of physical inquiry is of only minor importance. It is far more important and practical to explore the metaphysical implications within the lesson. Metaphysically, this parable is placed as it is within the chronology of lessons in order to emphasize the idea that our thoughts are automatically energized, within the subconscious mind, with a force that enables them to manifest real events and things within our personal realities.

Metaphorically, leaven is a symbol for *consciousness*. The reason there appears to be a beautiful foamy pattern to the structure of the universe, rather than a random pattern, is because the universe had a very important ingredient added to it when it was created. That in-gredient is *consciousness,* and it permeates every galaxy, every star, every planet, every organism, every cell, every molecule, every atom, and every subatomic particle. This living consciousness also extends to organized structures at many levels *above* and many levels *below,* as well. It extends upward into the superstructures of the multiverse and downward into the sub-subatomic realms.

Why is this important, and what can we do with this information? This "leaven," the consciousness that permeates every iota of the fab-ric of the universe, is important to normal people in their normal lives because it gives the universe a tremendously valuable tendency. And if we know this tendency, if we are knowledgeable in the law that de-scribes it, we can live and think such that we work *with* it and not against it. The most important tendency of the consciousness that per-meates the universe is best expressed as a corollary to the law: What you focus on expands.

Consciousness Responds to Consciousness

This matters to you in your life today. What matters is that if you are conscious of something and *stay* conscious of something, it will, like leavened bread, begin to *expand.* The consciousness, the leaven that permeates the universe around you—in your room, in your body, in the air you breathe—reacts to *your* consciousness.

If you think about what you lack by worrying about it and projecting vivid, emotionally charged images of failure, the conscious sub-stance permeating every aspect of the world around you will *respond in kind*: What you lack will expand, and you will find yourself even worse off. If you are lacking but concentrate and focus on the things you *have,* the substance that causes the expansion of your reality will *respond in kind* and what you have will increase. If you concentrate on the things you should be *grateful* for, the consciousness permeating the universe will respond such that more circumstances and things that will stimulate more *gratitude* are created.

If you have a health problem yet concentrate and dwell upon the parts of your body that are healthy, the healthy portions of your body and your life will increase. If you concentrate on the relationships of your life that make you feel close rather than lonely, the universe will automatically produce circumstances that will contribute to more and more intimacy. If you concentrate on the money you have, even if it is only the change in your pocket, the consciousness of the universe will respond and your world will rearrange itself to support circumstances in which you have more money.

It's a sobering thought really. And one that should compel us all to think and speak positively at all times. Think about it: Whatever you focus on expands. And you are almost always focusing on *something.* You are *always* causing expansion whether you know it or not.

ACTIVATING PARABLE LESSON 8

1. One of the very best things you can do to understand the impor-tance of this parable is to *learn how to work backward with the law "What you focus on expands."* This is done by taking a circumstance that is currently prominent in your life. It could be the fact that you

have a certain career, or a certain kind of relationship, or a certain kind of skill or a certain kind of lack or suffering. Now work backward and *see* how this circumstance expanded, how it became a larger and larger part of your life, *as you focused upon it,* concentrated upon it, dwelled upon it over many years.

2. Now you are ready to tackle a problem situation in your life. This can take a lot of courage and a great deal of honesty and integrity. For example, if you are in a bad relationship or have a particular type of health problem, *try to see* how *you contributed to the formation of this problem by thinking certain thoughts along the way.* Again, this can take an enormous amount of courage and honesty, but it can be done. And it must be done if you are to evolve. For evolution, in our terms, is in no small part the process of understanding how your thoughts produce the circumstances both good and bad in your life.

The discipline called science is, in the simplest possible terms, the orderly study of the processes of cause and effect. Working backward in an attempt to trace the origin of your circumstances in your past thoughts is actually a very *scientific* process that imparts a sense of order and comprehensibility to the process of expansion. Sometimes the process can be difficult. This is in part because some of the circumstances that have manifested and expanded within your life began as thought forms before you were born here.

There are many different constructs and models to explain where we were, who we were, and what we were before we came here, but one thing is widely agreed upon in the New Metaphysic and in New Thought in general. And that is that we came from *somewhere* before we got here and that we are going *somewhere* after we leave here. Infinite Intelligence is very efficient and would never waste a life and the soul that develops with it by simply terminating it when the body that houses it ceases to function. The soul goes on and, in due course, finds another way to express itself in another life.

Some of the things that you find as "reality" in this life, and that you *apparently did not choose* or otherwise create by focusing upon certain thought forms, were actually consciously chosen—*before* you came into this existence. How could you know such a thing? It may be easier than you might think. If you are really honest with yourself, you can ask, "Would that have been like me, to have chosen this hardship? Is the hardship actually helping me correct deficiencies in my soul that I know perfectly well need improving?"

3. Invite God into the process. Don't take this for granted. It is at once essential and enormously helpful. Ask him to help you be honest in your analysis of specific problems. Ask him to give you the courage and the energy to understand how you have created your own personal reality. Ask him to help you understand the reasons why you have chosen what you have chosen and the importance of what you are learning as a result.

4. Continue to examine situations in your life as they arise, on an ongoing basis from now on. Always work backward and try to see how your thought patterns contributed to what you see around you. Try to see how focusing on certain things, sometimes negative things, may have caused them to expand or persist.

———— ✒ ————

THE HIDDEN TREASURE

The Philosopher's Stone

MATTHEW 13:44

Again, the Kingdom of Heaven is like unto a treasure hid in a field; that when a man hath found, he hideth, and for joy thereof goeth and selleth all that he hath, and buyeth that field.

MAGINE, IF YOU WILL, that you are hiking in the country-side near your home. As you are walking along, you stumble on a rock. Picking yourself up, you notice that the rock is shiny. With your handkerchief you wipe the dust from the rock and find a massive jewel easily worth hundreds of thousands of dollars. You are stunned. What should you do? After mulling the situation over you make a decision. Even though you are sorely tempted, you don't want to be dishonest, so taking the precious rock is out of the question. Making the decision to avoid the unethical is your first split in the road. But then you think of something. There is, after all, an honest solution to the dilemma, the *high* road of the split point before you.

Off you go to the town in search of the land title office. Lo and behold, you find that the land is for sale. But there's a big problem, a stumbling block that may prevent you from succeeding by this high path. The land isn't cheap. The price for the tract of land is very high, even though the owner doesn't seem to be aware of the presence of the jewel. But you make another decision and take another split point. Instead of backing down and giving up—or worse, going back to pilfer the treasure—you put your entire estate up for sale. Everything goes—all the furniture, both of the family cars, your vacation cabin, and all of your toys and collectibles.

This is a most difficult task and incredibly stressful. But you persist. For even in your worst moments during this drastic process you know the nugget is so enormous, so rare that it is worth many times the money you will make liquidating your material possessions. In fact, you are so sure of this that you are not only confident, you are *overjoyed,* even giddy over the whole matter. However, you maintain a lot of secrecy. With the capital you have generated by liquidating your assets you make an offer on the land, and it is accepted. You take possession of the tract of land, walk out to the secret location, and take possession of the priceless commodity.

For some, the treasure represents, variously, the love of God, salvation, and/or a personal relation with Christ. These spiritual treasures are infinitely more valuable than any conceivable material possession. They are worth far more than the sum total of all your material assets. The teacher, at this level of interpretation, seems to be saying that we may indeed have to give up material possessions—or, at the very least, our attachment to them—if we are to attain the great treasure. But, we are reassured, when we finally take possession of the treasure, we will not only be satisfied, we will be overjoyed, for we will be saved and avoid an afterlife in hell.

At a deeper metaphysical level, the message of the parable is far more self-empowering. For the evolved soul, the hidden treasure is the core "mystery," the knowledge of cause and effect as it relates to thought forms and the power of manifestation. The hidden treasure is the Philosopher's Stone sought by seers and sages for ages, the catalyst that will turn the base into gold. The treasure is hidden within, in the "field" of consciousness, and is found through initiation into the mysteries. This initiation process is arguably the most important inflection point of evolution a human being can negotiate.

When a person becomes conscious that his thoughts have the power to manifest circumstance, to heal disease, to correct states of lack, she must agree to contain her discovery and honor the mystery tradition—and the process of initiation into its powerful secrets. Then, realizing that the knowledge of Mind is more powerful, *far* more powerful, than all that has already manifested in her life, the initiate focuses all her effort, all her will, all her energy and time into the mastery of the true processes of cause and effect.

The knowledge of Mind is a bit like a genie that can grant any wish. Because it can enable a person to acquire and sustain *any* desired state of happiness, it is infinitely more valuable than all existing material assets in a person's life.

ACTIVATING PARABLE LESSON 9

1. Make every conceivable effort to avoid any unethical behavior in your quest for the knowledge of Mind. Although this may seem as if it should go without saying, it cannot. For the unethical splits in our decision-making processes are often most subtle. The man in the parable could easily have taken the hidden treasure for himself

and no one would have ever known. The owner of the field didn't know the treasure was there on his land, but the land was purchased fairly and through normal, legal means.

We can obtain so many valuable things in this life by borderline and questionable means, yet in ways that we can never be "caught." But doing so will set us down the wrong path, into the wrong worlds, into the wrong personal realities, and the remainder of our quest will be tainted, and our lives demeaned in subtle ways that are often too difficult to understand at the time. But we can never cheat the universe. It knows everything. Our only alternative is to be perfectly ethical and honorable at all times.

If there is anything that you are saying or doing that is even slightly at variance with what we know to be truly fair, truly honest, truly high-minded, do not be tempted. Don't go down that road—for it leads to the wrong destination. Even though you might achieve initial rewards, you aren't getting away with anything. Your decision will catch up to you and destroy your quest. Make every effort in consciousness to do the right thing according to the other laws so clearly delineated by the teacher and other great masters at every juncture without exception.

2. Every time you come to a place in the road where you are presented with a choice of either attaining or keeping material advantages or attaining spiritual knowledge, make a *decision* to *choose* the spiritual over the material. Even though the initial result may be a loss of the material, the end result, the parable tells us, will be the attainment of something infinitely more valuable. The knowledge that will grow within you as you proceed in this way will, in the final analysis, be so much more valuable than anything that you have sacrificed on a world level that there can be no comparison. For

you will end up with a state of consciousness that will allow you to have everything good. You will end up happy, free, at peace with yourself, and in a world of *true* wealth.

3. Like the character in the parable, it is very important to keep your discoveries of the laws of mind to yourself. At least for the time being. So often we are tempted to go out and tell the world about what we are learning about the ability of our own minds to create better circumstances. And who can blame us? For it is indeed exciting. But the parable tells us to resist this temptation and to be quiet. Many experts agree that this will aid the manifestation process in many instances.

Later, when mastery has been achieved, only then will you be in a position to teach others. For now, realize that even though you may know a lot, you are not yet ready to teach. For now, *concentrate on yourself,* on learning more. Don't waste your energy trying to convince others because that is codependence. For now, at least, let those around you worry about themselves. Get yourself to a place of greater strength. Only then will you be in a solid position to help others.

The Pearl of Great Price

The Law of Perception

MATTHEW 13:45,46

Again, the Kingdom of Heaven is like unto a merchant man, seeking goodly pearls:

Who, when he had found one pearl of great price, went and sold all that he had, and bought it.

THIS IS THE SECOND PARABLE in which we are told of a man who finds something valuable and sells all that he has to buy that thing. And, as is the case with the parable of the hidden treasure, this parable has a basic, mainstream level of interpretation and a deeper, metaphysical meaning. The traditional interpretation is that the man is you. The pearl is an afterlife in heaven and not hell. Salvation—attaining one and avoiding the other—is, in many classic belief systems, the single most valuable "thing" that a person can find and then "purchase." The term "purchasing" in these belief systems is a metaphor for the attainment of a personal relationship with Christ and general adherence to the Ten Commandments and other religious doctrines. This level of interpretation is entirely valid and admirable in every way. For many people around the world, this approach works beautifully. It can help them create and structure a life that is much superior to the ones they might have chosen without such guidance.

Metaphorical or mystical levels of interpretation range from the simple to the complex. At the most basic level, the parable is a reminder that the mysteries we are learning about are unquestionably the most valuable things we can possibly learn about in this life. That, if necessary, we should gladly make considerable sacrifice to assure that we learn the mysteries, including the knowledge, being revealed in the parable sequence. And what is that knowledge? Clearly, we have seen through meticulous retranslation that the knowledge conveyed by the mysteries is knowledge of Mind—knowledge and expertise in the use of positive intentions to create better realities.

The pearl of great price, the treasure more valuable than any other, and worth more than the sum total of a person's entire array of possessions, is the knowledge of cause and effect. This, because the knowledge of cause and effect—the laws allowing the manifestation of thought forms into reality—allows a person to manifest amazing and very beneficial circumstances.

But the interpretation cannot of necessity end at this level. There is more. For we are working on the hypothesis that the teacher was an extremely brilliant and even "scientific" man—in that he was able to put together intricate and convoluted logical trains of thought. Simultaneously, he was gifted with mystical insights we can only begin to imagine. When combined, these two factors—his high intelligence and his more right-brained, visionary insights—may well have allowed him to understand far more than we would normally expect of a blue-collar worker in a simple agrarian society. To see how this is so, we need to closely examine the specific choices he made with regard to the elements of the allegory, primarily the choice of a "pearl" as the precious object.

PEARLS OF WISDOM

It is interesting to note just what a pearl is, from a biological perspective. A pearl is much more than a shiny object. It is a product of *organic growth*. The mustard seed and the leaven were used in previous parable lessons to illustrate processes of organic growth. Because of the universal law "as above, so below," we know that the principles of growth and expansion that the seed and the leaven illustrate operate at all levels of reality—all the way from the subatomic to the astronomical and all the way from the mental to the material.

So it is with the example of the pearl. The formation of a pearl illustrates critical organic principles at work in the formation of our personal realities via the splitting of universes. Consider a pearl from a biophysical perspective. It begins with a kind of "mistake," a bit of foreign matter—a piece of sand or debris—gets stuck in the soft tissue of an oyster. The debris becomes a strong irritant to the soft and unprotected membranes within the oyster shell and the oyster mobilizes to minimize this irritation. It begins to coat the irritant with layers of calcium.

Gradually, as months and years pass, more and more layers are added in a concentric fashion until a round, smooth object forms. This smooth pearl is much less irritating to the oyster and allows the organism to regain a level of ease. Under special circumstances, which are relatively rare, more and more layers are added to the pearl until it becomes very large. If its layers have been added in a perfectly round, concentric fashion, and if the layers have a special kind of luster, a pearl can be extremely valuable. A particularly rare and beautiful pearl is so precious that it can be worth the combined values of thousands of smaller pearls

A metaphysical pearl, then, is a creation, a life that has resulted from a person attempting to ease her own suffering, attempting to heal her own life of some type of challenging circumstance. A pearl is the wisdom gained from a prolonged and dedicated course of work with the laws of Mind, the laws of thought forms. The layers of the pearl are the years of effort, faith, and dedication in the face of setbacks and handicaps. The oyster that makes the pearl, including its sensitive tissues, is a person's heart, which remains soft through the process of repeatedly overcoming obstacles.

The heart of a truly evolved person will not harden in response to irritation, aggravation, and hardship. Instead it begins the work of transmutation, converting the base to the noble. Such a soul, taking this higher path in response to challenge, turns ugly and painful circumstances into beautiful things. Instead of hardening, a person taking this path, this fork in the road, will become a miracle worker, someone who turns the irritation, the debris, into a jewel. Such a person routinely and reflexively transmutes hate into love, deformity into beauty, depression into joy, and aggression into peace—just like the teacher. Working through these challenges gives a soul grace, flexibility, and a softness of heart.

A person, circumstance, or thing that has been so miraculously transformed is more valuable to the creator than anything else in the universe. In one sense, this means that *you* are the jewel, the most valuable thing in the universe, for you are a miracle. You have been transformed, without a doubt, if you have reached the stage where you are reading this book and your heart has deepened, softend toward others.

So the parable is telling you to believe, to have faith, and to persist in the face of any hardship, any aggravation, any setback, any handicap, or any negativity of any kind. It is telling you to remain trusting, innocent, softhearted, kind, and compassionate no matter how many times you are beaten down by the harshness of life. The parable is telling you that there is really no other choice. This is the only way to get to a beautiful reality, a reality in which *you* are beautiful, admirable, and *valuable*. The parable is telling you to make sure that you continue choosing the high road, the path less taken, as you continue to make decisions about the circumstances life presents along your way to the One.

PERCEPTION

There is yet another level of interpretation to this parable that comes from the phrase ". . . sold all that he had and bought it." The Greek word normally interpretated as "bought" is *heurisko*. This word stems from the root *heureo,* which means to "find, get, obtain, perceive, or see," according to *Strong's Exhaustive Concordance.* This would not seem to be a random choice of wording for a brilliant mystical teacher. "Perceiving" and "seeing" are of extraordinary importance to mystics and visionaries of all kinds.

The choice of this word strongly suggests the story is really not about the pearl but about the *man* who is finding and buying the pearl with his liquidated assets. It indicates that the man has transmuted all his material wealth into one thing, and that is the ability to *perceive* the pearl. First he finds the pearl. This means that he first learns of the existence of the wisdom and expertise in the laws of positive intention, the laws that enable miracles to happen. But learning of the exis tence of the laws and the wisdom that activates them will not suffice. What will be required, in the end, is a higher level of perception.

Perception is the ability to make sense out of the data, sensory and otherwise, that bombards us from our external worlds. It is an ability that is *learned* over many years of infancy and childhood, the ability to recognize and interpret what is seen and heard and sensed. It is the ability to put data together in such a way that it makes sense and is usable, practical. And this includes not only external sensory data, but internal, spiritual data, as well. A baby has not yet *learned* to perceive. A baby receives huge amounts of sensory data but has not yet learned how to put that data together so that it makes sense.

The parable is saying that we can learn of the laws, study them, write about them, teach them, and in every way appear to be an expert in their principles and usage yet remain outside of them and ineffective with them. To truly evolve, we will also be required to learn a new way of putting together and interpreting all the things we see and experience in the worlds around us. This shift in perception is alluded to extensively in *A Course in Miracles* and other highly evolved self-empowerment systems.

ACTIVATING PARABLE LESSON 10

1. If there is anything that is irritating to you, anything in your life that is apparently nothing but an annoyance, *shift your perception* of that factor so that you see it in a different light. *See* that irritant as a chance to make something better, to make a pearl. For the pearl that will result from your patience, your tolerance, your ability to keep your heart soft is the thing that you are really seeking.

2. Invite God into the process. Specifically ask him to help you perceive the "mistakes," the irritants, the hardships that rest within your heart differently. It is so very hard to do this when we are suffering. But you may rest assured that God will be ready and willing to help you shift your perception so that you can see things in a more positive light and transmute the base into the noble.

THE DRAGNET

Decisions and Discrimination

MATTHEW 13:47–50

Again, the Kingdom of Heaven is like a dragnet cast into the sea, and gathering fish of every kind;

and when it was filled, they drew it up on the beach; and they sat down, and gathered the good fish into containers, but the bad they threw away.

So it will be at the end of the age; the angels shall come forth, and take out the wicked from among the righteous,

and will cast them into the furnace of fire; there shall be weeping and gnashing of teeth.

THE END OF THE WORLD, the Armageddon, the Rapture. These are some of the most famous concepts in all of Christianity. They are the idea that the world will end at any time and in a spectacular way. At the end of the world, the virtuous will be lifted out of their homes and offices, even their automobiles on the freeway, and transported upward into the sky. The righteous or virtuous will be separated from the sinners, and the sinners cast into hell, where they will burn for eternity with no possible hope of redemption. Few concepts can strike such intense fear into the hearts of the faithful.

Fundamentalists, who take the words of the Bible very literally, believe the parable of the dragnet refers to and confirms these terrifying predictions. But did the great teacher really have such a negative view of the future of humanity, the future of life on earth? Or was he speaking at the level of deep metaphor, at a *mystical* level?

We know from the second and third parables that the Nazarene did not believe in the concept of hell. We know that "hell" is presented as a concept that the teacher talked about frequently by orthodox translations but it seems doubtful that he believed in it in reality. He made this clear when he explained very cogently that any lasting army or conspiracy of evil was logically impossible because a "nation divided against itself cannot stand." Any organized league of destructive entities would automatically destroy itself in time. And this has been confirmed over and over through history. All the great nations of evil eventually self-destruct while the great religions, the great beneficent religions, endure.

The teacher could not come right out and say this, however. Then, as now, church authorities and parishioners alike were extremely attached to profoundly negative concepts such as evil and the fiery end of humanity. Therefore, the teacher had to be extremely careful how he refuted such concepts and how he replaced them with more positive, healthy ideas. The parable of the dragnet is an excellent example of how this worked.

On the surface, there is something familiar and confirming for the fundamentalists, but there is a much deeper, mystical level of meaning for those who have transcended the negative emphasis of the traditional approach. Remember that when the disciples asked the teacher why he was teaching in parables, he replied, "because it is given to you to know the mysteries." So it will simply not suffice to accept a non-mystical interpretation for any of his carefully constructed allegories. We need to look deeper.

The ocean, the sea full of fish, represents what we now refer to variously as the subconscious mind or infinite intelligence, the "sea" of consciousness that looms beneath the level of conscious awareness. We have learned that the subconscious mind is like the hard drive of a computer, that it contains a vast amount of data, the sum total of all memories, all thoughts, all sensations, and all intentions—positive and negative. This enormous pool of information is so vast that we could think of it as being very much like the Library of Congress. The *conscious* mind, on the other hand, is like the monitor on a computer—it can display only one page, from one book from that library, at any one time. In this analogy, the universal mind is like the Internet. At the deepest level, the entire computer is connected to the vast sea of data that connects countless minds, countless consciousnesses together in the collective unconscious or Infinite Intelligence, God.

We also know from previous parables that many kinds of "seeds," or thought forms, in this collective unconscious can germinate, even though we do not consciously intend them to. This germination of "weed seeds" can happen in a more or less random or chaotic manner unless the germination process is managed properly.

Consider: There are thousands of weed seeds lying dormant in a cubic foot of garden soil. But they don't all germinate at once. Some may lie dormant for years, deep beneath the surface. Only when the proper conditions are present can a seed germinate. If the soil is disturbed by plowing or erosion, a deeply buried dormant seed may come closer to the surface. There it can receive warmth from the sun, oxygen and carbon dioxide from the atmosphere, and moisture from the rain and dew.

If all necessary conditions come into alignment, the seed begins to grow. Its cells divide, splitting again and again until the first embryonic leaves, or "cotyledons," form. Roots divide and proliferate, penetrating deeper into the soil, and a living, growing plant emerges into the light. This explains why weeds will continue to germinate for many years in your vegetable garden even though all emerging weed seedlings are carefully destroyed each year and no new weed seeds are added.

In the parable of the tares, a character is introduced called the "enemy." The enemy represents the ego that sows weed seeds—unintentional and undesirable thought forms—in the farmer's field while he is asleep, *via the subconscious.* The message is that the ego presents a potentially serious problem in that its dominance in a person's consciousness provides the perfect conditions for the germination and ultimate manifestation of chaotic and undesirable thought forms.

In the parable of the tares, we are told not to fight this process, not to try to consciously winnow germinating undesirable "weed" seedlings from desirable, intentional thought forms as they manifest. If we try to do this, we will only make matters worse. The task is far too complex, too impossible for a human being to perform effectively. Instead, we are told, we are to *let go.* We are to let our servants, our angels, our agents of God take over the process of cultivation that will allow only the desirable thought forms to continue as manifestations within our realities. In fact, whenever the teacher talks about "servants" or "angels" doing things, he is telling us that we can let go of our conscious control over these processes and delegate them to God.

The parable of the dragnet provides additional practical information on how to manage the chaotic thought "seeds" that permeate the subconscious. This is the mystical level of interpretation that we are seeking. To understand how this is so, let's take a closer look at the parable. What is a net exactly? It is a relatively transparent, porous de-

vice that can move through deep reaches of water with little if any resistance. Water, the substance, the fluid medium that contains everything within the sea, may pass unobstructed through the holes in the
net. However, anything suspended within the water will be caught
and collected. The fish within the sea represent the thought forms
within the subconscious, thought forms that behave in an *organic* matter, growing and expanding automatically. When the net is drawn to
the surface, all the collected organisms and objects will become visible.

The net, this parable tells us, is a feature of the Kingdom of Heaven.
This "feature" is another process, another characteristic, another personality trait that characterizes the behavior of things within the Kingdom of Heaven. The "net" is one of the automatic tendencies of this
ever-splitting conglomeration of infinite universes—and of our personal realities. The parable seems to be saying that one of the properties of this infinitely branching milieu of time and space and events is
an intelligent kind of *discrimination* that automatically provides us, the
fishermen, with a powerful and highly effective device for winnowing
desirable, altruistic, and intentional thought forms from undesirable,
lower, subconscious thought forms. This discrimination lies within us,
and if we are aware of its existence, we can call upon it to help us in
very valuable ways.

The ocean represents the subconscious mind, which holds vast
numbers of thought forms. Without the knowledge of cause and effect
all these subconscious thought forms are manifesting, all these seeds
are bearing fruit. The Kingdom of Heaven is likened unto a net that
can be cast into this chaotic milieu to draw to the surface, into consciousness, the array of thought forms looming beneath the surface.
Then, via the power of discrimination, that which is undesirable can
be intelligently separated from that which is desirable so that increasingly benevolent, weed-free "crops" begin to manifest.

Remember, however, that we are told by the parable of the tares not to attempt to separate thought forms that have already germinated. We are to leave those to God, we are to let go of them and know that Divine Intellgence will take care of them in its own way and its own time. This parable is talking about thought forms that are still within the subconscious, still within the sea, as yet unmanifested.

ACTIVATING PARABLE LESSON 11

1. Make a conscious decision to draw to the surface as many subliminal thought forms as you can. Ask God to help you in your process of discrimination. Ask Him to help you understand how certain thought forms are really not in your best interest.

2. If a thought form has not as yet begun to germinate and show its head within your reality, make every conscious attempt to neutralize it. This is not done by concentrating on it. That will only give it energy and cause it to expand. Negative thought forms are neutralized by dwelling on thought forms that are the polar opposite, positive intentions.

3. Neutralizing unmanifested subconscious thought forms is also done by asking God for his help. Many of these negative projections are simply too big for you to handle. However, the mere act of knowing that God can take care of them and acknowledging that he will be an irresistibly powerful help in the process.

THE UNMERCIFUL SERVANT

Perpetual Forgiveness

MATTHEW 18:21—35

Then Peter came and said to him, "Lord, if another member of the church sins against me, how often should I forgive? As many as seven times?"

Jesus said to him, "Not seven times, but, I tell you, seventy times seven.

For this reason the Kingdom of Heaven may be compared to a king who wished to settle accounts with his slaves.

When he began the reckoning, one who owed him ten thousand talents was brought to him;

and, as he could not pay, his lord ordered him to be sold, together with his wife and children and all his possessions, and payment to be made.

So the slave fell on his knees before him, saying, 'Have patience with me, and I will pay you everything.'

And out of pity for him, the lord of that slave released him and forgave him the debt.

But that same slave, as he went out, came upon one of his fellow *slaves who owed him a hundred denarii; and seizing him by the throat, he said, 'Pay what you owe.'*

Then his fellow slave fell down and pleaded with him, 'Have patience with me, and I will pay you.'

But he refused; then he went and threw him into prison until he would pay the debt.

When his fellow slaves saw what had happened, they were greatly distressed, and they went and reported to their lord all that had taken place.

Then his lord summoned him and said to him, 'You wicked slave! I forgave you all that debt because you pleaded with me.

Should you not have had mercy on your fellow slave, as I had mercy on you?'

And in anger his lord handed him over to be tortured until he would pay his entire debt.

So my heavenly Father will also do to every one of you, if you do not forgive your brother or sister from your heart."

ORGIVENESS—THE BOTTLENECK through which all must pass to enter the parable sequence and ultimately the Kingdom of Heaven. We discussed this classic and most challenging of all spiritual exercises in depth in the first parable, and a series of very specific sub-steps was outlined through which forgiveness can be thoroughly implemented. When you worked through that gauntlet of surprisingly difficult steps, designed to clear your mind and soul of all negativity toward others, you probably thought you were done with the issue. Not so. For apparently the teacher felt this critical spiritual process was so important to achieving competency with the great mysteries he came here to teach that he brought it up again, here at the auspicious position of parable number twelve.

Here we are taken even deeper into the realms of spiritual cleansing and purification and notified in no uncertain terms that we are far from finished with our release of existing negative thought forms. In this parable, we learn that the process of forgiveness will be an ongoing process and will, in essence, be perpetual. And would we not find this logical if we think about it?

You know from the first parable that the very first thing you have to do to attain the effective and powerful spiritual knowledge that will be conferred by implementing the lessons of the parables is to systematically identify and release negative emotions encapsulated in your conscious and subconscious minds. This makes perfect sense when you contemplate it. Before you can proceed with any project you first have to clean up the workshop. And the workshop in this instance will be your deepest mind, your deepest soul.

If the workshop is strewn with dangerous and destructive thought forms—resentments, fears, grudges, judgments, egotistical and self-serving notions—all continually and efficiently germinating dangerous and destructive circumstances within your personal reality, how can you possibly expect to proceed with orderly, positive, spiritual measures? Trying to move forward into the more advanced lessons of the mysteries under such conditions would be utterly absurd. It is of vital importance to accept the truth of this basic concept if you are to have the spiritual energy and conviction necessary to undertake the ongoing process of forgiveness.

The Kingdom of Heaven here is related to a king who forgives a man a huge debt. The man then goes out and finding a man who owes him a debt, fails to forgive him. Upon hearing this, the king then revokes the forgiveness of the man's debt, and he is once more right where he started, in a state of lack and torment. The king of the kingdom here is normally thought to represent God. And this is accurate, to a degree. But it is not the whole truth. If you have really been working the program and have carefully and systematically identified and externalized your negative thought forms, you have indeed been forgiven an enormous debt. But it is you who have brought about the release of your debt. You are acting here as your own agent of God, taking responsibility for your own role in advancing the work of God. Forgiveness of others' perceived debts to you automatically forgives *your* debts.

The Lord's Prayer entreats us to ask of Spirit, "Give us this day our daily bread, and forgive us our debts, as we forgive our debtors." The way this sentence is constructed is interesting. We can ask God to provide for us our daily bread—the symbol for sustenance at all levels—but in the same breath we are to remember that this can only occur if we forgive others their debts to us. The two things, sustenance and forgiveness, cannot be separated, which is why they are carefully placed within the same sentence. The two are part and parcel of the same psychospiritual process. The implication is profound and should not be glossed over. If you are going to have any measure of success, comfort, and material security in this world, you will have to release your resentments toward all others in your life.

But the parable drives home the point that, although we have made enormous progress in parable one by undertaking a thorough spiritual housekeeping, our job is not over. We are going to experience perceived offenses to our egos as life goes on. And we are going to have to continue the process of forgiveness indefinitely. It will not be enough to forgive others once. Rather, we are entreated to forgive oth ers seventy times seven. In other words, as many times as it takes as long as it takes, forever. Our job is not likely ever to be over. *We need to expect this and be ready for it.* Although we have made peace within ourselves and with others by undertaking the rigorous process of re-lease outlined in parable one, we should hardly be surprised or disap-pointed when the very same people we have so generously released offend us again.

We, after all, are human beings. Others are not perfect, nor are we. Others are going to *continue* to act and speak in ways that may not sit well with us and will cause us to experience powerful emotions of fear and anger. But the same will be true of us as well. It is easy to see the stick in someone else's eye but so very easy to miss the gigantic log in our own eye. We, too, will cause others offense through our words and actions. Therefore, we will continue to generate debts as we pro-ceed through life. We have to have some kind of *ongoing mechanism* to deal effectively with our all too human failings, or we cannot experi-ence any sort of ongoing sustenance through spirit.

The Kingdom of Heaven, the field of cause and effect within which we live and manifest, has an automatic tendency to be compassionate, to be "moved with compassion."

This compassionate bias of the laws of cause and effect is highly beneficial to us and can be used to correct enormous mistakes and en-ergetic debts. This bias can be harnessed and put to work in our lives with incredibly desirable consequences only if we become *automati-cally compassionate ourselves.* To the extent we tend to *automatically* for-give mistakes and debts others make in dealing with us, our own mistakes and debts are forgiven.

ACTIVATING PARABLE LESSON 12

1. Continue at all times, on an ongoing basis, every day and in every circumstance, to forgive others around you for their perceived insults, their unfairness, their shortcomings, and their wrongdoing. *Establish a permanent mind-set of forgiveness.* You will never be done with forgiving. For as soon as you are finished, the world will undoubtedly present you with something else that offends or harms you. That is just the nature of the world. If your mind-set is to complain or react defensively or aggressively, you will doom yourself to unhappiness, and you will not progress to the life you seek so earnestly in your spiritual quest.

2. The mind-set of forgiveness will allow you to rise from a state of inner turmoil and conflict to a state of peacefulness and harmony. This new and highly superior state of inner well-being is far more conducive to learning. For how are you to concentrate and master the intricacies of the mysteries if you are wasting vast amounts of psychic energy on arguments, petty disputes, and perceived injustices? The parable lesson tells us that this is not the way.

3. *Realize and believe, have faith, that as you forgive others on a daily basis, even on a minute-by-minute basis, that your debts are being forgiven.* As you continue to let the perceived wrongs of others go, your own wrongs, and rest assured there are many of them, will be let go. Think of the problems in your life, the perceived lack that you are experiencing as you are trying so hard to heal yourself and to create a better life. These things are the result of your own debts. It is fine to strive to create more for yourself, but if you are mired in this debt,

it is wholly unrealistic to expect to make much progress. At least half the process of getting to a better personal reality will be to have the debts that are weighing you down forgiven. Instead of devoting all your personal energy to getting more, concentrate more on freeing the debt that is keeping you down. And the parable lessons are crystal clear on how this is to be done: The release of your debts will be a direct function of your release of others' debts.

THE GOOD SAMARITAN

The Law of Compassionate Reflex

LUKE 10:29–37

"A man was going down from Jerusalem to Jericho, and fell into the hands of robbers, who stripped him, beat him, and went away, leaving him half dead.

Now by chance a priest was going down that road; and when he saw him, he passed by on the other side.

So likewise a Levite, when he came to the place and saw him, passed by on the other side.

But a Samaritan while traveling came near him; and when he saw him, he was filled with pity.

He went to him and bandaged his wounds, having poured oil and wine on them. Then he put him on his own animal, brought him to an inn, and took care of him.

The next day he took out two denarii, gave them to the innkeeper, and said, 'Take care of him; and when I come back, I will repay you whatever more you spend.'

Which of these three, do you think, was a neighbor to the man who fell into the hands of the robbers?"

He said, "The one who showed him mercy." Jesus said to him, "Go and do likewise."

IN THIS PARABLE, we are told of a man who is robbed, beaten, and left for dead on the side of the road. Before long a priest comes upon the man, but simply walks on by doing nothing. Next, a Levite walks by, also sees the man, and also walks on by doing nothing. Finally, however, a Samaritan happens to pass by. He sees the man and, according to standard translations, is "filled with pity." What he does next puts the other two men to shame. Not only does he help the man up, he finds him a place to stay in an inn. Finally the Samaritan gives the innkeeper some money for the beaten man so that he will have the means to continue on his way safely and securely.

This all sounds very good, but there is a serious flaw in this translation. It occurs in the sentence that says ". . . when he saw him, he was *filled with pity.*" The same translation defect surfaces in the preceding parable as well as in the translation of the miracle of the loaves and fishes. This defect is incredibly important to understand and correct, for without a proper understanding of what *really* happened, we cannot glean the practical information given in this crucial step. To clear matters up, let's take a closer look.

In the account of the miracle of the loaves and fishes given in Matthew 14:13-23, we are told that the first thing that happens in the miracle is that Jesus walks far out into the desert in an attempt to be alone, and enters into a state of deep meditation. He does this in an attempt to recover from the shock of hearing that his beloved mentor and friend, John the Baptist, has been beheaded by Herod in order to impress his girlfriend.

The second thing that happens is that he comes out of his state of meditation. As he does, he finds that he is surrounded by more than five thousand people who have followed him on foot into the empty reaches of the desert. At this point, the account in Matthew specifically states that he "saw the masses and was moved with pity." The Greek word traditionally translated as "moved with pity" is *splag-chnizomai*. Here is what the standard Greek to English dictionary in *Strong's Exhaustive Concordance* says about this important word:

> Splagchnizomai: to have the *bowels* yearn, i.e. figuratively *feel sympathy*, to *pity*:—have (be moved with) *compassion*.

It would in fact be acceptable to translate the word as "moved with pity," but this translation does not seem to accurately reflect what any enlightened being would really feel. Pity is a condescending and very codependent emotion, a sentiment wholly inappropriate for an advanced soul. This is a translation that would be more appropriate for medieval times, when codependency ran rampant through the existing church structure that dominated Christianity during its infancy and adolescence. And although such cutting-edge concepts as "codependency" might seem an anachronism in medieival times, nothing could be further from the truth. If codependency is defined as an attitude a person or society may adopt toward others, in which there is excessive concern about what other people are thinking and doing, and a preoccupation with wanting to change what others are thinking and doing, then the psychospiritual climate of the Middle Ages could only be described as profoundly codependent. It is important to remain cognizant of when the usual translations took place.

———————

Now, in our more spiritually evolved state, such a translation is unseemly and wholly inaccurate. The average spiritually minded person, at the turn of the millennia, is acutely aware of the problems inherent in codependency, and *eager* to avoid its rather obvious pitfalls. It hardly seems an excessive jump to move to the conclusion that the teacher was reasonably like-minded in his desire to avoid codependency and instead promote self-empowerment. With this in mind, it would seem far more logical and accurate to translate *splagchnizomai* as "*moved* with compassion."

Not to belabor this point, but the dictionary does not say the word means "felt" compassion. Because Greek is such an intricate language with many ways to express subtlety, there is another word that would better express "felt" compassion. But the author did not choose that word in describing the shift in attention that occurred as the teacher awoke from his meditation and focused his attention on those gathered around him. Instead he deliberately chose *splagchnizomai* because it is a more *active* word. The deliberate choice of the word *splagchnizomai* indicates the teacher was going one step further in his response to what he was *seeing* in those who were suffering before him—as he shifted his attention *from* himself *to* those around him. It indicates that he was *moved,* set into motion, into *action, as* he felt compassion. What is so profound about this is that the author did not use two words— one for *feeling* compassion and one for being set into *motion. Both* concepts are integrated into *one* word, as if to say that when an enlightened being *feels* compassion there is—or certainly *should* be—an automatic, immediate *reflex to do something.* Establishing this kind of *reflexive compassionate response,* and the mind-set that is part and parcel of it, is the second condition that must be established by all miracle workers and it is also a condition of supreme importance to someone studying the parable sequence.

Seeing what is going on with others, *feeling* compassion, and being *set into motion* are the three elements that make up the second condition of a miracle where the teacher fed five thousand. These very same three elements are incorporated into Luke 10:33: *But a Samaritan while traveling came near him; and when he saw him, he was moved with compassion.* The use of the word *splagchnizomai* here in parable number thirteen is no accident and gives us the practical take-home point that we can *use* to change our own lives for the better. We are being told that if we are to master the mysteries, particularly if we are to experience their miraculous *benefits* in our own lives, we will have to develop the reflex sequence of seeing, feeling compassion, and being *set into action* as an automatic and immediate reaction to any suffering that we perceive.

In other words, you have to develop an automatic tendency to pay attention to what is happening to others around you, and *at the very same time,* automatically and immediately take *some* kind of action. At this point it will no longer suffice for you to see something in the media about suffering and tragedy and simply continue to sit there "feeling pity." At this point, it will no longer do to simply sit there, say, "That's too bad." Those days are gone. From now on you will be expected to actually do something. Something. Anything.

My own spiritual adviser has given me one prayer to pray each morning before I arise, and it may surprise you to learn what it is. For in this prayer, I am to ask *nothing for myself at any time.* Instead I am to ask God for only one thing, and that is to help me get my mind off myself and onto others. This simple but often difficult task is the single most important thing I can do to assure that my own life goes smoothly. And it works perfectly.

On the days that I actually remember to say the prayer and say it sincerely, something wonderful and magical happens. Although I am still just as self-centered and egotistical as everyone else, things begin to spontaneously occur to *help* me take my mind off myself. People appear, situations occur in which I *have* to pay attention to others. Without the aid of such people and circumstances, the task of taking my mind away from my own problems and putting my attention onto the affairs of *others* might be next to impossible. The ego is so powerful and pervasive that to overcome it would require a will and a discipline far beyond that possessed by me—and most other average minds. The wiles of the ego are incredibly tricky, incredibly subtle, and will take over even the most sincere individual in very short order if there is not some kind of competent help. The good news is that if you *ask* for such help, you will get it. Always. If you ask to be a billionaire, Spirit may not be able to help you, at least anytime soon, as this is simply not one of its priorities. However, if you ask for help in being more attentive to the needs of others, and less selfish, Spirit will most certainly help you, always. Helping people become less egotistical and more helpful to one another is one of its priorities. But you have to ask. Be sure to ask. Spirit is not codependent, as has been made abundantly clear, and won't simply sweep in and help you. You have to ask or it is not authorized to do anything.

THIS PARABLE CONTINUES the lesson in the last parable—that the universe will treat us as we treat those who interact with *us* on a daily basis. But this parable is not a simple reiteration of any other lesson or parable anywhere. This story has its own personality, and a very distinct and well-delineated message. The essence of this particular lesson is that although you are strongly advised to have an automatic attitude of compassion and goodwill—that seems almost a given—you are also expected now to go *out of your way* to help others, even those you have no obligation to help. In this way the universe will go out of its way to help you, *even when it has no obligation to help you.* This is the building of *grace.* This lesson seems of *extraordinary* importance to the teacher because the next parable, the parable of the friend at midnight, elaborates on this idea of going out of the way as well.

It's all about things you already know about, in your heart, at least. This is basic information but may easily bear infinite reiteration: We can only give to ourselves. It is not possible to reach out to someone, to give someone help and not receive a gift in kind yourself that, if not equal, is ten- or a hundredfold in return—provided you are sufficiently conscious to perceive the return. Consciousness responds in kind to consciousness. Unfailingly. Our thoughts bear fruit, unerringly reflecting the intent behind them, the accounting system regulating the exhange of energy, our return, far more accurately than that of any human being. If we treat others well, even when we do not *owe* them anything, the universe will help us. It will even help us with our "weed seeds." If we consistently *notice* the needs of others and actually do something to help, the universe will automatically help us manifest our highest thought forms in a benevolent, prosperous manner even when we unintentionally sow negative thought forms.

ACTIVATING PARABLE LESSON 13

1. There are circumstances in *your* life, right now, that are a direct parallel to the circumstances presented to the good Samaritan. There are people around you in need that you are passing by. You need to be *very* careful and *very* attentive to pick this up, for in many cases it will appear that there is nothing wrong with what you are doing—or

more likely not doing. Like the priest and the Levite, the people who are passing by those in need won't be getting into any trouble or suffering any apparent negative consequences because of their neglect.

Neglect may even seem to be socially acceptable. Like the people in the story, you might easily feel that no one will notice, that there will be no consequences if you simply do the same thing that others are doing and quietly pass on by. And that is the bulk of your transgressions of the law at this point, neglect. You've long since passed the place where you were intentionally stingy or did much of anything, for that matter, intentionally malignant. Now it's all about what you simply *don't* do. So, if you feel in any way that you may have reached some kind of plateau and are failing to experience the kinds of distinct exciting advances that you used to have, you may have to take a hard look at what you are simply neglecting. These two parables are all about this precise subject.

It all comes down to this: Altering the course of your own life, your own spiritual journey, in order to help someone may very well be inconvenient in most cases. In fact, if you want to apply this parable, you can count on it. If you have your guard up, you are more likely to be able to pass the tests that are being presented to you. You are a busy person, you have places to go, responsibilities to attend to, and these responsibilities will be pressing and important for sure. That should not be mimimized. But all along the way you will be encountering people who have gotten themselves into trouble, sometimes in very subtle ways that are nonetheless very significant to them. They may not be beaten and bleeding on the side of the road. They may be perfectly well composed and have no visible signs of immediate suffering. That doesn't matter.

The parable is an allegory. There are many, many ways to be beaten and bleeding. The challenge will be for you to see, *with the eyes of Spirit, what is happening at the level of Spirit.* People can be spiritually beaten and bleeding, emotionally beaten, mentally beaten. You know exactly what this means. Your responsibility at this level of evolution is not to wait until you see suffering but to proactively *look* through the surface, to *find* where there is real suffering.

The very first thing you need to do to activate parable lesson thirteen is to *make a conscious decision to cultivate a deeply rooted reflex of compassion,* to take the mature spiritual responsibility, to *proactively* develop the skill to automatically *see and at once be moved with compassion.*

2. Realize you can fully expect to find, as you encounter the people in need you will certainly be encountering, that helping them may be expensive, time-consuming, and generally inconvenient, perhaps causing you to get in trouble because you have not attended to your *expected* worldy duties.

Who are these people? What are their circumstances? The answer is that you know. You already know, as you read, who these people are. Maybe you are passing them by physically—it could be the disabled vet with the sign at the stoplight—and it is inconvenient for you to stop. God forbid the car behind you honks. It could be the person in the next cubicle, the next seat on the plane, or at the checkout line at the supermarket, or any other mundane and apparently insignificant situation. But more likely is the tests will present themselves, are presenting themselves, via people *close* to you, people you are passing by in *consciousness.* The son or daughter, wife or husband, who wants you simply to *be* with them, to pay *attention* to them—but you convincingly rationalize at every opportunity that your attention is best kept on other things.

The ways that those in need may present themselves vary widely. And the ways that we can pass them by also vary widely. The story of the good Samaritan, after all, is a parable, and as such applies to all analogous cases. To activate this parable lesson, you need to begin now, today, to take the responsibility, the *initiative* to open your spiritual eyes and *see* the people who need your attention, your care, your kindness, your generosity. Then, it is your sacred responsibility to actually *do* something. Now.

3. Be *moved with compassion.* At this point in your spiritual evolution, seeing those in need and feeling compassion for them is no longer sufficient. *Far from it.* To progress through the mastery of the parable sequence and to mastery of the mysteries, you will have to begin *acting and in a more consistent, reliable, and rapid manner.* And not just once, or ten times, or even a hundred. It is required of you at this split point in your own evolutionary sequence to *make the conscious decision to act*—every time, always, and immediately.

IN THE HUMAN BODY, a reflex is something that happens *automatically, without* the input of the mind. When the doctor taps your knee with a hammer, a signal goes from the knee to your spine, is processed quickly there without any input from the higher parts of the nervous system like the brain, and goes back directly to the knee, which immediately jerks. This all happens before you can think a single thought. So must it be with your seeing and being moved. In order to proceed beyond this point you actually need to be that good at it, that automatic.

THE FRIEND AT MIDNIGHT

The Reflex of Compassion II

LUKE 11:5–8

And he said to them, "Suppose one of you has a friend, and you go to him at midnight and say to him, 'Friend, lend me three loaves of bread; for a friend of mine has arrived, and I have nothing to set before him.'

And he answers from within, 'Do not bother me; the door has already been locked, and my children are with me in bed; I cannot get up and give you anything.'

I tell you, even though he will not get up and give him anything because he is his friend, at least because of his persistence he will get up and give him whatever he needs.

So I say to you, Ask, and it will be given you; search, and you will find; knock, and the door will be opened for you.

For everyone who asks receives, and everyone who searches finds, and for everyone who knocks, the door will be opened."

---

*T*HIS PARABLE IS ONE of the most interesting in that it includes one of the most frequently quoted statements in the Bible, "Ask, and it will be given you." This statement is arguably the most lavish—and the most *mystical*—of all the promises we are given by the teacher. Normally, this famous statement is quoted by itself—as if it were a statement of truth unto itself. But it is not a self-contained truth. For the promise to become realized, it has to be understood, and *activated,* in context. And this parable shows us how.

How many times have we been in need and someone has told us to simply *ask God* to help us fulfill that need, telling us wisely that "everyone who asks receives." But this parable would have us understand this critical promise differently. If we are to get the promise to really *work* in our lives, we will have to do more than simply *ask.* What the parable says is that we can indeed ask for things and receive them, knock on doors and have them opened, but only if we do this *after* establishing very specific spiritual conditions. Therefore, any serious student of the parables would obviously be eager to understand and implement these spiritual conditions without delay.

The parable tells the story of a man who is visited by a guest late at night—"midnight," specifically. He wants to treat the guest with respect, he wants to help him, honor him, and feed him. But he cannot. For his own cupboard is bare and he has no food with which to feed the guest. But his *intention* is pure and selfless and genuine, so he *persists.* He is so focused on providing sustenance and comfort for the guest that he goes to a nearby house and knocks on his neighbor's door.

Now imagine, if you will, that this person is you, that it is midnight, and that you have to go next door to one of the neighbors living near you. How would this make you feel? Would you be expending a huge amount of personal capital to do this? One of the last things any of us wants to do is to wake up the entire household of a neighbor in the middle of the night. This would be most embarrassing and humiliating. It wouldn't necessarily hurt you or the neighbor in any serious way, but it would likely injure your *pride,* possibly evoke the disdain, however subtle, of the neighbor, and certainly put you in a state of indebtedness.

But the man of the parable has an intent so pure and so selfless that he *works through* his fear and his ego, and actually walks over to the neighbor's door and pounds on it. The neighbor is awakened. But he won't open the door. He tells the man that his family is asleep and that he simply can't open the door to allow a disturbance that will awaken his wife and children at such an awkward time. Surely this is utterly humiliating for the man. If you were in his shoes, you would probably stop at this point, wouldn't you? But the man persists even in the face of this terribly humbling state of affairs. If this were not enough, he humbles himself even further by asking to borrow three loaves of bread! He is asking a lot. In that time and place, three loaves of bread was no insignificant amount of food.

The parable tells us that although the neighbor will initially refuse to open the door and supply the requested food, if the man persists and continues knocking, the neighbor will eventually open the door and lend him the three loaves he has requested. The teacher then tells us that the same will hold true for you: that if you knock on doors they will surely be opened—*but the opening will be greatly facilitated if you are including the welfare of others in your search.*

The man isn't knocking on the door to get food for himself. No doubt he will share in the meal and have a great time with his guest, but that is not his primary *intent.* His primary intent is to focus on the well-being of someone else. He knocks on the door in order to take action to provide sustenance to increase *another* person's well-being.

Now we're getting somewhere. This brings up a concept best referred to as "integral need," that is so aptly illustrated in the miracle of the loaves and fishes. When that profound miracle was enacted five thousand people were stranded in the middle of the desert after they followed the teacher—with the intention of gaining spiritual knowledge. Eventually, the disciples find that it is getting very late in the day and that the masses are very hungry. They make an inventory and find that they do not have enough food. They ask the teacher to help them supply food for the massive crowd.

The food is then manifested by miraculously *expanding* the small amount that already exists in hand—five loaves and two fish. The point is that what is asked for is supplied to the disciples, but only because they are not asking for themselves. They have *seen* the masses, noted that they were hungry, and then are *moved* with compassion. They are set into motion and begin trying to help the large crowd. Their motive is unselfish. They have *integrated the needs of others* into their request. Furthermore, the miracle worker who produces the supply for the disciples and the crowd is not supplying it for himself, either. He, *too,* focuses on the needs of others.

The other important point here is that everyone who receives the food, masses and disciples alike, are not there for the purpose of receiving food. They are there for spiritual reasons, they are there with the primary intent to receive spiritual truth and knowledge. Therefore, their need for food, which would allow them to continue to stay with the teacher and learn more, is an *integral* part of their spiritual quest. They are in the desert with the teacher seeking Spirit. Now, with these conditions in place, Spirit has a *vested interest* in supplying the food necessary to sustain their quest.

In summary, the real message of the parable is that if you are to activate this most profound and direct of promises—that you *will* receive if you ask—you will have to do more than simply ask. You will also be required to be generous to others—even when it is completely inconvenient for you.

ACTIVATING PARABLE LESSON 14

1. At this split point in your personal evolution, it is required that you continue to shift your focus from yourself to others, from getting to giving, but at a new and higher level. Although you may already be helping others, and doing it reasonably well, parable fourteen will have you now go another step up the ladder. This will be difficult and may be painful at times, as it is for the host in the story. This is why the teacher simultaneously gives us the *requirements* for our more evolved behavior and the most lavish of all his *promises*: Ask and you will receive.

   To activate parable fourteen, so that you can ascend upward in your spiritual journey, you will now be required to go *out of your way* to give to others, no matter how *inconvenient* it is for you. To activate parable lesson fourteen, *become ready and willing* to proactively help anyone who presents themselves for need, *no matter how inopportune or malapropos the situation.* This parable is thus a continuation of, and expansion upon, the parable of the good samaritan.

2. Rest easy. Codependency will take care of itself automatically if you have followed all the parable lessons carefully. Certainly, there are ways that people can become *codependent* and unhealthy in their giving, but as long as you follow the rest of the parable lesson sequence, you will remain appropriate and your own life and reputation will remain secure. Neither parable thirteen nor fourteen tells

us that anything untoward happened to the generous givers. We can rest assured that our development will remain psychologically sound and healthy as long as we follow all the parable lessons to the letter.

3. *Know* that as you so activate the parable by shifting your mind-set and your actions, you have activated the greatest of all the promises. Know, believe, and *move ahead confidently* with the absolute assurance that you can now ask and receive. *Dwell* on this in your spirit and have faith.

THE RICH FOOL

The Law of Confidence and the Law of Circulation

LUKE 12:16–21, GALILEE

And he said to them, "Take care! Be on your guard against all kinds of greed; for one's life does not consist in the abundance of possessions."

Then he told them a parable: "The land of a rich man produced abundantly.

And he thought to himself, 'What should I do, for I have no place to store my crops?'

Then he said, 'I will do this: I will pull down my barns and build larger ones, and there I will store all my grain and my goods.

And I will say to my soul, "Soul, you have ample goods laid up for many years; relax, eat, drink, be merry."'

But God said to him, 'You fool! This very night your life is being demanded of you. And the things you have prepared, whose will they be?'

So it is with those who store up treasures for themselves but are not rich toward God."

He said to his disciples, "Therefore I tell you, do not worry about your life, what you will eat, or about your body, what you will wear.

For life is more than food, and the body more than clothing.

Consider the ravens: they neither sow nor reap, they have neither storehouse nor barn, and yet God feeds them. Of how much more value are you than the birds!

And can any of you by worrying add a single hour to your span of life?

If then you are not able to do so small a thing as that, why do you worry about the rest?

Consider the lilies, how they grow: they neither toil nor spin; yet I tell you, even Solomon in all his glory was not clothed like one of these.

But if God so clothes the grass of the field, which is alive today and tomorrow is thrown into the oven, how much more will he clothe you— you of little faith!

And do not keep striving for what you are to eat and what you are to drink, and do not keep worrying.

For it is the nations of the world that strive after all these things, and your Father knows that you need them.

Instead, strive for his kingdom, and these things will be added unto you as well.

Do not be afraid, little flock, for it is your Father's good pleasure to give you the kingdom."

THE TERM "SPIRITUAL LAW" is an interesting one. It implies that spiritual principles can be articulated in the same way as legal principles. And law, modern legal law certainly, can get remarkably detailed and specific. Often, when we read the way a modern law has been written, we find that there are many clauses and subparagraphs within that law. So is it in the spiritual realm. Spiritual law can also be detailed and complex and require multiple clauses and paragraphs to articulate correctly. This parable and the statements that flow from it represent an excellent example of this kind of detailed description of a spiritual law: the Law of Confidence—and the Law of Circulation, which is part and parcel of it.

There are different ways of summarizing the Law of Confidence and the subclauses that complete it. If we weren't careful, and lapsed into negative phraseology, we might be tempted to call the law described in this parable the Law of Greed. For the parable begins with the story of a man who appears to have fallen prey to this most insidious of spiritual enemies. But the parable's law and its clauses actually describe the power a specific *positive* thought form has to enable consistent and effortless material supply. And that thought form, the antithesis of greed, is *confidence*.

But the parable is somewhat complex. Although it certainly addresses the issue of confidence and trust, it also illustrates the Law of Circulation just as well. This is a law that tells us what happens when resources are allowed to move freely through one's life and one's world—and not hoarded.

> *The land of a rich man produced abundantly.*
>
> *And he thought to himself, "What should I do, for I have no place to store my crops?"*
>
> *Then he said, "I will do this: I will pull down my barns and build larger ones, and there I will store all my grain and my goods."*

In this case, a man has successfully created a state of superabundance—he has *more* than he can actually use, even more than he can save. He represents you, the student of the mysteries, when you have started to generate personal prosperity by activating the parable lesson sequence. What does the man in the story do with the excess? Instead of giving it away and allowing it to continue to circulate, he *hoards* it, storing it away in the belief that the surplus will protect him from further lack down the road. This gives him a *false sense of security.* He lets down his guard and regresses into celebration mode, believing euphorically that everything is all taken care of, that he has nothing else to worry about. But he *does* need to worry at this point. For the parable indicates that the man will need his soul "this very night."

The wording of the story implies that debauchery is not conducive to care and maintenance of the soul, that a soul indulging vainly in mere sensual pleasures is one that can quickly grow weak and spiritually unfit. It seems to warn us that when we begin to reap the benefits of our spiritual quest, our activation of the parable sequence, we will grow in riches. But that if we lose sight of what is really happening within the motion of the spiritual laws in play, we will stop relying on those laws and instead rely upon elements of mere material security. It tells us that if we make decisions to take this fork in the road, the fork that leads to reliance on matter over spirit, we will be setting ourselves up to face a serious test of some kind. Even enormous material holdings and reserves won't help you weather the storm that is about to hit you.

What could present such a test of the soul for you in your life? It could be anything. It could be the death of a child, a natural disaster, a physical disease, an emotional or mental condition, or any number of other difficult and painful circumstances. Indeed, it is only through the deep inner conviction and fortitude that a strong *soul* provides that we can survive such terribly trying conditions such as these. We can all cite numerous examples of materially wealthy people who have suffered great loss in spite of their apparent material security.

There is a priority clause to the laws illustrated. Failing to understand what should always come *first,* the man has put the cart before the horse. Rather than making the same mistake, you are admonished to strive first for the kingdom, *then* these things "will be added unto you." The recommended cause-and-effect sequence is clear and articulates the first element of the Law of Confidence: Strive *first* for spiritual knowledge and spiritual sustenance, and *then* the "things," these material elements of security, will be added unto you. If you prioritize the spiritual aspects of your life such that they come first, you can rest in perfect *confidence* that you will be taken care of materially.

The rich man's challenge is to realize that his soul is the part of his being that connects him with the Source of all his riches. And it is the part of his being that can allow him to freely release his abundance so that it circulates. A man without a soul will have no understanding of the other laws of abundance, the other mysteries, and be incapable of freely releasing energy and resources, secure in the knowledge that they will return ten- or a hundredfold in due course.

The soul is not a "thing" but a motion. The soul is a living, breathing *process,* and is taken to higher levels of evolution through actions, in this case the action of circulation. A miracle worker seeks not a single act of abundance but seeks to become a constant, ongoing, ever-expanding *process of circulation.* Abundance flows in because he works with the laws, and abundance flows out with confidence and ease. For a miracle worker, a master of the mysteries, outflow and inflow become one flow.

Imagine yourself standing in a stream up to your knees in moving water. Look downstream and see the water moving away from you. Now, simply turn around and look the other way. *Shift your perception.* See the water moving toward you. Realize that this process of flow, inward and outward, is the same river, the same flow. The miracle worker shifts his perception in every circumstance to see the true nature of the flow. A miracle worker then offers no resistance to either the inward *or* the outward flow of energy and resources through his life, through every circumstance great and small.

The parable tells us that the Law of Confidence will bring us real energy, real reasources, and thus real security if we will but activate it. But it tells us that this law is activated by *action,* by working seamlessly minute by minute within the great stream of circulation. Circulation in turn will generate abundance and ultimately *more confidence.* As the parable is activated, an upward evolutionary spiral develops, and the soul is lifted to new realms of understanding and personal power.

ACTIVATING PARABLE LESSON 15

1. To activate the Law of Confidence, you will be required to now shift your confidence from worldly security to spiritual security. Although you have no doubt made considerable progress in this area, it is apparently insufficient or you wouldn't be working so hard to increase your awareness and the overall quality of your life. *Make a conscious decision* to strive more diligently for confidence in spirit in every circumstance that life presents.

   Does this mean that you are to cancel your health insurance, take your life savings out of the bank, and cancel your retirement plans? Of course not. The parable makes no recommendation for the man in the parable to dismantle the security, the supply he has thus far assembled. It simply makes the point that relying *in consciousness* on such material backup—without "being rich toward God"—can be a major pitfall and impede your mastery of the mysteries. The parable is a lesson designed to increase your reliance on Spirit and not matter.

2. *List* on a sheet of paper every element that composes your physical

security. Your bank account, your job, the equity in your house, your insurance policies—everything you can think of that you rely upon to keep you safe in this world. Leave enough space beneath each item to write a few sentences.

3. Next, carefully *consider* each item in your list. *See* how each of these factors in your security system really comes *from God.* See that your job has really been provided by God and not human beings, that if you trace the energy in your paycheck back far enough and carefully enough, you will see that it truly originates with Spirit. Become conscious, meditating as long as is required, of the *Source behind the sources.* Then write a brief description of how Spirit is the real power behind each and every component of your survival system.

4. Finally, make a concerted effort to remember each and every day, referring to your list if necessary, what you have learned. *Cultivate a mind-set of ongoing confidence* such that changes at the worldly, material level of reality begin to weaken in their ability to upset you or worry you.

Shift your reliance from finite self, to infinite God.

Remember the teacher's classic question, "Can any of you by worrying add a single hour to your span of life?" Realize, now that you have shifted your reliance from matter to Spirit, that you cannot be let down, cannot be threatened, by people or things—as long as your confidence is coming from the right source, the source that can never dwindle or disappear. Feel the solid trust and optimism that this gives you. Relish it, expand upon it, and live abundantly within its protective arms.

5. Learn and use the Law of Circulation. Do not hoard the resources that come to you. As material supply flows in, maintain and *expand* your outflow of supply and energy. Know that the Law of Circulation is a subclause of the Law of Confidence. In other words, practicing the law of circulation will increase your confidence. And increasing your confidence will in turn allow you to progress with your mastery of the mysteries and the parable sequence—and lead you to everything that you can possibly need or want.

THE BARREN FIG TREE

The Law of Delay

LUKE 13:6–9, GALILEE

Then he told this parable: "A man had a fig tree planted in his vine-yard; and he came looking for fruit on it and found none.

So he said to the gardener, 'See here! For three years I have come looking for fruit on this fig tree, and still I find none. Cut it down! Why should it be wasting the soil?'

He replied, 'Sir, let it alone for one more year, until I dig around it and put manure on it.

If it bears fruit next year, well and good; but if not, you can cut it down.'"

IN MY FIRST YEARS of medical practice I worked in a tiny town in central Kentucky. One of my most interesting pa-tients was a man named John who owned a sawmill where he produced beautiful native hardwoods—cherry, walnut, oak, and sycamore. Some-times I would drive out to his isolated farm deep in the backwoods and peruse the numerous stacks of planks looking for especially well-figured ones I could use to make furniture.

John also owned an orchard and had made part of his living for years selling apples, apple cider, peaches, grapes, and other readily salable produce. One day I got to talking with him about an apple tree I had purchased and was about to plant on my own land. I told him how careful and thorough I was going to be, that I was going to dig a big hole and mix the soil from the hole with plenty of organic matter and lots of manure so that it would be abundantly fertilized.

But I could tell that I wasn't impressing the man a bit because he just started shaking his head back and forth. "No, no, no," he said, with his gentle twang. "That's a terrible way to treat a young fruit tree. If you fertilize a sapling like that, sure it'll grow really fast. But you'll ruin it."

"Now, how could that possibly be?" I queried. "How could fertilizing a tree ruin it? That doesn't make any sense."

"Well," he said, "the slower a fruit tree grows, the more fruit it will produce when it comes of age. That's just the way they are. I learned that the hard way a long time ago," he said. "Fruit trees are different than other trees. The more you prune them, the less you fertilize them with rich fertilizers early on, the *more* flowers will bud in the spring and the more fruit will form on the branches. And the apples will taste better, too, with a richer, more flavorful taste," he added. *Timing*, it seemed, was crucial in the process of fertilization.

I ALWAYS REMEMBERED this little bit of knowledge on the fine points of tree growth and thought it a wonderful analogy to explain the growth and development of human beings and their souls as well. It is common knowledge that people who grow up having to work through problems and overcome hardships tend to be deeper, more mature, and more compassionate than people who grow up with lavish advantages that prevent them from ever struggling, ever becoming strong in spirit and inner conviction.

We choose the problems we encounter in life consciously and with full knowledge of how difficult they will be. But we also know, when we choose these elements of the life we will live, how working through adverse conditions will affect our evolution as spiritual beings. Spiritual evolution, after all, is the ultimate reason we are here on earth in the first place, and our lives are designed with precision and care to offer us a framework for personal growth.

Trees provide a perfect metaphor to illustrate a wide variety of metaphysical principles and have been used by teachers for millennia. This parable presents a prime example. A man has a fruit tree, in this case a fig, planted in his garden. After three years he thinks that plenty of time has elapsed for the tree to have matured sufficiently to bear fruit. He goes out to inspect the tree but is badly disappointed. There isn't even a single fig on the tree.

He expresses his displeasure to the gardener and tells him that he thinks the tree should be cut down. Because it is not bearing fruit, he reasons, it is wasting the soil and other resources that could be used to produce a more abundant tree. But the gardener tells him to slow down and give the tree another chance. He tells the landowner that he is going to fertilize the tree and give it another year. Then, he says, if it has not by that time borne fruit, he will cut it down to make way for a new and better tree.

The fig tree is a specific, partially developed intention that has not yet manifested. It is important to note that a tree is chosen, as opposed to an annual plant, to illustrate the point. A tree, particularly a tree that bears fruit repeatedly, represents the concept of a larger and more elaborate thought form project. The fig tree in the parable has not manifested after three years so its owner asks the vinedresser what to do. The vinedresser tells him that the tree is not a failure, that it simply needs more attention, more time.

A fruit tree is a tree that bears fertile, seed-bearing structures. These seed-bearing structures can generate more trees. A fruit tree therefore represents *self-perpetuating thought forms.*

Remember that the teacher told us that these parables are about the mysteries, about secret knowledge conveyed by initiation. Ergo, in this context, the vinedresser represents a teacher helping the initiate cultivate a thought form project to its completion as manifested reality.

An elaborate thought form may have to be cultivated for quite some time. The bigger it is, and the more complex its elements, the longer it will take to germinate and mature to its fruit-bearing stage. Without a teacher's reassurance and guidance, the parable seems to say, we may never persist long enough to be able to put the *cause*—thought—together with the *effect*—the manifestation.

ACTIVATING PARABLE LESSON 16

1. Examine the thought forms that you are cultivating in your life. Realize that there will be two distinct phases in their development. In the initial phases, Divine Intelligence may not apply too much "fertilizer," too much external help, too much of the Law of Increase to your project, for that would not be in your best interests. You might manifest something quickly, but it would be grossly inferior to what could manifest if a degree of patience and restraint were exercised. If you are getting anxious in the early phases of working with a specific thought form project, relax. Realize that everything is still on

course. To activate the sixteenth parable lesson, *begin by making a conscious decision to choose the path of patience* with your project.

2. If you have worked with a certain thought form project for a respectable interval but are not noticing any significant progress, it may *now* be time to consider adding fertilizer. What will be this fertilizer as it applies to your daily, modern life? Consider: Fertilizer is the waste product of animals. But because of the beautiful symbiosis of the plant and animal kingdoms, animal waste—things like carbon dioxide and manure—is something that makes plants more fertile, i.e., more likely to grow and bear fruit. Conversely, plant "waste," such as oxygen, is pure life energy for animal life forms.

Your "fertilizer" may therefore come from the lowest effluvium of your life, the detritus—material and spiritual—that you are trying to jettison. For a miracle worker, nothing must be wasted, not even waste. The miracle worker is a transmuter, a being who makes it her business to metamorphose the base to the noble—the way animal waste might be converted into life-giving fertilizer via the process of composting.

Think about it: If you were to take your lowest thought forms, your doubt, your fear, your anger, your resentment, and transmute them such that all the vast psychic energy that is tied up in them is now freed and redirected toward your positive intentions, what would happen? Needless to say, the psychic energy now available for your positive thought form projects would be massive. You could use this newly freed energy to surge ahead in profound ways.

We already know from the previous two parables that we are being required to shift our reliance from matter to spirit, and from doubt to trust—to cultivate a mind-set of confidence. We also know from other parables that, via the powerful process of forgiveness and other means, we are supposed to be releasing negative psychic energy, resentments, and "debts," and attempting to convert them to more positive, more productive thought energy anyway. This is a parable that is activated especially when the student of the mysteries finds herself experiencing a developmental plateau. To activate parable sixteen during such a plateau, redouble your efforts to turn your negativity into useful, positive intention.

3. Understand the Law of Delay. Normally we find the delay between the conception and implementation of a thought form and its manifestation to be aggravating and annoying. And perhaps it is. But it is essential at this point in your progression toward mastery to understand the delay process and work *with* it. To begin with, if not for the delay process, you would have destroyed yourself long ago. Be realistic: How many of your angry, terrified, violent thought forms would have destroyed you or others had they immediately manifested?

Spirit has blessedly built a *protective delay factor* into the universe to prevent such tragedies, and if not for it, the human race would literally never have survived and developed to its current level of development. This delay factor works like this: The more *selfish* your overall mind-set, the *longer* the delay you will experience in most of your projects. The more *unselfish* your mind-set, the more you tend to naturally focus on others and their needs in a healthy, non-codependent way, the *shorter* the delay you will experience. This is why a highly evolved soul such as Christ was able to manifest things almost instantly—the water into wine, for example. His degree of evolution was a direct function of his tendency to be concerned with those around him and not with himself. When a human being has reached such a state of selfless mind-set, he or she is now "safe" and can be entrusted with advanced powers of creation because it is impossible for any truly selfless person to even think a negative thought form.

And the previous parable lessons contribute to the development of such a safe personality as well. When a person is able to effectively and efficiently *forgive* others automatically and with perfect consistency, that person will be virtually incapable of projecting a negative harmful thought form. Such a person no longer has a need to have the safety delay factor and it is gradually shortened. A persona with a delay factor that has been so diminished is referred to by others as a miracle worker.

But there is another powerful variable at work in the delay factor, and that is patience. The Law of Delay works such that the more patience a miracle worker is able to exercise, the shorter the delay. The more impatience, the longer the delay. To activate parable sixteen, make a concerted effort to examine your thought form projects and honestly identify any instances of impatience. List these on a piece of paper so that you can clearly contemplate how they may be lengthening the delay processes you are experiencing.

4. Invite God into your situation and ask him specifically to take away your impatience, and to help you in your conscious efforts to substitute the more positive and more effective attitude of patience.

5. Ask *your teacher.* If you find yourself experiencing a developmental plateau and everything seems as though it is stalled out, ask your teacher what he or she thinks may be happening. The teacher is likely to suggest that you now "add fertilizer," to inject your posi-

tive intentions with more psychic energy. If you don't have a teacher, *don't believe it*. When the student is ready, the saying goes, the teacher *always* appears. To activate this parable, *recognize* the teach-ers who will always be present in your life when you need them and then maximize their ability to help you by asking them their opinion and following their advice.

THE GREAT SUPPER

The Law of Generality

LUKE 14:15–24, PEREA

Then Jesus said to him, "Someone gave a great dinner and invited many.

At the time for the dinner he sent his slave to say to those who had been invited, 'Come; for everything is ready now.'

But they all alike began to make excuses. The first said to him, 'I have bought a piece of land, and I must go out and see it; please accept my regrets.'

Another said, 'I have bought five yoke of oxen, and I am going to try them out; please accept my regrets.'

Another said, 'I have just been married, and therefore I cannot come.'

So the slave returned and reported this to his master. Then the owner of the house became angry and said to his slave, 'Go out at once into the streets and lanes of the town and bring in the poor, the crippled, the blind, and the lame.'

And the slave said, 'Sir, what you ordered has been done, and there is still room.'

Then the master said to the slave, 'Go out into the roads and lanes,
and compel people to come in, so that my house may be filled.
For I tell you, none of those who were invited will taste my dinner.'"

I HAVE COUNSELED MANY PEOPLE over the years in thousands of private sessions, both in person and over the
phone. We talk about all kinds of things, solve all kinds of problems,
and I love this work more than any other that I do. One of the most
common questions I am asked about the process of manifestation has
to do with specificity. Many of my clients tell me that they have taken
courses on manifesting better circumstances in their lives, and that
one of the most common recommendations they are given is to be extremely *specific* in the use of thought forms. People are often told, for
example, that if they are looking for a soul mate, they should ask very
carefully and systematically for precise and well-defined *specifics*—
color of eyes, color of hair, height, weight, individual personality characteristics, occupation, hobbies, and so on.

One woman so advised came to me and told me that she was having a really bad problem with the manifestation process. "I got the
guy," she said, "and I got almost every specific thing I asked for."

"So," I mused, "what's the problem?" I thought I might know how
the story would end.

"I forgot to add *single* to the list," she moaned.

Another woman told me a nearly identical story but lamented that
she had neglected to add the quality *sober* to her list. I myself experienced the same situation when I first started working with standard
manifestation techniques, affirmations, visualization, "treasure maps,"

and so forth. I decided that what I wanted was to be a very busy doctor. That I thought would be fantastic. What a life that would be, I thought. I'll feel so wanted and needed and respected and I'll be able to do so many people so much good.

We must be very, very careful in this regard. When my manifestation finally materialized, I got all the things I had specifically desired. I found myself really starting to get busy. And busier. And busier—until I finally found myself one of only three doctors working a very underserved county in an underserved area of the country. I was one of three doctors serving more than seventeen thousand patients. And now I was having to do shifts of twenty-four and even thirty-six hours. Once I even had to work a total of seventy-two hours with only a very few, short naps.

I got what I had specified. I was busy. But I had forgotten to add something important to the list: Happy. To my deep dismay my manifestation had brought me a great burden and a great misery.

So it is with the manifestation process. The parable of the great supper, in Luke—along with a slightly different version of the parable found in Matthew called the marriage of the king's son—illustrates this critical principle very clearly. The people originally invited to the "feast" are those who were *expected* to come. We send out thought forms with specific expectations as to what will result, what will manifest. But *the more specific our expectations* the harder it is to accomplish the manifestation. This is a clause within the Law of Delay: *The more specific your requests, the longer the delay may be. The more general your request, the shorter the delay.*

With each specific demand we limit the ways the universe can accomplish the goal, the feast, which represents a state of fulfillment, happiness. With each specific request we tie the Universe's hands a little bit more, limiting the routes through which our request may be processed and fulfilled. The parable tells us that when this kind of specific approach fails and that which we *expected* fails to manifest, we are thus advised to "kill" those specific expectations, to relinquish them, in favor of more general thought forms. Generality frees the universe to take many paths to achieve the desired end state. When that happens the wedding hall will be filled—the desired state manifested.

For example, a man tries to manifest a relationship. But he tries to include too many specific details. His life mate is a certain height, has a certain personality, a certain color of hair, a certain figure, and so on. The universe can of course find and supply such a woman, but if many things have been specified, many women will be eliminated from the pool of possibilities and few will remain. It may require a lot of time for the universe to line everything up such that one of these relatively rare women appears in the man's life. Even when she appears, he may well find that he is not happy.

It would be much better for this man to try inviting something more general into his life—like being "happy in a relationship." Now the universe has a much larger number and variety of women who will fit the bill. The manifestation can happen much more *quickly*. But more important, the man ends up with what he really wanted in the first place, and that is to be happy.

ACTIVATING PARABLE LESSON 17

1. To activate the Law of Generality, examine all your thought form projects. What are you really *expecting*? What have you really *invited* into your life? Are you visualizing a *successful wedding* as the

end result, or are you visualizing *specific guests* and thus trying to manipulate the process unnecessarily? Realize that you don't have the knowledge or expertise to be specific at this point in your evolutionary development. Who are you to try to control the process by which your dream manifests? This parable would have you take a fresh look at what you are trying to accomplish.

2. Redesign your thought form project. If you are trying to obtain something specific, it is absolutely critical that you understand what is *behind* that specific thing, what it is you really want. If you want a car, for example, meditate upon the car until you realize what it is you want *from* the car. *In most cases what you really want from things are certain feelings.* A feeling is a word psychologists use to describe the sum total of a person's experiences in a given situation—the bodily sensations, the emotions, the mental thoughts—all of these put together compose a feeling. A feeling is thus the essence, the *spirit* of any circumstance.

   We may want "a car." But we have to understand what is behind the car. We have to realize that we want it because it can bring us security, freedom, excitement, and fun. Redesign your current thought form projects so that they will bring you the *feelings* first. Let the rest remain more general. Turn the project over to the great designer who knows better how to get you to your desired goals.

3. *Reprioritize.* Even though these kinds of feelings, these kinds of spiritual essences are what we *really* want, we too often put the cart before the horse, the matter *before* the spirit. Put spirit first, we are told, and *then* all these things will be added unto you. To activate

this parable lesson, make sure you understand what the true priorities are in your quest. Put first things first.

4. *Lower your standards.* That's right. You heard correctly: Lower your standards. The man invited all the high-society people to his celebration but ended up with an empty hall. All too often I counsel people who have set standards so high that they have made things very difficult to manifest. Doing this is often unnecessary and inappropriate. It is another way of being too specific. You may be trying to manifest a job, a soul mate, or a house that is nearly perfect. Not only have you paid little attention to identifying the feelings you are wishing to experience, you have made foolish decisions regarding what it will take to achieve the feelings that are your real desire.

It is so often the case that such individuals end up with nothing because they have tied the hands of the universe so tightly that it has few if any ways to bring about the manifestation.

This is not to suggest that you should lower your moral or ethical standards, per se. Rather, it is to suggest that you might be much happier than you ever thought with a lot less than you ever thought. It is to suggest that you reevaluate what you are trying to achieve to see if it is possible for you to have a great time, a great life, with much less than you are asking for. You don't need perfect *things* to make you perfectly *happy.* Such thinking is fundamentally flawed.

Letting go can be a little tricky and divine guidance is in order. *Invite God into the situation and ask him specifically to help you be happier with less.* Infinite Intelligence is always eager to help with this kind of task and will go out of its way to help you. The end result is that you will find your heaven more quickly and *enjoy* it much more.

In theory, you could be happy with almost nothing. That is entirely within the realm of possibility. Contemplate any dissatisfaction or perceived lack in your life right now. Realize that if you could somehow *want* much less that most, perhaps all, of this dissatisfaction would dissipate in short order. Consider revamping your entire mind-set such that it becomes a priority to desire less.

THE LOST SHEEP

The Law of Independence

LUKE 15:3–7

So he told them this parable: "Which one of you, having a hundred sheep and losing one of them, does not leave the ninety-nine in the wilderness and go after the one that is lost until he finds it?

When he has found it, he lays it on his shoulders and rejoices.

And when he comes home, he calls together his friends and neighbors, saying to them, 'Rejoice with me, for I have found my sheep that was lost.'"

I T IS A WONDERFUL STORY. Perhaps you've heard it: The story of *The Hundredth Monkey,* as told in Ken Keye's classic book of the same name. It goes like this:

In 1952, something most fascinating was observed in the Macaca fuscata, a Japanese monkey that had been observed by wildlife experts for many years. At that time scientists started feeding the wild monkeys on the island of Koshima by leaving them sweet potatoes in the sand. This was a big hit. The monkeys really liked the sweet potatoes. However, they had a bit of a problem. They hated the sand that covered the potatoes and this seemed to dampen their eating experience greatly.

That's when things started to get interesting. One of the monkeys solved the sand problem. An 18-month-old female the scientists had named Imo learned that if she took the potatoes over to a nearby stream and washed them, that the sand easily disappeared leaving a clean, delicious snack.

That was certainly an act of brilliance. No monkey had ever washed a potato before. This monkey thought in a way that was completely and totally different from all the other monkeys in history. She was an original and knew how to think for herself. She had failed to blindly imitate the behavior of the rest of the colony, all of her forebearers. As a result, she made a breakthrough that would have a profound effect she could not possibly have fathomed.

And although the new washing technique was sheer genius in monkey terms, what she did next was even more profound. She taught the technique to her mother. In short order, their playmates also learned the new technique and they in turn taught it to their mothers.

Over the next six years, every young monkey on the entire island learned the technique.

Finally, a kind of critical mass of knowledgeable monkeys was reached and something utterly amazing happened. Colonies of monkeys on other islands and the mainland troop of monkeys at Takasaki-yama began washing their sweet potatoes.

Author Keyes interpreted this true story to mean that it takes an exact critical mass of human beings that know something before that item of knowledge catches fire and spreads automatically through the populace.

But there is another interpretation to what happened. It might be called *The Millionth Monkey*. This title refers to the fact that the monkey who made the breakthrough, the one that completely shunned convention and thought for herself, was one in a million. And it is that one-in-a-million human being who makes all the difference in our world.

The traditional interpretation of this parable is that if you become "lost," God will find you. He values you and your life, your soul, so much that he will go far out of his way to find you and save you. In this interpretation the Shepherd is normally thought to represent Jesus. His act of returning a lone lost sheep to the fold is depicted in countless popular religious paintings and images.

But this interpretation has a serious flaw. A very viable case can be made that this interpretation simply cannot be the one the teacher intended. For if the analogy is carefully followed, it would seem to indicate that when the Shepherd leaves the ninety-nine sheep to run off after the hundredth sheep that has been lost, the ninety-nine are left completely vulnerable. No sane Shepherd would risk the welfare of ninety-nine sheep in order to save a single sheep. No sane caretaker of any kind, caring for anything, would leave ninety-nine charges vulnerable in a potentially lethal environment filled with predators to save a single charge. Unless, of course, there is something highly unusual about that one particular individual.

Surely there must be some other interpretation. One that somehow explains how the hundredth sheep, the one who leaves the rest of the flock, is valuable enough, special enough to warrant leaving the entire remaining flock vulnerable. And that explanation brings us to the famous story of *The Hundredth Monkey* or, as we will rename it, *The Millionth Monkey*.

THE BENEFICIAL MUTATION

In nature, evolution, *true* evolution—where a species actually changes into a new species—occurs through what are known as "beneficial mutations." A beneficial mutation results from an alteration of the genetic structure of an organism, an alteration that results in a new kind of organism. The new species resulting from such a beneficial mutation has improvements that allow it to *adapt and survive* better than members of the original species.

A mutation that is beneficial and not harmful is actually very, *very* rare and is likely to occur in most species once in thousands or even tens of thousands of years. It is so rare, first, because mutations in general are rare, and, second, because 99.99 percent of those few mutations are *lethal* to the organism—because it leaves it *less fit for survival.* Organisms with such harmful mutations fail to survive and reproduce and naturally die away. It is only when a beneficial mutation occurs that results in *better* adaptation to the environment and subsequent survival that a new and more highly evolved species reproduces and begins to overtake the old species.

These very rare and precious beneficial mutations are, to the Creator, of incalculable value, the product of tens of thousands of years of patience. A being, an intelligence such as that being we refer to as God, who embodies the very essence of creation itself, would value such a creation as an artist might value the very finest masterpiece of an entire era of his life.

As above, so below. The evolutionary principle of the beneficial mutation also applies beautifully and very powerfully to other levels of existence as well. For example, the principle applies to human belief systems, cultures, religious traditions, scientific realms, financial realms, and almost every other kind of system involving many individuals.

What the principle of beneficial mutation says is that every once in a while a person comes along who thinks completely differently from all the other members of his or her system. That person is the one who thinks up the new original ideas, paints the radically innovative paintings, writes the book or paper with the breakthrough, seminal concepts, develops the technique or invention that works better than anything ever conceived before.

One can call to mind all the greats. For all of them were great directly by virtue of the fact that they did or said or thought something so radically different from anything that had ever been done or said or thought before. The millionth monkey is Einstein and the theory of relativity, Newton and the Calculus, Franklin and electricity, Edison and the light bulb. The millionth monkey is van Gogh painting in a way that no one had ever remotely before conceived and clearing the way for modern art as we know it. The millionth monkey is Beethoven, Shakespeare, da Vinci, the Wright Brothers, Mozart, Dylan Thomas, John Lennon, Debussy, and . . . Jesus. If ever there was a beneficial mutation, it was Christ himself.

And remember, our job is to imitate him. Our job is to follow his footsteps, at least on a spiritual basis. Our job is to do "even greater works than these."

ACTIVATING PARABLE LESSON 18

1. Take a hard look at your life. Are you a sheep, following everyone else blindly with the typical herd mentality? Are you worried about

conforming, thinking the way others think, doing things the way other people do things—just because they are doing it that way? Just because everyone is doing something one way hardly means that this is the best way. Nothing could be further from the truth. As we saw in the case of the Millionth Monkey, the one monkey that did everything completely different from the other 999,999 monkeys was the one that finally figured out how to do things the *right* way. The odd monkey, the one that was "weird," was the one that led all the others to a *better* way of living.

2. *Begin now to look for ways to think and act out of the box.* You need not make a fuss over this or attract undo attention. Keep things mostly to yourself. All the great geniuses, the people who have been able to break away from the pack, had a tendency to keep their newly germinating ideas mostly to themselves, to work on their own quietly. Take a fresh look at the ideas you have had that may have been discarded because they were too "outlandish," too "weird," too "strange." Don't worry about these labels. In fact, they may be words that flag ideas that are actually beneficial mutations. Realize that words like "weird" are words for thoughts and actions that don't blindly follow the herd mentality. Granted, all things "weird" aren't beneficial. Neither are all mutations. But all beneficial mutations are "weird" by definition.

3. You already know things that you could do to think and act for yourself. Now, take the leap. Leave the herd and have the courage to act on your own. The parable tells us that you will be fine in due course. Although you may go through a phase in which you appear "lost," *Spirit will ultimately take care of you.* In fact, Spirit will think you so valuable that it will go to *extraordinary measures* to assure

that you are safe and supplied as you help it create and implement new and beneficial ideas, new worlds, new realities with new power and effectiveness.

4. When you get to parable number twenty, the prodigal son, which is two parables ahead, compare the message of this parable to its message. The idea that we should consider doing things that are peculiar, unusual, or even the polar opposite of what the herd is doing was apparently very important in the teacher's eyes. For he repeats and elaborates upon this notion through the parable sequence.

The Lost Coin

The Law of Potential

LUKE 15:8—10

Or suppose a woman has ten silver coins and loses one. Does she not light a lamp, sweep the house and search carefully until she finds it?

And when she finds it, she calls her friends and neighbors together and says, "Rejoice with me; I have found my lost coin."

In the same way, I tell you, there is rejoicing in the presence of the angels of God over one sinner who repents.

The parable of the lost coin is the second in a series of three parables about something that is lost and then found. However, this parable is different from the other two because it talks about an apparently *inanimate* object that is lost. The lost sheep and the prodigal son are alive and capable of making decisions that cause them to be "lost." But a coin cannot make decisions. Or can it?

It is important to understand what a coin is. A coin is something that represents potential energy. This is always the case with money. If you trace any piece of money back to its source, you will find that it represents a human being's time and energy. Even monetary sums that represent "commodities," such as gold, really represent human time, attention, and energy, for such commodities require time and energy to grow, harvest, mine, or refine. As a symbol for time and energy, money thus represents *potential,* potential that can be used to do many different important things, even the miraculous.

So, the lost coin of the parable really represents a person's misplaced, forgotten, or mismanaged potential. It is a symbol for some part of your life force, your talents, or your abilities that has been neglected or forgotten. Ultimately, the coin represents the *consciousness* that underlies the life force and the talents you are considering.

What the parable is telling us is to be like the woman in the story. To pay attention to our potential, not to take it for granted or otherwise exhibit poor stewardship. For who among us has not neglected some element of our potential? The lesson is that we have to be extremely careful of the abilities that we have been given. We need to be acutely aware of our true capabilities, all of them. We need to take inventory of all our skills, all our potentials, so that, like the woman in the story, we know what we have lost and become appropriately concerned. We need to be so concerned that we are moved to action.

When the woman in the story becomes aware that she has "lost" some of her potential, she begins acting, she is set into motion rather than simply falling into idle lament. The action she takes, sweeping the entire house, is telling. Sweeping the house is her way of doing everything possible to be extremely thorough, extremely diligent. Her awareness of the loss causes her to do everything in her power to examine everything in her life to recover the precious potential.

But the lesson doesn't end there. When she recovers the lost energy, she becomes appropriately elated. It should not be a small matter to come to the awareness that you have found or recovered an impor-

tant element of your true potential as a human being. The parable in-
structs us to enter into a state of joy, and to *share* this joy with others.
Apparently, it is not enough to be happy within ourselves. Sharing the
happiness and relief with others will powerfully reinforce the process
of recovery and solidify its effects so that they are more stable and
permanent. If we tell other people who are near and dear that we have
neglected a certain talent or ability, if we make a big deal about it, we
are far less likely to fall back into a state of neglect again.

The final sentence of the story is traditionally translated such that
it would seem to strongly support the idea that the teacher thought in
terms of "sin" and "repentance." But we need to take a closer look and
more accurately translate the orginal Greek terms to understand the
real meaning. The word "sin" really means "to miss the mark." A sinner
is therefore someone who has not achieved their true potential, which
is the real goal, the real "mark." The word traditionally translated as
"repent" or "repentance" is the Greek *metanoeo,* which *Strong's Concordance* tells us means "*to think differently afterwards, to reconsider.*"

The parable is telling us that we need to make a change in our consciousness. It will not be enough to be aware of the loss of potential,
our inadequate stewardship, or to find it and rejoice with others.
What will really be required is that we make a critical shift in our perception, our perception of ourselves.

ACTIVATING PARABLE LESSON 19

1. *Make a written inventory* of all your potential assets, all the things
   that you are capable of doing, all your talents, your abilities, your
   strengths. You may have done this before, but the parable is asking
   you to take a quantum leap forward in the inventory process such

that it is *extremely thorough and comprehensive*—analogous to "sweep-ing your house" top to bottom. Don't neglect anything, don't take anything for granted. Like the woman in the story, get down to the very floor, the base of your consciousness, and examine every cor-ner, every nook and cranny, so that you make absolutely sure that you aren't leaving anything out.

2. *Meditate* upon the components of your potential that you are not using, not maximizing. *Dwell* on these things, so that you are truly recovering them in consciousness. *Stay* with this until you are *acutely aware* of the loss and the recovery. You may be experiencing some kind of lack, some kind of incompleteness, some kind of un-desirable situation that seems to require more spiritual energy, more miracle energy, than you possess. Realize that in reality, you may in fact possess enough energy, enough potential to accomplish the manifestation or healing that you need. It's just that you have "lost" or misplaced the part or parts of your potential. When you suc-cessfully find and gather together and use your lost potential you may very well find that it is quite sufficient to get the job done. It is your responsibility at this level of spirituality to make a con-certed effort to maximize *every iota* of the vast spiritual energy that you possess as a son or daughter of the great creator.

3. *Share* your feelings and your new awareness with others who are important to you. Make sure that you verbalize completely and thoroughly how you have neglected your potential.

4. *Celebrate* the process of recovery. Make a big deal out of it. Have a gathering or a dinner to rejoice in the fact that you have become aware of the potential you have wasted and will now maximize.

This will powerfully reinforce the entire process. When you have made your discoveries "public," it will be more difficult to lapse back into a state of inadequate stewardship.

5. Be aware that God will be rejoicing with you, as well as your guides, your angels. All these action steps will catapult you into a new state of personal power and go a long way to helping you solve any problem you are working on, manifest any dream or thought form project you are working with. For to reach the state you long to achieve you will have to use every iota of your abilities, your talents, and your potential.

THE PRODIGAL SON

The Law of Entanglement

LUKE 15:11—32

Jesus continued: "There was a man who had two sons.

The younger one said to his father, 'Father, give me my share of the estate.' So he divided his property between them.

Not long after that, the younger son got together all he had, set off for a distant country and there squandered his wealth in wild living.

After he had spent everything, there was a severe famine in that whole country, and he began to be in need.

So he went and hired himself out to a citizen of that country, who sent him to his fields to feed pigs.

He longed to fill his stomach with the pods that the pigs were eating, but no one gave him anything.

When he came to his senses, he said, 'How many of my father's hired men have food to spare, and here I am starving to death!

I will set out and go back to my father and say to him: Father, I have sinned against heaven and against you.

I am no longer worthy to be called your son; make me like one of your hired men.'

So he got up and went to his father. But while he was still a long way off, his father saw him and was filled with compassion for him; he ran to his son, threw his arms around him and kissed him.

The son said to him, 'Father, I have sinned against heaven and against you. I am no longer worthy to be called your son.'

But the father said to his servants, 'Quick! Bring the best robe and put it on him. Put a ring on his finger and sandals on his feet.

Bring the fattened calf and kill it. Let's have a feast and celebrate.

For this son of mine was dead and is alive again; he was lost and is found.' So they began to celebrate.

Meanwhile, the older son was in the field. When he came near the house, he heard music and dancing.

So he called one of the servants and asked him what was going on.

'Your brother has come,' he replied, 'and your father has killed the fattened calf because he has him back safe and sound.'

The older brother became angry and refused to go in. So his father went out and pleaded with him.

But he answered his father, 'Look! All these years I've been slaving for you and never disobeyed your orders. Yet you never gave me even a young goat so I could celebrate with my friends.

But when this son of yours who has squandered your property with prostitutes comes home, you kill the fattened calf for him!'

'My son,' the father said, 'you are always with me, and everything I have is yours.

But we had to celebrate and be glad, because this brother of yours was dead and is alive again; he was lost and is found.' "

*T*HE PARABLE OF THE PRODIGAL SON is one of the richest and most fascinating of all the parables, second only, perhaps, to the parable of the sower. It conveys a beautiful and very useful lesson at its most superficial level: If you have gone "astray" it is never too late for you to come back home, back to the good, back to the light, back to God. Even if you have said and done things that you believe are shameful or unforgivable, you will not only be accepted back into God's graces if you seek to return, you will be welcomed back with enthusiasm and great joy.

And who among us would deny that this is true, that this is most certainly consistent with what we know about God? We know that God's mind-set is one of absolute compassion, forgiveness, gratitude, and profound love for us his beloved children. Deep within, we know that there is nothing we can ever do to alienate God from us. We may leave him, but he could never leave us. No matter where we find ourselves, no matter how far from home, we can return with surprising ease, once we have come to the proper state of humility and acceptance.

This is true at an internal level as well, at the level of consciousness. No matter how far off center we have veered, we can get back to a state of centered clarity with greater ease than we might expect. If we find ourselves, during a stressful day, regressing to a less than enlightened state of mind, we should not think, "I'm so far off center that there's no point trying to get back now, here in the thick of things. It's going to take so much effort that I'll have to wait until I get off work and can get to the gym or my yoga class or my meditation room to work on this."

The parable indicates instead that returning home, to our clear, loving, grateful, and centered space, will be easy—*at any time and under any circumstances*—once we have become conscious of the need to return and make a humble, heartfelt attempt to get back. The parable tells us that when we make such a sincere effort we will not only be able to achieve our center, we will find our place of higher consciousness to be even *more* stable and enjoyable than we might normally expect. *The elevation of consciousness will be proportional to the degree of our humility* in accepting the fact that we have fallen off the mark, and proportional to our degree of sincerity in seeking a higher state of mind in the midst of things.

Many times during my typical workday as a physician, I stray like the prodigal son, away from my home, my center. We all have a home, a place of calm and solidity deep inside. For me, that center is a place in which I am grateful for my work, for my health, for my beautiful nation, for the incredible systems of healing knowledge that inform and serve us, for my patients who look to me for guidance with such trust and faith, and for my family.

In that place, even the plant hanging in the sunny window behind the patients' chair is a thing of profound beauty and wonder. When I am in my center, even the most mundane and difficult detail seems a blessing, a wonderful gift. The parable of the prodigal son reminds me of what can happen when I wander from this home, into a place where I squander the capital of this elevated consciousness by indulging my self in pointless and petty ways. I quickly find that I end up feeling far from my real self, far from the calm and confidence of the garden, far from God.

But when I am able to catch myself, when I wake up to what is happening and make a concerted effort to get back to the proper mind-set, centered in the present moment, centered in gratitude, I get a kind of "rush." Like the prodigal son's return, my return to the present carries with it a sense of celebration. The father, in the parable, is the real me, the centered me, the me that is in conscious contact and union with the One. The wayward son is the small me, the ego, which forgets who it really is. It's always great to get back home, this parable tells us, and it will always be a lot easier than we think. In fact, the parable clearly seems to indicate that the universe will have *a strong predisposition to help us come back in*—once we humble ourselves. If we take but a single step toward God, it is said, he will take ten toward us.

Contemplating the symbolism yet more deeply along these lines, we see that the parable of the prodigal son is a metaphor for the evolution of conscious events during formal meditation. Meditation was best defined by the Indian sage Patanjali thousands of years ago in his timeless series of Aphorisms. Meditation is the control of the "waves of thought," specifically the lengthening of brain waves so that they are longer and smoother. This process is routinely observed by neurologists when they perform an EEG or electroencephalogram.

Effective meditation and control of the thought wave requires the practice of *concentration*—the process of shepherding the ever-widening *concentric* waves of thought back to their central point of origin. During meditation, thoughts that have wandered away from the center of stillness are drawn back and *focused* via concentration. The mind is like a muscle. If it *practices* concentration it develops *stronger powers* of concentration. When thoughts wander away from the center, a mind so developed has the power to focus and maintain an unbroken, unshaken flow of attention onto a single point. This kind of single-pointed attention, referred to by various names, is extremely useful and arguably the single most powerful attribute of a miracle worker.

If the parables are all about you, and what happens inside you as you progress along the path, then the prodigal son is obviously the thought form that strays from the center. It is the wave form propagating itself outward. Such a decentralizing idea or sensory impression quickly takes on the convincing illusion of a separate conscious event and we become lost in it. Meditation reverses this systematically. During meditation one is not lost in thoughts. One establishes a *detached observer status* such that thought forms are simply "watched."

Neurologically, the act of *observing* a thought as a thought uses very specific centers of awareness in the prefrontal lobes. Man is the only animal with a brain sufficiently complex to allow it to watch itself thinking. Separating away from a thought form and watching it from the separate neurological vantage point of the prefrontal lobes brings the thought form under control and back to the center. As more and more thoughts are steadily and consistently so "observed," the observer, the true center, the true consciousness, is strengthened until it ultimately dominates the field of consciousness. The mind is so centered. Did the teacher know about these matters? Of course. This information can be articulated with many terminologies from various cultures and traditions, but it all amounts to the same basic idea: Meditation and concentration-focusing exercises and activities, whether those of a shaman, a priest, an Indian ascetic, a Catholic monk, a Zen master, or any other number of examples, develop one-pointedness. The one-pointedness is achieved by the gathering of thoughts to a central point over and over and over and enables all sorts of intuitive, intellectual, mystical, healing, and even physical "powers"—abilities to do extraordinary and beneficial things.

The parable of the prodigal son tells us that no matter how tenacious a wayward thought form, no matter how willful or pervasive, no matter how convincing and distracting, it can be brought back home to the center with the powerful tool of meditation.

Thinking Out of the Box

One of the things about the parable of the prodigal son that has troubled people for centuries has to do with what happens to the good son, the son who stays with his father from the beginning and does everything that is good and industrious and prudent. This son feels a lot of very justifiable pain over his father's reaction at the conclusion of the story. Although he has done everything that is *expected* of him all along, he is left feeling somewhat violated, disappointed, and threatened.

If we were to leave our interpretation of the parable at the traditional level where the prodigal son represents a lost soul being welcomed back into the kingdom, an internally consistent analogical interpretation would indicate the following: that after all the recent converts are welcomed into heaven with fanfare, all the good, and righteous, and clean-living consistent people in this world will be left feeling short-changed. Such a superficial interpretation suggests that a person who has just recently atoned for terrible transgressions will get all our heavenly father's attention at the great reunion, as well as the metaphorical reward of the "fattened calf," and that people who have spent their whole lives being good will feel resentful of this.

This makes no sense and would lead any logical person to wonder if there might be some other interpretation. If you think about it, the only way a true interpretation of this metaphor can make sense and demonstrate internal consistency is by showing that the apparently wayward son is in some way spiritually superior to the son who stays and does what is expected of him.

Such an interpretation can indeed be found. In it, the prodigal son represents Jesus himself, and others like him. Consider for a moment what this man was really like. He was brought up in a very traditional family, with traditional values, and within the ancient and well-structured religious system of Judaism. And yet he "disappears" for a number of years in his late teens and twenties and is engaged in activities that none of the authors of the Gospels seem to want to tell us about for some reason. He then reemerges, now disseminating teachings and truths that are completely and totally different, new, and original—his *synthesis* of Judiasm, Essene influences, and the Kabbalah.

In many cases the ideas he thus presents are so different that they are actually considered dangerous by the powers that be. In time the "deviant" nature of his ideas is found so extreme by the rest of his society that an attempt is made to eradicate them by executing him in the most brutal way available.

Christ is the prodigal son. He is telling us about something he learned by living his own life. He is the one who had sufficient individuality, sufficient *originality* to break out of his establishment and find his own way. If this interpretation is correct, it means that during his lost years, Christ went off into other cities, other lands, and lived the life of a normal young man, eating, drinking, having relationships with women, exploring, and experiencing new and different teachings. In time, he found that such worldly pleasures, although *apparently* desirable, did not, in the final analysis, lead to a state of true peace and fulfillment. In due course, he comes home.

At the beginning of the parable, he is at home, which represents the *thesis* in his evolutionary process. When he travels to a land far away, he reaches the *antithesis*. When he finally returns home, he achieves a state of *synthesis*. This state of evolution, the parable tells us, his homecoming, his success, can only be achieved *after* breaking out of the box and following his own heart into the world.

When he returns, his return is to his father, his home. His return is to that state of perfect love and lavish abundance that lies within us, at our center, our true home. There, in the light of eternal wisdom, it is seen that the good son, who represents those who only do what is *expected*—those who are fearful of change, fearful of individuality, who act like everyone else, those who can take no risks, who cannot experience life vigorously and with courage—ends up with less reward in the end, the parable tells us.

Granted, the "good" son is still doing reasonably well—he still seems well respected and has a job and a beautiful vineyard. But there is no glory in his position. In other words, the parable seems in no way to imply that there is anything wrong with being the stodgy son. It simply asks us to consider if we are living a limited, fearful life, never allowing ourselves to experience all the joy and pain available to human beings. It asks us to consider if we would do better following our own hearts instead of the expectations of our family and our society.

How many contemporary self-help teachers, books, and systems try to tell us this very thing? That if we will only trust in ourselves and have the courage to ignore the limitations of others, to think our own way, create our own creations, follow our own dreams, live our own lives—that this will lead us to our true success, our true self, our true life, our true home?

As we saw in the parable of the lost sheep, there are scores of obvious examples in which great men and women did something completely different from everyone else, something that others said was impossible or ill advised, and ended up inventing or creating something that brought them enormous recognition. How many examples can we find of people who had the courage to think completely out of the box who became leaders, people who inspired others, people who saved others, people who enlightened others? How many great musicians, artists, and writers made it to the top of their profession for the very reason that they were originals, because they thought and acted differently from everyone else?

The parable thus has an important message for you. It is telling you that if you are contemplating a project or endeavor of any kind that is very important to you, that you would be wise to follow your heart. If you must split away from your established world literally or metaphysically in order to be your true self, then so be it.

Psychologists have known for years that all successful people are good risk takers. This parable is telling you to have the courage to ignore the codependent, fearful expectations and limitations your friends and family would have you accept. They will listen to your dream and shake their heads sadly. But this dynamic teaching story directly from the master tells you to listen to your instincts, to take some intelligent risks, and follow your dream anyway. The parable is telling you that if you take your leap of faith you will be taken care of in the end, even though you may appear to fall flat on your face along the way.

ENTANGLEMENT

Although we have already found enormous depth and utilitarian guidance within this deceptively simple little story, there is still more depth to explore. Remember that the teacher told us that he was teaching us in parable because it was "given us to know the mysteries." As we said in the introduction, the greatest mysteries in all of science today are what are referred to as the great quantum mysteries. We know now that if we develop our study of the world to the extremes we find today, we come up against a wall of mystery. The more we know about the universe, the more we find that at its core, it cannot be explained, that things happen that are truly mysterious.

Could Christ, during his states of enlightened meditation, have arrived at the same wall of mysteries? There doesn't seem to be any compelling or convincing argument to indicate such a state of realization was impossible. If a person was at once highly intelligent *and* highly adept in meditation and concentration, it seems entirely within the realm of possibility that there could be an intuitive realization of fundamental concepts such as the "great quantum mysteries."

Granted, a person unversed in the language of mathematics and without instrumentation such as particle accelerators might not be able to understand the specifics of quantum mechanics and quantum mysteries. But it must be remembered that the quantum mysteries apply not only to the subatomic realm but *to all levels of reality.* As above, so below: Like other great universal principles, the profound principles illustrated by the quantum mysteries operate not only at the subatomic level, but at macroscopic and astronomical levels of reality. Theoretically, then, the mysteries would be accessible at the everyday levels of reality Jesus worked with.

The parable of the prodigal son demonstrates Christ's knowledge of one of the great quantum mysteries referred to as "entanglement." Entanglement is a mystery so profound that it stymied Einstein during his entire lifetime. Even the greatest intellect of the twentieth century struggled unsuccessfully with the concept of entanglement, and none of our other brilliant minds has ever been able to solve it.

In a nutshell, what the concept of entanglement says is that, in certain instances, a pair of particles can be formed that are "entangled," or linked together—even if they are many miles apart. In fact, the theory predicts that two entangled particles remain linked even if they are millions of light-years apart. Even more astonishing, the linkage of the two particles is such that if a property is changed in one of the particles, that same property is *immediately* changed in the other particle—no matter where it is in the universe. The change is absolutely *instantaneous* even if dozens of galaxies separate the two particles.

The problem is that this is utterly impossible. It is impossible because nothing can be instantaneous across many light-years, according to the theory of relativity. Nothing can travel faster than the speed of light, much less instantaneously. So it is veritably impossible for the change in the first particle to be *transmitted* across vast expanses of galaxies instantly to the second particle. And yet scientific experiments indicate that the changes are, in fact, transmitted instantly.

The whole matter was so disturbing to Einstein that he referred to the process not as entanglement but as "spooky action at a distance." In other words, if this whole concept is a bit baffling to you, don't feel bad. Even Einstein, with his stunning command of scientific concepts, couldn't come up with anything better than "spooky action at a distance" to describe this great mystery.

AT ITS DEEPEST LEVEL, the parable of the prodigal son describes the mystery of entanglement and tells us that it is not confined to the subatomic realm. Following the dictum of "as above, so below, and so below, as above," the phenomenon of entanglement described so beautifully in the parable applies to the splitting of entire personal realities, entire worlds, entire universes. Most important, it applies to your own life as you are living it right now. For the phenomenon of entanglement is something that you can actually take advantage of in very practical ways to improve your life and the lives of others in your world.

If that sounds somewhat confusing, unlikely, or just plain strange, good. It is all of those things, and more. Welcome to the wall of mysteries. But fear not. For although it is true that there is much about the matter of entanglement that will remain a mystery for everyone at this time, there is much about it that can be explained and understood. In the next section we will go over some highly simplified concepts from physics that will help you understand the powerful principle of entanglement and how to put it into use in your own life.

Quantum Physics in a Nutshell— for the Non-science Major

Dear reader, if you will be willing to engage in a brief and highly simplified review of some basic scientific facts about the atom, this will prepare you to understand the phenomenon of entanglement more adequately. To begin with, every atom is comprised of a nucleus, which is surrounded by tiny bits of energy called electrons. For the most part, the components of the nucleus are protons and neutrons. The electrons orbit around the nucleus like tiny planets. And, like the various planets orbiting the sun at different distances, the electrons can orbit the nucleus at different distances, in what are referred to as "orbitals."

What is important to understand is that it doesn't take much energy for an electron to occupy an orbital that is close to the nucleus. Therefore, when electrons orbit around the nucleus in an orbit that is close to the nucleus, they *carry* a relatively low amount of energy. However, if an electron in a low-energy orbit has energy added to it, it can jump up to a higher energy orbit that is farther away.

It is most interesting to note that the electron is very particular about the *amount* of energy that it can accept in order to jump to the higher energy orbital. If there is too little energy, the electron will not absorb it and will not jump to the higher orbital. If there is too much, that will not work, either. The exact and precise amount of energy that is required to boost the electron to a higher orbital is called a "quanta" of energy. The higher energy orbital is called a higher "quantum state." This is the origin of the term "quantum" physics.

Again, with an aim to understanding the phenomenon of entanglement, let's look at a specific example of how this can happen, how energy can be added to an orbiting electron in order to get it to jump to a higher quantum state.

Imagine in your mind's eye a nucleus, and around it an orbiting electron—much as the earth revolves around the sun. Now imagine that a ball of energy, a photon, is approaching, ready to strike the orbiting electron.

A photon is a tiny packet of light and contains one quanta of energy. As the photon strikes the electron, it transfers to it its single quantum packet of energy and "disappears." Now the electron has too much energy to stay in the lower orbital. It jumps up to the higher orbital.

Let's follow what can happen for just a bit more. What can happen now, in the simplest possible terms, is the exact reverse of this process. In the reverse process, a photon with the extra quantum of energy can *release* the extra energy in the form of a photon. When the photon containing the energy is emitted from the electron, the electron no longer has enough energy to keep orbiting up in the higher orbital. It now falls back to its original lower energy orbital or "quantum state."

This is where things get really interesting, for it is in this way that an entangled *pair* of electrons can be emitted from a single electron. In certain circumstances, the electron can be coaxed into emitting two photons instead of just one as it falls back down to the lower energy orbital. And, as you may guess, when the pair emerges from the electron, each contains exactly *half* of one quantum of energy. These two new special photons are not separate. They are actually a kind of team, a very special pair that is said to be "entangled."

Photons, like the other tiny components of atoms, can have a number of individual characteristics physicists call "properties." The simplest way to understand this is to imagine the photons are like, say, individual men or women. Each of the individuals has certain properties. They could be short or they could be tall. They could be happy or sad. They could be thin or fat. They could have a blue hat or a red hat.

An *entangled* pair of such individuals has exactly *opposite* characteristics. If the first individual in the pair is short, the second in the pair will be tall. If the first entangled photon is thin, the second will be fat. This is just the way things are. When two photons are emitted simultaneously from a single electron, their characteristics must be opposite, mirror images of the other. Moreover, if one of the characteristics is *changed,* that same property in the other particle must change, too. This means that if one individual is observed to have a red hat and the hat is changed to a blue hat, the hat on the other individual *must instantaneously and automatically change to a red hat,* so that the pair continues to exhibit precisely opposite characteristics.

If that sounds peculiar, it is. But it gets even stranger. For the two entangled particles can be *separated* by vast distances and will *still* exhibit exactly opposite characteristics. In fact, the two particles can be separated by hundreds of thousands of light-years and they will still exhibit their perfect opposite relationships. Even if one particle is on one side the universe and the other is fourteen billion light-years away on the other side of the universe, observing one particle to be "blue" will automatically "cause" the other one to become red, instantaneously. Faster, even, than the speed of light.

As Above, So Below
As Below, So Above

The parable of the prodigal son begins with a single man. The man fathers two sons. As they arise from the same father they are deeply entangled at multiple levels. They share highly similar genetics. And they have been *raised* in the same family, sharing nearly identical environment conditions. They are further entangled by their upbringing and their intimate association with each other through childhood.

The stage is set. Now, one of the two wants to leave, to go far away and seek a new and different life. His path, his reality, will split from his entangled brother's path. The energy to accomplish this is available from the father and is represented by the inheritance in the story. The father relinquishes the inheritance by dividing it *equally* between the two boys. The brothers then separate, each going his own way.

Consistent with the "as above, so below" dictum, this is precisely what happens at the subatomic level. Each entangled "child" particle receives exactly half the available energy—which is one "quanta" of energy—as it is emitted from the "father" electron.

Entangled particles are linked such that each particle has the exact opposite properties of the other particle. So it is with the two sons: One son wants to stay, the other wants to leave. One son is steadfast and prudent, the other unstable and wild. One son is a hard worker, the other lazy and unproductive.

Although we know that entanglement has powerful applications and implications at an atomic level, we are being told by the teacher that the phenomenon of entanglement applies in many instances to people, to events happening now in our daily lives. We are about to learn something about the entanglement of people that will help us, that will make a difference in our lives, something we can actually use. And it is this: *The opposite may hold the key.*

As you progress along your own path, your own way, *don't let the difference worry you.* As is the case with entangled particles, what you will *become,* and what you will *manifest* along the way may be so different from the status quo, from what is *expected,* that it will be the complete *opposite* in some instances. Don't let this deter you in any way. Move ahead confidently. Simply realize that, like the prodigal son, you may have to cycle through your own *antithesis* before you can achieve your ultimate *synthesis.*

In fact, and this is the most valuable point of all, it may very well be that when you are trying to solve a problem that has not been solvable, or trying to create something that no one else has created, you should *look very specifically at the exact opposite* of what everyone else is doing. For the exact opposite may hold the key.

Consider successful investors. Very often they will determine what everyone else is doing—what everyone else is buying—and do the exact opposite. The majority of investors do what everyone else is doing, thus buying stocks that everyone else is buying *when* they are buying them. As a result, they often end up buying high and selling low, at best breaking even. The "contrarian" *purposely* does the exact opposite. The contrarian thus ends up buying the stocks everyone else is selling and selling the stocks everyone else is buying. As a result, she ends up more often than not buying low and selling high.

The spiritual greats exhibited this principle as well. Take Gandhi, for example. When everyone else was advocating violent upheaval and protest—the only seemingly logical course of action—this genius did the exact opposite, doing something that appeared strange and unworkable: Gandhi acted with complete *nonviolence,* with no force whatsoever, and taught all his followers to do the same. As a result, he was able to free his country and bring it to an entirely new level of peace and prosperity. The same can be said for the Dalai Lama.

To activate the twentieth parable lesson, consider any problem you are experiencing, any plateau you seem to be stuck upon, and ask yourself: What would I do if I were to take a completely different approach? *What would happen if you were to think and act in a way that was completely opposite of what is expected? Now, it may well be that the exact opposite of what is expected is entirely inappropriate. But the very act of considering something so radically different can very often open the mind to startling and very workable solutions when you've gotten to a point where you feel "stuck."*

ACTIVATING PARABLE LESSON 20

1. Follow your heart. Follow your own personality. Don't be afraid to "leave the security of home" and the certain "success" that it offers. If you take your own path you may, in the end, far surpass the expected level of success that you will achieve by simply doing what is expected of you.

2. Know that your decision to take your own road may separate you from all you love, all that provides security and certainty—but only *temporarily.* Because of the law of entanglement, you will be ultimately reunited with everything dear to your heart, but in a new way, a different way, a better way than you could ever imagine.

3. No matter where you may find yourself on your path, realize that you can never be separated from your home or from your family. Your true father, your true mother, your true home will always be "waiting" for you, eagerly awaiting you. Realize that you can al-

ways, always go "home" again. Whether you have been separated for a matter of years, or simply separated from your true self, your true center, for a matter of days or hours, it is never too late. You can always find your way back to the place you belong. And it will be so much easier than you might think.

4. The key is so simple but so terribly effective. The key is humility, the same potent attitude the teacher wanted you to work on so hard in the first of all the parables. Humility is the doorway, and the destination. And it isn't really all that difficult, either, if you will but make a conscious decision to embrace it. It is a beautiful and simple law, that if you become humble, you can make your way successfully through anything, and solve problems that before seemed utterly impossible. One of the best ways to activate this multi-layered parable is simply to shift to a state of humility whenever you seem lost.

THE UNJUST STEWARD

The Law of Conservation

LUKE 16:1–8

Jesus told his disciples: "There was a rich man whose manager was accused of wasting his possessions.

So he called him in and asked him, 'What is this I hear about you? Give an account of your management, because you cannot be manager any longer.'

The manager said to himself, 'What shall I do now? My master is taking away my job. I'm not strong enough to dig, and I'm ashamed to beg—

I know what I'll do so that, when I lose my job here, people will welcome me into their houses.'

So he called in each one of his master's debtors. He asked the first, 'How much do you owe my master?'

'Eight hundred gallons of olive oil,' he replied. The manager told him, 'Take your bill, sit down quickly, and make it four hundred.'

Then he asked the second, 'And how much do you owe?' 'A thousand bushels of wheat,' he replied. He told him, 'Take your bill and make it eight hundred.'

*The master commended the dishonest manager because he had
acted shrewdly. For the people of this world are more shrewd in dealing with their own kind than are the people of the light.*

*I tell you, use worldly wealth to gain friends for yourselves, so that
when it is gone, you will be welcomed into eternal dwellings.*

*Whoever can be trusted with very little can also be trusted with
much, and whoever is dishonest with very little will also be dishonest
with much.*

*So if you have not been trustworthy in handling worldly wealth,
who will trust you with true riches?*

*And if you have not been trustworthy with someone else's property,
who will give you property of your own?"*

THE PARABLE OF THE UNJUST STEWARD is one of the most
complex of all the metaphors constructed by the teacher. The
metaphorical elements are numerous: A rich man, his manager, the
possessions, the job at stake, the debtors, the debts, the world's "own
kind," the "people of the light," the curious commendation of the "dishonest" manager, and the "eternal dwellings"—all of these metaphorical
components relate to one another in a complex web, a symbolic field
rich with potential. But this symbolic field is also rife with ambiguity
and easily subject to confusion. For this reason, the best way to look
at the parable and unravel its deepest levels of meaning is to do so
statement by statement.

*Jesus told his disciples: "There was a rich man whose manager was ac-
cused of wasting his possessions."*

At first glance, the parable would seem to be about stewardship and about lessons to be learned about waste. This should not be surprising. We know that the Universe is extraordinarily precise in its use of resources and that it abhors waste of any kind. The biochemical and physiological mechanisms that allow life to exist on earth are one of the best and most important examples of the importance of efficiency.

Just as it is said to be theoretically impossible for an organism such as a bumblebee to actually fly with the wings and muscles it has, life itself is theoretically impossible. By most reasonable theoretical estimations, the exquisitely ordered systems of trillions of synchronized cells and intracellular organelles in our own body that can orchestrate themselves, cooperate with one another, and repair themselves for decade after decade are extremely improbable from a mathematical and biophysical standpoint. The universe is hardly weighted in favor of order. Far from it. It is actually heavily weighted toward disorder and disintegration via the all-pervasive and irresistible forces of *entropy* acting at every level of reality.

So, how *do* living organisms negotiate this massive field of dynamic entropy and chaos? They do so by their sheer efficiency, their sheer ability to extract and use energy with such an extraordinarily tiny amount of waste. At the very core, the very soul of all life is a deep cellular, even molecular, preoccupation with efficiency, and an extreme aversion to waste of any kind.

Thus, a truly thorough sequence of lessons on the use of thought forms to change reality in a successful way would be expected to contain a dedicated lesson on the subject of waste. But waste of what precisely? Possessions? The Greek word normally translated as "possessions" is *huparchonta*. Surely the most obvious translation of this word has to do with possessions, specifically, according to *Strong's Exhaustive Concor-*

dance, "things *extant* or *in hand*, i.e. property or possessions." But *hu-parchonta* may also be used more generally to refer to "substance."

We know from the parable of the leaven that the fabric of reality, from the subatomic realms to the astronomical, is permeated with a "substance" similar to yeast permeating a matrix of bread dough. Though undetectable, this substance, when subject to attention/intention, causes *expansion* to occur. Thus, whatever we focus on expands.

If we are reading this parable correctly, it would seem to be telling us that this expansible "substance" is a kind of resource, a resource that is ultimately God's property and not ours. We are its steward. The parable tells us that God does not stand over us micromanaging the way we use this powerful substance. It tells us that Divine Intelligence largely leaves us alone to manage its use. And this is comforting. For it tells us the God being so described is not a codependent, dysfunctional God who feels he needs to control us, but rather a healthy God who is wise in knowing that his children need to do their own homework in order to make real learning.

So he called him in and asked him, "What is this I hear about you? Give an account of your management, because you cannot be manager any longer."

The manager said to himself, "What shall I do now? My master is taking away my job. I'm not strong enough to dig, and I'm ashamed to beg—

I know what I'll do so that, when I lose my job here, people will welcome me into their houses."

So he called in each one of his master's debtors. He asked the first, "How much do you owe my master?"

"Eight hundred gallons of olive oil," he replied. The manager told him, "Take your bill, sit down quickly, and make it four hundred."

Then he asked the second, "And how much do you owe?" "A thou-sand bushels of wheat," he replied. He told him, "Take your bill and make it eight hundred."

The manager in the story is you, of course. And the account you will have to give is the account of how you are using this field of en-ergy and thought, how you are using its tendency to respond to your thought forms and positive intentions—as God's steward. The parable seems to be telling you how to deal with this accounting process when you may have failed to manage "substance" at an optimal level. And like it or not, you will not have likely been quite perfect in your man-agement. Who among us would claim that we are anywhere near be-ing able to manage all our thoughts, all our vast potential, with perfect faith, perfect integrity, and with perfectly pure, positive intention? We are only human and cannot hope to achieve perfection, at least not anytime soon. So the parable tells us how to deal with this issue, how to work with it so that we end up doing well in our accounting—in spite of our negativity, resentment, discouragement, and moments of weak faith.

This is a good thing, too. For the parable indicates that if we will be judged purely by our management record alone, we are going to be in big trouble. If, by the accounting system of the universe, we were to be compensated precisely for our record—with no mitigating factors—our position as steward should be removed. We're really that bad at things, if truth be told. But there is a way out.

Enter, once again, forgiveness. What the parable tells us is that we can undo much of our record, much of the harm that we have caused by our numerous resentments and negative projections, if we will but forgive others who owe debts to God. This is a new kind of forgive-ness that has not as yet been covered by any other parable lesson. It

means that from time to time you will find yourself in a position to forgive others' debts, debts they owe to God and to other people besides
you. The parable says that when you find yourself in such a position,
you are advised to be generous and reasonable and compassionate.
This will result in a much more lenient standard being applied to *your*
accounting.

Situations to which this principle may apply vary widely. Take, for
example, a man who marries a woman. Later he finds that a man with
whom she had a previous relationship owes her a great deal of money.
On an energetic level, this man also broke her heart and left her in
great pain for many years caring for her child all alone with no help.
The new husband has every right to be incensed and finds that because of the laws in that state they can sue the man from the previous
relationship and exact a significant toll from him. In this case, the
debts are not owed to the new husband, yet he is in a position to be
either harsh or lenient in directing the powers that be in their treatment of the irresponsible lover.

There are many variations on this theme. In other circumstances,
the debts that are owed are to God, to your country, or to your society, for some kind of unethical behavior. At times you find yourself in
a position to influence, in some way, the degree of severity by which
the debtor is treated. Although the circumstances may vary widely,
the take-home point remains the same: When you find yourself in this
kind of situation, *be careful.*

Although you may feel that the debts a person owes one of your
loved ones or your company or your god are terrible, and that it would
be completely fair, completely justifiable to come down hard on the
debtor, *think twice.* When you are in a position of power, a position of
stewardship, realize that the master who oversees you will be most interested in the way you treat others who are indebted to him. The

parable indicates that we are, in essence, authorized to forgive others their very debts to God and to others.

For the debts that we contemplate in such circumstances are just that, contemplated debt. They are something in our heads, mental constructs, and thus varieties of resentment. The parable is telling you that these *perceived debts* of others have to be cleared from your head, right along with the debts others have incurred to your self, as discussed in parable lesson one.

> *The master commended the dishonest manager because he had acted shrewdly. For the people of this world are more shrewd in dealing with their own kind than are the people of the light.*
>
> *I tell you, use worldly wealth to gain friends for yourselves, so that when it is gone, you will be welcomed into eternal dwellings.*

At first glance this statement appears somewhat mercenary: "use worldly wealth to gain friends for yourselves," as if the teacher is telling us that we somehow can and should "buy" friends for ourselves. But this is not the message. As the overall message is about forgiveness, this statement means, in context, that you should be ready and willing at all times to forgive others their material debts. In this way, you will be using the material wealth that is at your command, which is really God's property, wisely—*in God's opinion.* Unlike the man in the previous parable who stored all his wealth away in barns where it could not circulate and benefit others, a person following the admonition of this parable would instead circulate wealth to reduce debt, and to increase trust, goodwill, and friendship in his world, his reality.

> *Whoever can be trusted with very little can also be trusted with much, and whoever is dishonest with very little will also be dishonest with much.*

Recall the enigmatic statement in the section of the parables called the Key, which is contained as an explanatory passage within the parable of the sower: To him who has will be added more, and to him who has little, even that will be taken away. The above statement at the end of the parable of the unjust steward echoes the statement in the "key" embedded in the parable of the sower, and makes it a bit more specific. The statement indicates that what God considers trustworthy in the management of his wealth, his resources, his substance, is not what a worldly rich man would consider trustworthy by any means.

A worldly rich man normally insists that his managers go after every penny that is owed to his estate. A worldly rich man would probably demand interest as well. But this rich man, who represents God, is the polar opposite. This rich man considers proper management to consist of the *forgiveness* of the debts owed to him. If we are reading the parable correctly, it is telling us *that forgiveness is our duty as stewards* and we will actually be held accountable to forgive.

> So if you have not been trustworthy in handling worldly wealth, who will trust you with true riches?
>
> And if you have not been trustworthy with someone else's property, who will give you property of your own?

ACTIVATING PARABLE LESSON 21

1. Examine your life carefully—and be proactively on the lookout on an ongoing basis from now on—for debts over which you have a degree of control. Be particularly aware of such debts that are not owed directly to you but to loved ones, to your company, to your religion or country, or to Spirit. Realize first of all that the debts that

you are perceiving are largely in your mind, that they are things that you have thought. Realize that because they are mental constructs—mere ideas—that you have the power in many instances to erase or reduce these debts by mentally and emotionally forgiving them.

2. Reduce the debts over which you have control. This is good stewardship. As you forgive you will, in essence, be spending God's resources wisely and in the way he intends. As you forgive, you will clear your own mind and be better able to expand the goodwill of Spirit.

THE RICH MAN AND LAZARUS

The Law of Compensation

LUKE 16:19—31

There was a rich man who was dressed in purple and fine linen and lived in luxury every day.

At his gate was laid a beggar named Lazarus, covered with sores and longing to eat what fell from the rich man's table. Even the dogs came and licked his sores.

The time came when the beggar died and the angels carried him to Abraham's side. The rich man also died and was buried.

In hell, where he was in torment, he looked up and saw Abraham far away, with Lazarus by his side.

So he called to him, "Father Abraham, have pity on me and send Lazarus to dip the tip of his finger in water and cool my tongue, because I am in agony in this fire."

But Abraham replied, "Son, remember that in your lifetime you received your good things, while Lazarus received bad things, but now he is comforted here and you are in agony.

And besides all this, between us and you a great chasm has been fixed, so that those who want to go from here to you cannot, nor can anyone cross over from there to us."

He answered, "Then I beg you, father, send Lazarus to my father's house, for I have five brothers. Let him warn them, so that they will not also come to this place of torment."

Abraham replied, "They have Moses and the Prophets; let them listen to them."

"No, father Abraham," he said, "but if someone from the dead goes to them, they will repent."

He said to him, "If they do not listen to Moses and the Prophets, they will not be convinced even if someone rises from the dead."

THE PARABLE OF LAZARUS AND THE RICH MAN has for years posed a difficult problem for teachers and students of the New Metaphysic. On the surface, the parable seems to indicate that, *without a doubt,* Jesus believed in an eternal hell. And it seems to un-ambiguously indicate that he was *adamant* that his followers know the specifics about it. The story seems to tell us that simply being rich is a very perilous state of affairs, that being wealthy could easily qualify a soul for harsh judgment and harsh consequences in the afterlife. Finally, it seems to indicate that there is an unbridgeable gap between the dead and the living and communication of any kind between them is forever barred.

We should always be most respectful and open-minded about these kinds of traditionalist approaches. All viewpoints have a purpose and a place in the evolution of this world. But with this said, it must also be added that a case can be made that the sheerly literal approach is somewhat illogical and brings us to some conclusions that don't seem to add up. For example, that the dead in heaven can view those who are being eternally tortured in hell. If you think about it, a heaven in which billions of horribly tortured souls are clearly visible as they writhe in agony isn't much of a heaven, is it?

There is a deeper, more subtle, and very viable level of interpretation of the parable of Lazarus and the rich man. To reveal this layer of meaning, the parable is best unraveled one step at a time. It should be noted at the outset that this parable is not like the other parables in that it conveys a lesson that is more political than metaphysical. It is a parable that does not contain a direct or specific message or lesson directly relevant to the use of thought forms.

To begin with, the parable is set in a part of the Gospel of Luke that is largely concerned about money, and the power and potential money possesses to generate both good and bad circumstances. Our story begins with a rich man who wears purple clothes, specifically *busos,* a Hebrew word that refers to very expensive Egyptian cotton. Purple, according to most biblical authorities, indicates that the wearers are either wealthy, elevated in the hierarchy of the priesthood, or both.

Enter a beggar named Lazarus. This is a common name throughout the Bible and means "one who has been helped by God." Lazarus is apparently so sick and disabled that he cannot ambulate himself and is "laid" passively at the gate of the rich man. This seems a good option for him, because the rich inhabitants of the estate will see him repeatedly when they pass in and out of their property. Perhaps, the beggar hopes, one of them will take pity on him and he will be saved. He is so poor, so down and out, that it is his fondest hope that he may be given the scraps from the rich man's table. However, it is important to note that the parable does not specifically state that Lazarus is necessarily a good or righteous man. Nor does it specify the rich man as evil.

Apparently, we are led to believe, the rich man does *not* help the man. The dogs do. Although they would normally provide security for the estate in such a situation and likely attack the beggar, they show their superiority to the wealthy people by licking the poor man's wounds. Although this sounds strange in the context of our modern culture, dog saliva has antibiotic and other healing characteristics and was used in ancient times as an important curative modality. Archae-ologists once uncovered a site in Israel where 1,300 dogs were buried in individual plots at a place believed to be an early version of a spa or alternative therapy center. The dogs thus represent the presence of es-oteric healing energy and guidance through the beggar's most difficult, and terminal, rite of passage.

The dogs also represent unconditional love. Anyone who has ever had a good dog can tell you that a dog is capable of more perfect un-conditional love than almost any human. There is even a saying in the Hindu tradition to the effect that the dog is the only animal that can completely bypass the human state of incarnation on the way to the One. This is because the dog is capable of reaching perfect selfless love and devotion just as he is. And that is the real goal. The point of this life is not to reach a state of more complex and esoteric mental knowledge. Far from it, for complex mental processes can actually im-pede our progress at certain evolutionary periods. The goal of this life, as the parable sequence clearly indicates, is to reach a state of perfect selfless love, service, and faith. The dogs are hardly present in the story by accident or as an afterthought.

The parable then tells us that, after a period of time, both the beg-gar and the rich man die. The beggar is carried to Abraham's bosom while the rich man goes to hell—proof positive that the teacher be-lieved in hell and wanted to warn us about it. Or is it? Let's look closer.

The Greek word normally translated as hell is *hades.* Note that this term is *not capitalized* in the original Greek text. A capitalized "Hades" is a term from Greek mythology and refers to something completely different, specifically the god of the netherworld, who was *also* the dispenser of earthly riches. The capitalized Hades can also refer to a shadowy abode of the dead, similar in some ways to the Judeo-Christian "hell."

By contrast, the non-capitalized *hades* originates from the Greek *eidos*, which means "to see or to know." The true, more mainstream interpretation of the non-capitalized *hades* here, according to the Greek to English dictionary, is "*the unseen*" or "*the unknown*." The original text doesn't seem to say anything at all about "hell," per se. It actually seems to indicate that the selfish rich man—who had everything but didn't lift a finger during his earthly life to help the dying—goes to an unseen, or unknown state.

Furthermore, the traditional translation of the term "torment" in this unknown place is a gross simplification. Actually the word normally translated as "torment" is the Greek *basanos*. And the primary meaning of this word isn't "torment" at all but rather, "*touchstone.*" A touchstone is a hard black stone formerly used to test the purity of gold and silver. Also called a Basanite, a touchstone is an imperfect black jasper or black flinty slate, originally brought from Mount Timolus in Lydia, and therefore called *lapis Lidius*. An object could be rubbed on the touchstone, and depending on the color of the mark that was left behind, the amount of gold contained in the object could be determined. The mode of trying the fineness of a material with such a stone was called "touching."

The many ancient forms of alchemy sought to transmute the base into gold. The stone thought able to catalyze this most desirable reaction was the so-called Philosopher's Stone. But alchemy as well as all the mystery traditions also sought to transmute base *reality* into golden *reality*, on many intricate, higher planes—via, of course, the use of positive intention, positive thought forms. The touchstone evolved, in part, as the standard that was used to see if the alchemist, the mystery student, had succeeded. The products of his trasmutational experiments could be tested by a touchstone. In metaphorical terms, a touchstone is therefore the standard used to see if the product of a light worker's endeavors is truly higher than the original state, truly golden.

In summary, *hades* is an unknown state, while a touchstone is a known state, a standard *against which* the unknown may be evaluated. In other words, the rich man enters into a state of uncertainty. This state of unknown or uncertainty is a state in which his purity is being tested and determined. His soul, although deficient in certain areas, is still golden, that is not in question. The only thing in question is *how* golden? This is a far more positive and helpful interpretation of the fate of the rich man and one more consistent with contemporary concepts of the afterlife.

The beggar, by contrast, is carried by angels to Abraham's side. The beggar ends up in a known state, for Abraham is used as a wellestablised standard of righteousness, of familiar and confirmed moral and ethical refinement. This state needs no touchstone to confirm its purity.

It is important to keep in mind that within the symbolic field of the parable format, the death of both men is a kind of *figurative* death. There are different ways that we can go through "little deaths" along the way to the one. A particularly harrowing life transition may provide the impetus for such a "dying" experience. But focusing in even more closely on the fabric of personal reality, we find that we can even die to our selves on a *momentary* basis, perhaps with a simple sigh as we resign ourselves quite sanely to simply letting go of ego, letting go *control* of some difficult daily situation. Don't sell the teacher short. His stories had many levels of meaning, many levels of practical application.

But Abraham replied, "Son, remember that in your lifetime you re-
ceived your good things, while Lazarus received bad things, but now he
is comforted here and you are in agony.

And besides all this, between us and you a great chasm has been
fixed, so that those who want to go from here to you cannot, nor can
anyone cross over from there to us."

In Ralph Waldo Emerson's famous essay on *Compensation* we are
told a great deal about the way in which one state in the world will
eventually and inexorably lead to its opposite. There is a pendulous
quality to life. Emerson was so certain of this that he cheerfully explained that whenever he was down and out or people had ravaged his
reputation in the press, he became particularly *optimistic*. For he knew
that if he simply persisted in doing the right thing, he could be *absolutely certain* that the laws of the universe would lead him to be perfectly compensated as the pendulum inexorably swung to its other
extreme. He knew without a doubt that the negative state was a sure
harbinger that everything was about to shift, that the thesis state
would soon and surely evolve to its antithetical state, and he would
end up in great shape.

This parable is telling us that if we are in a state of well-being,
wealth, or glorification that we had best have our guard up. That if we
are not conscientious and careful, this *known* state of well-being or *security* may evolve to its opposite, antithetical state of *unknown* supply or
insecurity. Conversely, it tells us that if we are in a state of deprivation
and discomfort and disease, we will ultimately end up in a perfectly
compensated state of known wealth, known well-being, a state of security and ease. *If* we work with the kinds of esoteric healing and unconditional love that the rest of the parable sequence advocates. This

notion of inevitable compensation is nearly indistinguishable from Taoist concepts and from the concepts of the Greek philosopher Heraclitus, who held that this entire world was the result of the perfectly reliable interplay of the great opposites, or *logos,* as he referred to it.

The parable is thus an important lesson on how to work with this great interplay of opposites, the Tao, the world that is always changing, shifting to a different state. What it is saying is that we can learn to navigate and flow with this great interplay of opposites in an intelligent way—that we can learn to "surf" it, if you will—as opposed to being helpless, passive victims of its ever shifting currents. The technique for accomplishing this is fairly simple.

To begin with, if you find yourself in a state of relative wealth and ease and well-being, do not, under any circumstances, ignore or neglect those who are having a hard time. If you do, the parable lesson tells us, you can be absolutely certain that your lack of concern will be perfectly compensated and you will end up in a dark, unknown state that is far less pleasant.

On the other hand, if you find yourself in a state of lack, suffering, and disease, it is very important that you enter into a state of unconditional love and avail yourself of every kind of esoteric healing that you can. If you do, you can be certain that your state of consciousness will be inevitably and perfectly compensated as the tides of the world shift and you are carried to a state of known abundance, a state of security.

ACTIVATING PARABLE LESSON 22

1. *Make an accurate assessment of your current state* within the great interplay of opposites. Are you in a state of security and ease, like the

rich man, or are you in a state of insecurity and lack? This is not a one-time procedure. The lesson is a metaphor for something we need to do *regularly* in consciousness.

2. If during any assessment cycle you find that you are doing relatively well, carefully ask yourself: Am I ignoring those in need around me? Am I failing to see and be moved with compassion? If you find yourself within a state of relative lack and insecurity, ask yourself: Am I using all the tools of esoteric healing that are at my command, all the techniques for living outlined in the parable sequence? Even though I am suffering and uncertain, am I cultivating a state of unconditional love?

3. Meditate on the process of compensation as it applies to your current situation. Realize that, according to the parable, there is more to the movement of the Tao than an impersonal, uncontrollable motion from thesis to antithesis to synthesis. The lesson indicates that there is actually a more evolved way to view our place in this great interplay than as victims who simply have to flow along, who simply have to resign themselves to inevitable and sometimes painful changes.

    The lesson indicates that if we see and are moved with compassion while in a secure state we can avoid, to some degree, the inevitable degradation of that state into a state of uncertainty and insecurity. It also indicates that if we are in a state of lack and insecurity that we can navigate and use the inevitable tendency of the world to continually shift to its opposite state by using the esoteric tools of conscious healing and unconditional love.

4. Make a list of everything you can possibly do to actually set the laws of compensation in motion in your favor. Be comprehensive and don't neglect anything.

5. *Act now.* Do something. *Do whatever it takes* to stop thinking about the laws of compensation and begin setting them in motion in your favor by doing everything you have listed in step four.

---◆——✧∕✧——◆---

THE UNPROFITABLE SERVANTS

The Law of Service

LUKE 17:5—17

And the Apostles said unto Jesus, increase our faith. And he said, if
you had faith as a grain of mustard seed, you might say unto this
sycamine tree, "Be you plucked up by the root, and be planted in the
sea; and it will obey you."

But which of you, having a servant plowing or feeding cattle, will
say unto him, "By and by, when he is come from the field, go and sit
down to meet?"

And will not rather say unto him, "Make ready now, I may dine,
and clothe thyself. Serve me, until I have eaten and drank; Only after-
ward shall you eat and drink?"

Does he thank that servant because he did the things that were
commanded of him? I doubt it.

So likewise when you have done all those things which are commanded you, say, "we are unprofitable servants: We have done that
which was our duty to do and are no better than slaves."

power: The state or quality of being strong: strength, vigor, brawn,
brawniness, might, muscle, potency, power, puissance, robustness,

sturdiness, toughness. The ability to change things, to act, to accomplish things in an effective way.

E MAY NOT LIKE to come right out and admit it in so
many words, but we all like power. Power is the ability
to do things, the ability to *change* things. When you think about it, we
spend a vast portion of our lives seeking various forms of power. It is
said that knowledge is a great power. And we spend many, many years
educating ourselves and learning new skills. Money is power and we ex-
change untold hours and years of our lives for this precious commodity
so that we can use it to shelter ourselves, clothe ourselves, feed ourselves, entertain ourselves, and heal ourselves. And we all like forms of
power that are especially *potent.* Forms of power that are very potent require very little effort to apply in order to produce very large effects.

With that said, everyone should be particularly interested in the
parable traditionally known as the parable of the profitable servants.
For it describes a power that is incredibly potent, a power that is within
our reach, a power that is our birthright and our responsibility to claim
and to develop. It is a power called faith, and the teacher tells us that it
is so potent that even a single speck of it in its true form, its pure form,
can cause enormous changes in the realities we find ourselves within.

We have things in our modern world that are enormously potent
that serve to illustrate this principle nicely. Take, for example, purified
plutonium. In its highly purified state, plutonium is so potent, so powerful that it can do things that truly defy human comprehension. Even
a small ball of plutonium contains enough energy to power an enormous city with all its myriad lights and machines and circuitry for
years. This potency was described by Einstein in his most famous

equation, $E = mc^2$. What this equation means is that the power in a tiny piece of matter is so potent that it equals the very speed of light, 180,000 miles per second. In fact, the power in a piece of matter is so powerful that it equals the fantastic speed of light, not multiplied times a thousand or even ten thousand, but *squared—times 180,000!*

The parable of the profitable servants begins by telling us of a power every bit as potent as the unspeakable atomic power coiled within the atom, the very fabric of reality. And that power the teacher calls "faith." The word normally translated as "faith" is the Greek *pistis.* This word has a number of shades of meaning including "conviction" and "assurance." It is derived from the root *peitho,* which means, among other things, "to wax or become *confident.*" Conviction and confidence are states of mind that the modern dictionary tells us are "free from doubt." Therefore, for our purposes, "faith" is a mind-set that is free from doubt.

Faith is therefore much like a substance, such as plutonium, that has been refined, or freed, from impurity. In its purest and rarest form, faith is a state of mind from which all contamination by doubt, misgiving, uncertainty, equivocation, and lack of conviction has been refined away, leaving only pure and absolute confidence. This purified conviction, we are told, is powerful beyond our comprehension and is capable of inducing remarkable changes in physical reality itself.

None of this would seem particularly new or surprising to the average student of the New Metaphysic. We are all aware, at least at a theoretical level, that faith in its most purified state is irresistibly powerful. But what we may not know is what the teacher next tells us about this principle. For he immediately tells us that if we are to increase our faith, if we are to continue the process of refining our faith and so "increasing" it as the disciples put it, we have to understand the principle illustrated in the story of the unprofitable servants.

The parable describes a servant who works for his master all day in the fields doing what is expected of him. This is his normal day's work and he understandably expects his normal compensation, which is generically described as "eat and drink," i.e., material sustenance, material supply. However, the worker is surprised to find that on this particular day the master wants him to work overtime. Instead of being able to relax and eat dinner as expected, he has to continue working, serving the master.

Only when the additional work is completed can the worker sit back and receive his expected compensation. When he does, he feels that the situation is entirely unfair. He complains at this point, saying, in effect, "We are unprofitable. Even though we have done what is required of us, and even *extra* work, we have not 'profited' by taking home *more* than our usual reward. And therefore we are little better than slaves, who work for nothing."

The question at this point is "What does this have to do with faith?" What does this have to do with learning how to obtain and refine that most powerful and potent of all spiritual tools? The lesson of the parable is that in order to obtain faith and in order to refine it to its purified and ultimately potent state, we are going to have to *work*. What the parable is saying is that purified faith, that most desirable of all spiritual mind-sets, is the result of *action,* and not necessarily of thought processes.

If we are going to increase our faith, purify our faith to miracle-working potency, we are going to have to get used to the fact that our work for Spirit, for God, is not a nine-to-five affair. In essence, our work for the Universe will never be done. If we think that it will be done, if we expect that it is only a part-time arrangement, we are going to end up believing that we are unprofitable, that we have been somehow "ripped off" even when Spirit takes care of us and gives us our daily bread—the sustenance we need to maintain ourselves on the physical plane. This feeling of being somehow "cheated" will disrupt the on-going purification process and send us back to a state of spiritual impotency.

On the other hand, if we resign ourselves to the fact that we are permanently on God's time clock, morning, noon, and night as well, we will have taken an enormous step forward. We aren't doing right things, helping others, helping God part of the time, we are doing it all of the time, 24/7. In this state of perpetual diligence we are not to be constantly asking, "What's in it for me? Where is my reward?" If we lapse into that kind of selfish thinking, we again disrupt the refinement process of our faith and harm ourselves immeasurably. We will re-ceive our reward. Like the workers in the story, we will receive our compensation, our daily bread, a reliable flow of material and spiritual sustenance. And that is a good thing.

But the parable tells us that if we achieve a mind-set of perpetual service we will get something infinitely more valuable than material sustenance, or expected "wages," and that is real faith. And this faith that will arise from our attitude of continual service can then be used to do *anything*. This faith can be used to heal an incurable disease, cor-rect a frightening state of financial lack, amend a broken relationship, or any number of other *apparently* impossible things and is thus infi-nitely more valuable than our expected "pay."

Don't look for your return where you always expect. Realize that although your normal forms of compensation may at times remain sta-ble, even though you are working overtime for God in consciousness, your faith is steadily increasing as a function of your service. And your faith will in due course enable you to do things for yourself that will surpass your wildest dreams.

The word traditionally translated as "serve" in the parable is the

Greek *diakoneo,* which means to be an attendant, to wait upon, to act as a deacon or minister. The message of the parable, then, is clear: Adopt an attitude of continual service and you will develop the power to work miracles, a power so strong that you can tell a massive tree to move and it will move. And if anyone would know, it would be the teacher. His works were so profound that we are still discussing them today.

ACTIVATING PARABLE LESSON 23

1. Make no mistake about it: The wording of this parable indicates that it is rendering up a powerful piece of knowledge, one of the core mysteries, one of the secrets of secrets. The secret is that purified faith has the ability to alter the very fabric of reality, to generate beautiful, interesting, and prosperous new dimensions, new realms of freedom and joy. The parable tells us that ounce for ounce, the power of faith is as potent as atomic energy.

   Perhaps we do not yet understand the import of this. To activate this lesson, begin by *meditating* on the awesome power of a mere handful of matter to light up a vast city with its billions of points of light, for hour after hour, day after day, month after month. Meditate until you are in a state of awe and respect.

2. *Resolve* to learn the mysteries of faith. Resolve to practice faith, to attempt faith, to trust the power of faith. Resolve to do *anything that it takes* to master this most desirable of all the spiritual traits, to refine it again and again and again until it is completely free from any doubt. To continue activation of this parable lesson, *resolve to choose faith,* to focus on the growth of your faith, to keep the practice and

development of your faith a *top priority* in your life. Keeping the development of your faith as a top priority will automatically cause you to choose the right forks in the road so that you will end up where you really want to be.

3. *Make a conscious decision* to develop your faith by learning to develop a mind-set of service. This is nothing new. Although there are many different ways to say it and teach, in many different languages and spiritual traditions over the millennia, it all boils down to the same thing: If you adopt and maintain an attitude in which you are focusing on serving God and others, you will automatically refine your faith into its purest and most potent form.

Resolve to ask in every situation that manifests within your life, "How can I be helpful, how can I be of service, in this particular circumstance?" This is the Law of Service: Service generates faith. Faith generates power. Power enables happiness, pleasure, joy, security, beauty, health, wealth, and love.

THE IMPORTUNATE WIDOW

The Law of Persistence

LUKE 18:1—8

Then Jesus told his disciples a parable to show them that they should always pray and not give up.

He said: "In a certain town there was a judge who neither feared God nor cared about men.

And there was a widow in that town who kept coming to him with the plea, 'Grant me justice against my adversary.'

For some time he refused. But finally he said to himself, 'Even though I don't fear God or care about men,

yet because this widow keeps bothering me, I will see that she gets justice, so that she won't eventually wear me out with her coming!'

And the Lord said, 'Listen to what the unjust judge says.

And will not God bring about justice for his chosen ones, who cry out to him day and night? Will he keep putting them off?

I tell you, he will see that they get justice, and quickly. However, when the Son of Man comes, will he find faith on the earth?'"

_T_HIS PARABLE BEGINS with a statement that would indicate it contains very critical information on the practice of prayer. And prayer, without a doubt, is a matter of supreme importance to any spiritual person, then or now. It is still the primary way a modern light worker—a _miracle worker_—communicates with the source of all knowledge, all power, all good, and all supply. And it is when the channel to God's power is open that we can receive it. We are told that we are going to learn something that will motivate us to proceed with prayer, to _persist_ in our efforts to communicate with God and our higher selves—even in the face of adversity, discouragement, and setback.

Enter the judge, an interesting and perplexing character. To understand the role of the judge in the story we have to realize what a judge really is, what a judge does. A judge is someone who has the power to make decisions that will profoundly affect the lives of those who come before her. And this is the case regardless of whether her decisions are "right" or "wrong." It doesn't matter if a judge has honor, or scruples, or even whether a judge is intelligent enough to understand the problems before her and solve them in a logical, equitable manner. What a judge pronounces at the end of the case determines the fate of those who have come before her.

The judge represents the illusion of the material world, this "hard, cold reality" within which we operate on a daily basis. Every day, every minute of our routine lives we "come before" the power of this immense matrix of matter, energy, space, and time. On the surface, at least, the often erratic "realities" of this world "decide"—or at least _appear_ to decide—our fates. Like it or not, and hard as it is to admit sometimes, even the best practitioner of the New Metaphysic repeatedly lapses into this sort of subtle "victim consciousness."

It is perilously easy to "buy" the illusion that it is our external circumstances that "cause" our problems and that we are, to a large degree, dependent upon its whims, upon the often illogical and grossly unfair "decisions" it hands down to us in the way of hardship, setback, accident, and unlucky breaks. It is easy indeed to regress into subtle forms of victim consciousness.

But as we ascend in evolution, we begin to know that the real truth is that this is a backward way of thinking. It gradually dawns on us that in truth, this reality responds to us, to our thoughts, to our positive intentions, and to our prayers. The truth is that our conscious and unconscious thought patterns have generated and will continue to generate the worlds we find ourselves within, acting out the dramas that we have set up for ourselves so that we may learn more about the truth and practice its powerful ways.

In the story, a widow—who represents a human being who has experienced hardship, lack, and injustice—comes before a judge. This judge is a particularly indifferent judge. He fears neither God nor men, meaning that his thought processes and decisions are affected by neither a sense of spiritual rightness nor care or compassion for human beings. But the judge turns out not to be so all-powerful after all. Although the widow at first receives no justice, no favorable ruling that will improve her life, she *persists*.

And as she persists, the judge's weakness is revealed. He begins to realize that the woman is not going to give up and that he is going to have to continue dealing with her entreaties. And that is work for him, a kind of inconvenience. So, in due course, he relents to her tenacity and renders her a favorable ruling. Her perseverance brings her justice.

The message is clear: The hard, cold, impersonal realities that you find yourselves within have a bias built into them. That's what the parable is really all about. As was the case with the parable of the leaven and the parable of the mustard seed, we are being told about a personality trait of the universe, an automatic tendency built into the fabric of reality that we can use to our advantage, as miracle workers following in the teacher's footsteps. The bias described in this parable is *a tendency for the material world to yield to persistent positive intentions.*

The parable is telling us that the world will "give up" in resignation and render us a favorable outcome if we will simply repeat our requests, if we stay on its case, if we intend, if we *insist* that it cooperate knowing that right is on our side—now that we have activated the other parable lessons within our lives. And this is something we desperately need to know. For though the world *appears* in every way to be more powerful than we are, the secret truth is that it is actually weak, just like the lazy judge in the story who finally gives in to the persistent widow's entreaties because he doesn't want her to "wear him out." The truth is that the apparently powerful currents of circumstances, people, trends, finances, politics, and environments that swirl around us so impersonally have a weak spot—*an automatic bias to yield to persistence.* We need not give in to victim consciousness anymore.

And would we not *expect* to find a parable specifically devoted to the quality of persistence? All modern experts on achievement and success invariably cite simple persistence—the ability to continue positive intention in the face of apparent failure—as one of if not *the* single most important element of a successful mind-set. The presence of a parable devoted to persistence simply confirms that we are on the right track in our parable interpretations.

ACTIVATING PARABLE LESSON 24

1. According to the parable, the very first thing to make straight in preparation for the process of prayer is to pull yourself out of any type of victim consciousness with regard to your current life situations. Any undercurrent of thinking that attributes problems to chance or to "hard, cold reality," *and not to the self,* should be honestly identified and admitted. Write down the ways you may have lapsed into victim consciousness, however subtle.

2. After the admission, *ask God* to help you maintain a state of trust during your prayer time. *Trust* that the laws are real, that we really do have the power to change our lives for the better via changes in our consciousness.

3. *Pray and meditate on the power of persistence.* Realize at the deepest possible level that "hard, cold reality," as undeniably powerful as it is, can be overcome by the specific mind-set of persistence—assuming, of course, that the groundwork has been properly laid by activating and living the other parable lessons. Understand that, according to the lesson in parable twenty-four, the laws of time and space are weighted such that they yield when confronted with pure persistence, in conjunction with purified faith.

4. To complete activation of the twenty-fourth parable lesson, *ask God to help you—invite him into the situation.* Don't make the mistake of skipping this critical step or taking anything for granted. Specifically *ask* God to help you develop and exercise spiritual persistence. Know that he will gladly help you, that it is in his own vested inter-

ests that you continue to work with positive intention and for you to succeed in your efforts.

5. *Persist.* There is no shortcut here. Just do it. Whatever you are working on, *keep* working on it. Don't back down. Don't give up. Don't stop.

    Just keep going.

—◦⟋⟍◦—

THE PHARISEES AND PUBLICANS

The Law of Humility

LUKE 18:9—14

To some who were confident of their own righteousness and looked down on everybody else, Jesus told this parable:

"Two men went up to the temple to pray, one a Pharisee and the other a tax collector.

The Pharisee stood up and prayed about himself: 'God, I thank you that I am not like other men—robbers, evildoers, adulterers—or even like this tax collector.

I fast twice a week and give a tenth of all I get.'

But the tax collector stood at a distance. He would not even look up to heaven, but beat his breast and said, 'God, have mercy on me, a sinner.'

I tell you that this man, rather than the other, went home justified before God. For everyone who exalts himself will be humbled, and he who humbles himself will be exalted."

*T*HIS PARABLE TURNS OUT to be one of the simplest. It is yet another parable that gives instruction regarding a critical mind-set that must be cultivated in order to achieve mastery of the mysteries. That mind-set, humility, is a virtue recognized by nearly every religion on earth as essential to spiritual growth and success in life. And it should be abundantly clear to anyone who has read and paid attention to the messages in the parables that the teacher thought this mind-set to be incredibly important to anyone seeking mastery of the mysteries—and the powerful abilities that come with mastery.

The particular lesson about humility that is conveyed in the parable of the pharisees and the publicans is one of the most important paradoxes in all spirituality, and is most directly and simply stated as the Law of Humility: "He who humbles himself will be exalted." The wording is critical. It clearly states that bringing the ego down to earth, down to a more accurate size, is something a person must do for *him- or herself and that this powerful psychospiritual act carries with it enormous rewards.*

It is one thing to be humbled by apparent "circumstance"—and that can be a good thing as well, in certain cases. But this parable is telling you to take the *initiative,* in the absence of humbling circumstances, to *proactively* bring your ego down to earth. If you remain at a station of evolution in which external circumstance is required to humble you, you have not yet arrived at the level of evolution described in this parable. At this point in your development it is important to take the *responsibility and initiative* to monitor yourself and do whatever is necessary to remove undue self-importance.

At this stage of your learning process, it is important for you to devote sincere and concerted effort to preventing inflated states of ego and promoting modesty. Without such efforts, every external circumstance that appears to exalt you will only feed your ego and you will be in danger of believing yourself to be much larger than you really are. If you remain in this stage of development, don't be surprised if external reality *forces* you to get back to a realistic self-concept. It's a bit dangerous to live this way.

Only the person who takes it upon herself to take an accurate personal inventory on a regular basis can hope to achieve the mind-set recommended by this parable. And, because this is a sequence of lessons that leads to mastery of the mysteries, we can safely assume that a self-regulated ego is one of the essential components of the miracle mind-set that confers the ability to change the world in beneficial ways just like the teacher did.

It is critical to note that this lesson is not targeted at everyone. It is designed specifically for people who are confident of their own righteousness and who look down on others. The specific wording of the parable does not specify that seeing yourself as a "sinner" is necessary or appropriate for everyone. What it says is that it *is* appropriate for you *when* you have allowed yourself to indulge in a *subtle state of superiority toward others.*

ACTIVATING PARABLE LESSON 25

1. Begin to work with the Law of Humility by making a written inventory of every conceivable way that you are feeling superior to others. Carefully and systematically list each and every person close to you in your home life and your social circles, each person you interact with regularly at work, and at school, and at your place of worship. Make an honest self-evaluation of your attitude toward

each person. Is there any way in which you feel better, more knowledgeable, more spiritual or politically correct than this person? Write down your honest self-evaluations as they pertain to each entry on your list.

2. *Specifically invite God into your self-evaluation.* Ask him to help you realize that all of us are mere children in the eyes of Spirit, that we are much like students in an elementary school, and that being a grade or two ahead of someone else is preposterously insignificant. Ask God to help you realize that many of the parameters in which you feel superiority are really not important in the cosmic scheme of things—and that you really have no certified or sanctified qualifications to support the notion that you are more correct in your thinking and behavior anyway. *Ask God for humility.*

3. As you did when you made your resentment inventory in parable one, include institutions, political parties, nations, races, or religions for which you may feel a righteous superiority.

4. Begin *acting* differently to the people for whom you have harbored superiority. Begin *treating* them differently. Humble yourself to them, perhaps by simply speaking *to* them in a friendly, nonjudgmental way and speaking *of* them in positive terms. Remember the parable of the friend at midnight and replace your attitude of superiority with an attitude of helpfulness. To continue activation of this parable lesson, begin now to *proactively consider* ways to *help* those you come in contact with. It is much more effective to *replace* your feelings of superiority with helpful attitudes and actions than to simply deny or repress them.

5. Pay *particular* attention *to people and circumstances with which you are experiencing conflict and tension.* Very often a shift in perception and a shift to an attitude of helpfulness will defuse an otherwise dangerous and unpleasant state of interpersonal conflict and allow all concerned to progress with the real work. You are going to need all the energy and attention you can possibly muster to manifest your dream, to heal yourself or others, and to create a better world. Part of how this inventory works is to simply make you aware of the vast amounts of psychic energy you are wasting on useless and destructive attitudes so that you can free it for use on more constructive issues.

6. For people who have become less than humble *without* committing the "sin" of adopting an attitude of superiority to others, a concept known as right-sizedness is more appropriate. When a person is right-sized she is appropriately humble. She realizes the full extent of her faults but, at the same time, has an accurate sense of her virtues as well. None of us is either all bad or all good. We are just human beings and possess both weaknesses and strengths.

   There are cases in which we may have come down too hard on ourselves and need to bring our self-opinion back up to a more accurate level. A sense of appropriate worthiness is required if we are to precipitate the kinds of circumstances and supply that will promote health and happiness.

THE LABORERS IN THE VINEYARD

Tunneling

MATTHEW 20:1–16

For the kingdom of heaven is like a landowner who went out early in the morning to hire men to work in his vineyard.

He agreed to pay them a denarius for the day and sent them into his vineyard.

About the third hour he went out and saw others standing in the marketplace doing nothing.

He told them, "You also go and work in my vineyard, and I will pay you whatever is right."

So they went. He went out again about the sixth hour and the ninth hour and did the same thing.

About the eleventh hour he went out and found still others standing around. He asked them, "Why have you been standing here all day long doing nothing?"

"Because no one has hired us," they answered. He said to them, "You also go and work in my vineyard."

When evening came, the owner of the vineyard said to his foreman, "Call the workers and pay them their wages, beginning with the last ones hired and going on to the first."

The workers who were hired about the eleventh hour came and each received a denarius.

So when those came who were hired first, they expected to receive more. But each one of them also received a denarius.

When they received it, they began to grumble against the land-owner.

"These men who were hired last worked only one hour," they said, "and you have made them equal to us who have borne the burden of the work and the heat of the day."

But he answered one of them, "Friend, I am not being unfair to you. Didn't you agree to work for a denarius?

Take your pay and go. I want to give the man who was hired last the same as I gave you.

Don't I have the right to do what I want with my own money? Or are you envious because I am generous?"

So, the last will be first, and the first will be last.

*T*HIS HAS ALWAYS BEEN one of the most curious parables of all. It concludes with the famous enigmatic statement widely quoted in a variety of contexts:

"So, the last will be first, and the first will be last."

Because this statement comes at the end, it appears to summarize the moral of the story, and would certainly seem to be very important. However, many scholars think that this a sort of "mistake." This position is summarized by the definitive source *The Interpreter's One-Volume Commentary on the Bible* (Abingdon Press, Nashville) as follows:

The concluding comment . . . blunts the point of the parable by draw-ing attention to the irrelevant fact that those workers who came last are paid first. The saying floated freely in the tradition and may have been attached to the parable because of the purely verbal connection with the order in which the workers are paid.

In other words, in traditional terms there is an important moral to the story, which we will look at shortly, but the fact that the workers arriving last got paid first is utterly irrelevant. In other words, the *tim-ing,* per se, has nothing to do with the moral. And what is the "moral" of the story. The moral, from a traditional, conservative, or fundamen-talistic viewpoint has to do with a concept known as "grace." Grace is an enormously important concept in conservative Christianity and is a central doctrine upon which other doctrine depends, to one degree or another.

Grace refers to the generous gifts that God may bestow to us, gifts that are wholly *unearned, even undeserved,* and thus "above" the laws of cause and effect—what would be called the Laws of Karma in the East. In traditional ideology, we have all received many such gifts and are likely to continue receiving them, even though as humans, we make se-rious errors in thought and deed. The concept of grace is that Spirit is so generous, so loving that sometimes it simply bestows us with bless-ings, *just because it loves us*—as a parent might give a beloved child a present one day, even though there is no particular reason to do so.

And this may well have been one of the levels of meaning the teacher intended. Grace is the name for all the good things we are given by God. Like a good parent, God tries to be fair and equitable. He can't have favorites. He loves us all equally. And so his gifts can be equal for both saint and sinner alike, for those who have come lately and for those with long-standing devotion. The common concept of grace suggests that it doesn't matter how *many* good works you have done or how *difficult* they were, it doesn't matter how *long* you have been in the church, how many dollars you have tithed—you will receive your grace, your freely given good, in equal measure with your neighbor.

It's a nice concept. But in a way, the more you think about it, the more unfair it is. Many people believe that the concept of grace is just a fudge factor, one of the concepts traditional theology has had to come up with to explain things that don't make any logical sense, things that are otherwise wholly unfair and unjust.

Many traditionalists believe the parable has an additional, deeper level of meaning. They believe the parable of the vineyard laborers is telling us how we will be rewarded after our deaths, or even after the apocalypse—the end of the entire world. In this context, the parable seems to be saying that everyone who has served the master of the vineyard—God—will be rewarded generously in the end, but that this generosity will be bestowed equally to all who have accepted Christ as their savior. In the end, it won't matter whether you have just entered the fold or have been there your entire life.

The moral seems to be aimed at people who have lived long lives of "sin" and neglect. It seems to be telling such people who are contemplating conversion that they shouldn't be deterred a bit by the fact that they are coming late to the game. It suggests that they will not only be accepted but that they will perhaps get some kind of spiritual bonus *because* they have had the courage and faith to accept salvation at such a late moment.

This is a beautiful concept but it has some serious problems. This interpretation implies that if you are an extremely dedicated, faithful, self-sacrificing individual and have practiced your faith for an entire lifetime, you will reap exactly the same reward in the end, in heaven, as other Christians who have only recently converted. If carried to its logical extreme, it means that a person could lead a life of horrendous crime, violence, and abuse affecting hundreds or thousands of individuals for many decades yet still receive the same rewards as a saint— provided he or she satisfies the requirements for salvation before death. This will be true even if the conversion takes place an hour or a minute before death, and, according to the last controversial statement in the parable, the equally measured reward will be bestowed to such a recent convert *before* it is bestowed to the saintly person!

In other words, if a person living an entire lifetime of destructive, malignant behavior converts to the faith, confesses her sins, and accepts Jesus as her savior a mere minute before death—or before the apocalypse—she will be admitted to the same echelons of the Kingdom of Heaven as the person who has led the exemplary life. *And,* she will be admitted *ahead* of those living long lifetimes of love and self-less service. Those holding to this interpretation seem to be able to shrug off the amazing and even absurd unfairness of this by simply saying, "That's just the way grace is. That's just the way God is."

But could there be another interpretation? One in which all the pieces seem to fit logically, including the last peculiar statement about timing, which, within the context of the traditional interpretation, doesn't seem to make a bit of sense and is thought by many scholars to simply be an error? Could we perhaps find an interpretation that not only integrates the last statement but shows how *the timing of grace* is actually very logical and very practical? Could we find an interpretation that goes even further and satisfies the law "As above, so below," one that seems consistent with science? Finally, could there be an interpretation that would even go so far as to explain some important aspect of *quantum* reality?

The Race

There is, in fact, an interpretation of the parable of the vineyard laborers that will satisfy all the above questions. It is logical, practical, universal, and all the pieces fit without fudging anything or glossing anything over. In order to understand this interpretation, however, a little preliminary work will have to be done to review a few basic concepts of Newtonian, or "normal," physics. Don't worry, we'll make this review extremely simple and take it one step at a time. If you are not scientifically inclined, do not be concerned, for the concepts we will look at are quite direct and will lead you to something wonderful and fascinating.

To begin with, let's look at a very ordinary situation—a tennis ball rolling over a small rug in your living room. We do an experiment with this ball. In the experiment, a spring-loaded mechanism, like one in the launcher of a pinball machine, pushes the ball with a certain exact amount of force—an amount that is equal every single time the ball is pushed over the carpet. We sit at one edge of the carpet and pull the plunger, the spring releases, and the ball rolls over the carpet to the other side.

Now imagine that we put a barrier in the middle of the carpet, a hump—something like a speed bump in a road. Now, using the spring-loaded launcher, we push the ball with the same force that we used when we pushed the ball across the carpet when there was no bump. In this experiment, we have made this "speed bump" carefully so that it is just high enough to *barely* stop the ball. The ball rolls toward the bump but is only able to get about 90 percent of the way up the bump before it stops and rolls back down toward you. The spring will not give the ball enough energy, enough "push," to get up and over the bump. No matter how many times we try, if we have set this experiment up correctly, the ball is always prevented from rolling over the barrier and getting to the other side of the carpet.

Now imagine that you are going to set up a little race between two tennis balls rolling across the same carpet. In this race, you have not one but *two* spring-loaded launching devices pushing *two* tennis balls across the carpet at exactly the same time. The finish line for this race is the wall on the other side of the room. When the two balls are fired across the carpet at the same time with exactly the same amount of force, they roll with exactly the same speed and get to the "finish line" at exactly the same time.

But you introduce a special condition in the race you are going to run. In your experimental race, one of the two balls will roll directly across the carpet with no bump, while the other ball has a severe disadvantage: The second ball will have to roll up and over the speed bump in order to complete the race. To make matters even more unfair, the ball that has to roll over the speed bump is given only about 90 percent of the energy it would need to get over the speed bump.

You sit at one edge of the carpet and release the two equal springs, and the two balls roll toward the wall on the other side of the room. About halfway to the finish line ball number one whizzes over the surface of the carpet with no bump while ball number two encounters the speed bump. Which of the two balls reaches the finish line at the other side of the carpet first?

IF YOU CAN GRASP this simple experiment, you are now ready to understand the following physics experiment that demonstrates one of the five great quantum mysteries, a phenomenon known as "tunneling." This experiment was done by a man named Raymond Y. Chiao at the Department of Physics, the University of California at Berkeley, who became quite well known in the physics world because of it. In the most basic terms, Chiao set up a race between two photons, two little pieces of light. In this race, he made absolutely sure that both photons started off at exactly the same time, just like the two tennis balls. He didn't want one of the photons to get even the slightest head start because that would make it hard to tell who the real winner was. In addition, he made absolutely sure that both photons had exactly the same amount of energy, the same amount of "push," just like the two tennis balls.

The end point in this experiment was a special instrument that provided a perfectly even "finish line" for both of the racing photons. This finish line also provided an amazingly accurate clock that would *time* the two photons down to a femtosecond—one quadrillionth of a second—so that the real winner could be determined with spectacular precision.

But there was one thing that was very unfair about the race—in the same way the race between the two tennis balls was unfair. Chiao put a barrier in front of one of the photons. This barrier was exactly like the speed bump the second tennis ball had to roll over. In other words, Chiao made the barrier just a little bit too "high" for the second photon to "roll over" with the amount of energy it would be given at the starting gate.

Certainly, this barrier would present a very unfair advantage for the first photon. The first photon would be able to proceed freely to the finish line with no interference whatsoever. For all purposes, this presented *such* an unfair disadvantage that the second photon could not possibly get up and over the bump at all and would, in theory, *never* make it to the finish line.

Now, imagine that you are watching the race. The two photons wait at the starting blocks and the starting gun is fired. Off they go. And they are exactly neck and neck as they head down the race-course. Soon they reach the point in the racetrack where photon number two encounters the barrier. The first photon continues on at the speed of light with no interference whatsoever. The second photon starts to head up the side of the bump, but it soon becomes apparent that it will not have enough energy to make it over. It would appear that the first photon will be the sure winner.

But that's not what happens. Instead of the expected outcome, something incredibly weird happens, something that makes absolutely no sense at all, something that seems in every way to violate the known laws of the universe: Instead of being rebuffed, *as it gets about 90 percent of the way up the bump* the second photon suddenly *disappears.* Then, to make matters even weirder, it suddenly *reappears* on the other side of the barrier—as if it had "tunneled" through the bump, tunneled through matter itself. As if that weren't strange enough, you notice something very odd. The tunneling photon not only makes it through the barrier but it does so *instantly. No time at all elapses as it tunnels through the barrier!* The photon makes it to the other side of the barrier, appearing to tunnel through both space and time.

As you now assess the progress of the race, you see that photon number two is not only still in the race, it is actually *ahead* of the unimpeded photon, which is still traveling at the speed of light. And, sure enough, according to the special timer you are using, the second photon reaches the finish line faster than the speed of light, reaching the finish line *before* the photon that had no interference at all along its racecourse. . . .

So, the last will be first,
and the first will be last.

Einstein once said of the strange phenomenon observed in quantum physics that if you understand quantum physics, you don't yet understand it. But if you get to the point where you run up against a wall of mystery that baffles you and runs completely counter to all your sensibilities, you now are beginning to understand it. So, if you cannot comprehend what happens in the experiment above, if it baffles you and gives you an odd feeling, great. *Now you're getting it.* Welcome to another great quantum mystery, *tunneling.*

But how do we know the experiment was done properly? Maybe this was just an illusion, an artifact of an improperly designed experimental setup. Any reasonable person would consider such experimental error as the most likely explanation for the irrational and paradoxical nature of the race results. But this most certainly does not explain the results of the race. The fact is that we know for *certain* that instantaneous tunneling occurs because it happens every day in everyone's life. Designers of electronics components and electronics devices have been not only observing the phenomenon of tunneling but actually using it to make common electronic devices for decades. You have scores of such components scattered through the appliances and gadgets in your house, your car, and your office. Common electronic components such as transistors and diodes use tunneling routinely to control the flow of electrons through various kinds of specially constructed barriers. So, the question is not whether tunneling actually happens, the question is "*How* can tunneling possibly happen?"

Tunneling Below, Tunneling Above

This is all very interesting but, you may well ask, what does it have to do with me and my life? Tunneling may be useful in electronics but, aside from that, what relevance does it have in my daily life and what spiritual implications could it possibly hold? And why would the great teacher go to the trouble of composing an entire parable about the issue? The answer is that the dictum "As above, so below, as below, so above" applies to the phenomenon of tunneling just as it applies to all the other quantum mysteries and all the other scientific priniciples we have looked at.

In the parable of the fig tree, we talked about the fact that in the right circumstances a fruit tree that is not fertilized will actually "gain" on a fruit tree that has been fertilized—in the sense that it will, in the end, produce far more fruit, and fruit of a better quality. When we talked about that parable, we also pointed out that the same is true for people. In some instances, a human being who has to work through hardships and problems will actually "gain" on a person who has the "fertilizer" of wealth and effortless living.

It is the person who has to overcome barriers who ends up having a deeper character and more compassion and understanding for others and ends up achieving these critical spiritual characteristics sooner. Spiritually speaking, such a person makes it to the "finish line" far ahead of the others. Because the finish line, the whole purpose of this life, is not to gain wealth, or to gain power, or to gain fame, or to gain recognition. The purpose of this life is to gain character, spiritual depth, and compassion—the ability to love selflessly and freely.

So, THE FINAL STATEMENT in the parable of the vineyard laborers now falls into place nicely without being forced or fudged. "So, the last will be first, and the first will be last," the irrelevant statement about timing that is often thought to have been added after the fact by someone other than Jesus now becomes logical. And to make things even tidier, this logic extends to the concept of grace.

There is no explanation of why the photon with the barrier is transported instantaneously through or "beneath" the fabric of time and space, through a kind of "wormhole" that allows for faster-than-light travel. Such mysterious transport might just as well be called miraculous transport. The photon with the barrier has only so much energy so it cannot "earn" the passage through the barrier; it does not "deserve" its instantaneous transport. So, it could be said that it is "grace" that allows the mystery to happen.

So it is with our lives. Sometimes we encounter barriers, problems, setbacks, hardships, challenges, disabilities, diseases, disappointments, and losses. And these barriers can seem impossibly high, impossibly formidable. Often, there is no logical way that we are going to be able to surmount such obstacles.

The parable is telling us that we just have to try. If we try, even though we don't have quite enough energy, quite enough merit, quite enough talent, quite enough time, or quite enough knowledge to get through a given situation, if we try and persist and have faith we will not only make it, we will actually gain on the competition.

The finish line in the story is the end of the workday. The reward for arriving there is a certain amount of money. The money is made equal in the story in the same way that the finish line is made equal in our experiments. The barrier in the story, the barrier to getting paid, is the amount of time spent in the field. The workers who arrive early have no barrier to getting paid the expected amount, no barrier to reaping the expected rewards. The workers who arrive later that evening are the people who don't have sufficient merit, sufficient energy, sufficient talent, who don't have sufficient time on the clock to make it to the "finish line" of the paycheck. But they sign up anyway, they begin work, they try, even though it would appear in every way that it will be impossible for them to earn the same generous paycheck as the others.

The moral of the story is that no matter how daunting the obsta-

cles we encounter along our paths of evolution, we will receive the supernatural, the mysterious, the *miraculous* benefits of "grace" if we try
as hard as we can, if we persist with faith. The moral of the story is
that if we do the best that we can, we will not fail. We may not succeed in the way our egos define success, but in spiritual terms we will
not only fail to fail, we will be *ahead* in the end.

And when is the "end"? That is most difficult to say. For our lives
are never really over. There are many races, many obstacles, many
speed bumps, many finish lines, and many rewards. It is our challenge,
our responsibility as spiritual journeyers, to see through the obvious
and perceive the barriers for what they are: opportunities to get ahead
of the game.

The Splitting of Realities

The parable of the vineyard laborers has one more level of meaning,
and we would be remiss if we were not to look at it carefully. As we
know, the vast majority of competent mainstream physicists now believe that our realities, our universes, are constantly *splitting*. Every
time a conscious being makes a conscious decision, a new universe
splits off from the parent universe. In due course, everything that *can*
ever be possible becomes *real* somewhere in some universe.

Furthermore, if we may reasonably assume that the same laws of
the universe were operating in the days of Christ as they are now, we
may also reasonably assume that the teacher knew full well of this crit-
ically important splitting process that would seem to be at the very
center of reality and of enormous practical importance to the light
worker. And it would be no stretch to believe that if this were in fact

so, the teacher would have wanted to share with us everything he could to help us understand the splitting of realities and to use them to create better realities.

The phenomenon of tunneling is a manifestation of the splitting of realities. At the beginning of a photon "race" two photons are launched with equal energy down two different "forks in the road." This is the split point. And as these photons race down the track, they show us what happens in the two universes within which each now resides. One universe is "easy" and one "difficult"—with an insurmountable barrier. One universe evolves down one path while the other universe evolves down another path. In the universe with the obstacle, evolution appears to slow, to be impossibly impeded in some way. And then, it suddenly takes a jump, a quantum leap, up to the next level.

What the parable says, from a practical standpoint, is that as you proceed through your life, today, wherever you live and doing whatever it is you do on a day-to-day basis, you will be presented with analogous split points. These will manifest as a series of decisions that you will have to make. You will be tempted in many cases to take the path that appears to simply be the easiest. But you should think carefully, choose carefully. For the path that simply appears "easy" will not necessarily be the path that will get you where you want to go in the most efficient way.

The parable tells us that if we are conscientious—if we have faith, and integrity, and the courage to try—even though one path may appear to be far more difficult, we will be helped along it in ways we cannot understand. If we give it our all, that alone will suffice in many cases. That's all we have to worry about, moving ahead, persisting, giving it our best effort, *acting as if* we have enough energy, enough impetus. When we do, we will receive the aid of *grace*—the miraculous, mysterious kind of help that will allow us to get through the situation in ways we cannot possibly foresee or even understand.

ACTIVATING PARABLE LESSON 26

1. *Meditate* upon your past. List two or three apparently insurmountable setbacks, challenges, or disadvantages that you have worked through in the past. These could be daunting physical, financial, emotional, mental, spiritual, or other kinds of barriers that appeared at the time to be impassable, or unsolvable.

   See how those barriers, in the end, actually were part of the process ultimately necessary for you to get where you are today. See how they actually *helped* you attain a higher attitude of humility, love, compassion, and service. Understand how you ended up achieving these most valuable of spiritual attitudes—which are the real goals in this life—where others, who had no such barriers to work through, perhaps did not.

   Make sure that you work at this until you find one or more good examples where, as you moved forward, grace entered into your life and helped you overcome your barriers and challenges in ways that you did not anticipate and could not explain from a logical perspective.

2. Look at the projects that you are working on in your life today, the things you are trying to create and build, the dreams you are striving to manifest, the situations you are trying to heal. List each of these on a piece of paper. Next to each, list the primary barrier or barriers that seem to stand between you and attainment of your cherished goals, anything that would seem to give you an unfair dis-

advantage, anything that seems to be slowing you down, anything that would seem to be especially challenging to overcome along your way.

3. If any of these barriers seem particularly difficult or even insur-mountable, *meditate* upon them one by one. *Realize* that each of these barriers could be an opportunity for you to use the principle of tunneling described in parable lesson twenty-six. *See* that if you resolve to move ahead in spite of these difficult obstacles and chal-lenges, the conditions have been set that can allow grace to enter into the picture.

4. *Invite God into the process.* Ask him specifically to help you have faith, faith in his generosity, faith in his undeniable tendency to kick in and provide unexpected and often miraculous assistance. Ask him to provide you with his help, his gifts, his grace. Promise in return to do what you can from your end, to the best of your ability, con-tinuing to move forward, continuing to work with the entire se-quence of parable lessons.

5. *Thank God in advance,* for the grace that you know in your heart, in your higher spirit, can enable you to overcome any barrier.

THE TWO SONS

The Law of Action

MATTHEW 21:28–32

"What do you think? There was a man who had two sons. He went to the first and said, 'Son, go and work today in the vineyard.'

'I will not,' he answered, but later he changed his mind and went.

Then the father went to the other son and said the same thing. He answered, 'I will, sir,' but he did not go.

Which of the two did what his father wanted?" "The first," they answered. Jesus said to them, "I tell you the truth, the tax collectors and the prostitutes are entering the kingdom of God ahead of you."

THE PARABLE OF THE TWO SONS is one of the simplest of the parable lessons. Not all the parables require lengthy explanations. Sometimes the teacher opted for straight, simple, direct messages. In this story there are two sons. One says, with his words, that he will do something. The other says, with his words, that he will not do something. The son who verbalizes that he will do something does not, and the son who verbalizes that he will not do something does.

The master, in the story, is far more pleased with the son who ends up actually doing what needs to be done.

The message of this parable is clear and unequivocal and uncompli-cated. It is specifically designed to teach one important principle. And it is an enormously important principle for sure. The lesson is that al-though words, such as we use in affirmations and prayer, are important and powerful, they don't hold a candle to the power of action.

The message is designed to remove any doubt in our minds that while considering various strategies and plans that apply to your thought form projects, you should put action far ahead of any sort of words. It is a good thing, even a necessary thing at times, to speak pos-itively about what you intend to do. We all know that putting what we need into words is an essential part of the miracle worker's game plan. But all too often we rely too much on words and too little on action.

The teacher was a man of action. Certainly he taught and spoke in eloquent and powerful ways. But if we really look at his life, we see that he was also a man who *did* things, a man who *acted,* a man who *worked hard.* We see him healing people from dawn to dusk on many days.

A person who has not yet evolved, not yet mastered the mysteries, waits for the world, and *then* acts. By contrast, a miracle worker pro-ceeds with action regardless of what the world shows him to be "real." A miracle worker doesn't wait for the world because he knows that the world is really waiting for him, waiting for him to direct it with positive intention. A miracle worker knows that all the principles learned so far in the parable lesson sequence are true. That the fabric of reality does re-spond to thought, that reality is permeated with a "substance" that causes it to expand in response to thought. A miracle worker knows that proceeding with action, taking the leap of faith and moving ahead proactively, with faith, and humility, and *persistence,* is more powerful than any words and can literally alter physical reality.

ACTIVATING PARABLE LESSON 27

1. At this point in your evolution, you are being asked to stop thinking about it, stop talking about it, and start *doing* it. This may sound elementary, but it can be very tricky. What you have to do to activate this parable lesson is to first *list* everything that you could be *doing* to move forward with your dream, your healing, but are *not*.

   Your entire life, your entire thought form project can be completely stopped, completely hung up because of a single, solitary snag. It will not suffice to do *most* of the things that are required to move forward; you will have to do *all* of them.

   Perhaps there is that one call you have to make but cannot quite bring yourself to do because of shyness, or inertia, or fear. Perhaps there is an application you need to fill out, a difficult conversation you need to have, a person you must forgive, a difficult and mundane job you have been putting off—it could be anything. What is critical is that you *identify* the snag or snags that are holding you back.

2. *Write* these uncompleted tasks down on a piece of paper and put your list in a prominent place where you can see it every day.

3. *Resolve now* to complete each of these unfinished tasks forthwith. *Set a time* when you will do each of the tasks. Make sure the time you choose is a point of *high energy*, when you have had a good night's sleep and won't be distracted by peripheral issues. *Write down* the time that you have chosen to begin acting.

4. *Invite God into the situation.* Ask him directly to help you focus on the tasks at hand, to have the energy necessary to work though the

mental and emotional blocks that have been preventing you from getting started. *Thank* God in advance for helping you see the task completed. Know that grace will enter into your life if you proceed toward your stumbling blocks *as if* you had enough energy, enough talent, enough intelligence to make it through. *See* yourself happy, and confident, and with a new sense of accomplishment and freedom now that the task has been finished successfully.

5. Stop thinking about it and *do it! Execute* the list of unfinished tasks.

———— ❦ ————

THE WICKED HUSBANDMEN

The Law of Perception I

MATTHEW 21:33–44

"*Listen to another parable: There was a landowner who planted a vineyard. He put a wall around it, dug a winepress in it and built a watchtower. Then he rented the vineyard to some farmers and went away on a journey.*

When the harvest time approached, he sent his servants to the tenants to collect his fruit.

The tenants seized his servants; they beat one, killed another, and stoned a third.

Then he sent other servants to them, more than the first time, and the tenants treated them the same way.

Last of all, he sent his son to them. 'They will respect my son,' he said.

But when the tenants saw the son, they said to each other, 'This is the heir. Come, let's kill him and take his inheritance.'

So they took him and threw him out of the vineyard and killed him.

Therefore, when the owner of the vineyard comes, what will he do to those tenants?"

"*He will bring those wretches to a wretched end,*" they replied, *"and he will rent the vineyard to other tenants, who will give him his share of the crop at harvest time."*

Jesus said to them, "Have you never read in the Scriptures: 'The stone the builders rejected has become the capstone; the Lord has done this, and it is marvelous in our eyes'?

Therefore I tell you that the kingdom of God will be taken away from you and given to a people who will produce its fruit."

THE PARABLE OF THE WICKED HUSBANDMEN, another word for farmer, holds one of the very last lessons in the powerful sequence of lessons. Its message contains a final admonition, a final word of advice to all people who are "farming the vineyard," who are working this fertile milieu of cause and effect that unerringly and inexorably turns thought into reality. And the parable contains extraordinarily advanced mystical information on the Law of Perception as it pertains to the development of the soul. This parable and the parable of the ten virgins, which follows this parable, form a pair, a two-part message on the subtleties of *perception*. To understand this critical piece of the puzzle correctly, we need to examine the two parables point by point as they unfold.

To begin with, the teacher paints a picture of what may be going on in your life now, late in the sequence, assuming you have mastered the other lessons. At this point in your progress, the story indicates, the set of circumstances that you will find around you may be comfortable and successful, and will tend to have three critical elements: a wall, a winepress, and a watchtower.

The wall represents protection. If you have done everything that has been so far suggested, you will now be in a state of protection, secured against external negative influences. You will be safe. And you will have appropriate and healthy boundaries with other people and with the world around you.

The winepress is a mechanism by which the fruit that manifests in response to your creative efforts can be transformed into its final useful and tradable form—into actual "product," if you will. A winepress does not perform this transformation automatically and without effort. It must be operated, it must be worked. The winepress therefore symbolizes any infrastructure that has developed within your life that allows the fruits of your thought form projects to be transformed into their final form. The winepress may represent, for example, a business that operates within your life and allows you to convert your creative energy into things with practical and even monetary value, or it could represent your job, an artistic studio, or a career path.

The watchtower is a vantage point, a vantage point that has been deliberately constructed, deliberately developed. In the strictest sense, it has been built by the landowner. But in its truest sense, the tower has been built by *you,* the higher "you," for all the elements within these teaching stories are things that are happening within you, within your creative universe. The watchtower is your ability to perceive, your ability to intuit at a higher level.

Your natural powers of perception have improved and become far more sensitive and accurate—*heightened* in the watchtower of your soul—as your spiritual growth has proceeded along the precise guidelines the parable sequence has delineated. From a watchtower, things that are happening at a distance can be observed. We are now able to see farther and more clearly, able to sense things in advance, able to discern circumstances and events more quickly and more accurately than we ever have before, able to connect increasingly distant causes together with the effects that they produce.

In other words, if you have followed the lessons that have been so carefully laid before you, you will, at this point in your personal evolution, "have it made," so to speak—at least in some areas. You will find yourself living a life that is, in some ways, more secure and profitable. And you will be simultaneously blessed with *wisdom,* which is the power to perceive what is *really* causing things to be as they are. The ultimate mover in your circumstances are your thoughts, of course. But your thoughts are often separated in time from the effects that they produce—there is often a delay between the time they are launched and the time they crystallize within your reality. It is only with increasing wisdom, increasing vision, increasing intuitive perception that we can put the thoughts together with their sometimes distance effects.

The parable indicates that this state of success will hold no small degree of peril for your soul. It is telling you that as your material circumstances become more comfortable, you will have an automatic, and very human, tendency to forget what is really causing things to be as they are. You will have a tendency to forget that the true source of your wealth, your comfort, and your success comes not from you—the small, egotistical "you"—but from the larger you, the "you" that is connected to, one with, Spirit. Although you have been instrumental in the positive developments that have transpired, via your free will and positive intention, you are still "renting the farm," you are still a tenant, still but a steward managing the resources of the real "landowner," your higher self, as it reflects and represents the One.

At this point, certain things are going to happen. Representatives of God, spiritual messengers of one kind or another, will begin to appear. These representatives, in whatever form they manifest, will be sent to "collect," in some way, the portion of your increase that belongs to the true owner. If the premise of your new understanding of these parables is correct, the most important level at which these

things will occur will be internal. As is the case with the other parables, this story is describing something that will be happening inside,
within yourself.

The messengers, the representatives of Spirit, may be parts of your
self as well. They could be parts of your self that are still connected directly to the "owner," Spirit, the true Source. These "representatives"
will be your higher consciousness, your conscience—the part of you
that always knows what is really going on at the highest level. The
parable is telling you that your higher self will be intruding on your
consciousness, that high, elevated, spiritual thoughts will begin to
come into your conscious awareness, thoughts that will be asking you
to divert some of the fruits of your labors and your success, some of
the powerful energy that has manifested deep within, away from your
lower self and back to your higher self. These "representatives of
Spirit" may indicate in some way that they need you to divert some of
your time, energy, and most important, your attention, your higher
concentrated thought forms, out of your personal life and into the
world of Spirit, where they are extremely useful in the projects of Divine Intelligence

If the parable is correct, you may begin to reject these higher
thoughts, these higher requests for energy. When these thoughts come
into your mind, you will want to "kill" them, sometimes in an obvious
sort of way, but more often in a very subtle and insidious way—more
through simple neglect than through deliberate negative intent. Even
though you will remember and periodically become aware that your
higher self, the part of you that is one with the source, needs to be fed
and maintained, you will have a strong urge to push these recollections
back down into the unconscious realm, and fall back into a state of spiritual indolence.

And who would deny that this is indeed something that happens within us all the time? If our external reality has improved and become very comfortable, we have a very human and very reliable tendency to want to delay or completely forget our Spirituality, and to simply kick back and enjoy things as they are.

When you meditate, a variety of thoughts comes to the surface of your mind where you will become conscious of them. Some of those thoughts will be of a lower nature and some will be of a higher nature. If you are comfortable and secure on the material plane, it will be very easy for you to sublimate, to push down into the unconscious realm, thoughts that are reminding you to pay attention to Spirit, feed Spirit, thoughts reminding you to do all that is necessary to maintain your progress forward.

Certainly you would be tempted to say that this will not happen to you, that you will *always* remember that it is Spirit that actually got you to the place you are now enjoying as you grow in energy, knowledge, and material security. This parable is telling you that to become *overly confident* of your spirituality in the face of material comfort is naive and very dangerous. The temptation to forget who you *really* are, what you are *really* doing, and what *really* sustains you will, in reality, be enormous. To fall into a state of denial regarding this universal temptation would be an enormous mistake.

This parable is reminding you now, near the end of the sequence, to examine your self very closely and with great honesty. Are you *really* aware of the fact that you are but a steward, a mere tenant, or are you simply giving lip service to this notion? It is one thing to *say* that you are aware of the danger and another to be *aware* of the danger. And it is yet another thing to actually *do* something about it. You are not doing what will be required of you to sustain your position of comfort and security by simply saying that you know who you are. You need to give God his due, both at a material level by *tithing*—this is surely one important level of the parable—but also at a mental level by remaining acutely aware of your true place in the scheme of things—by mentally tithing to him, as it were.

If you fail to stay sufficiently conscious of the reality of your life and your place within the world as stewards of the resources under your management, Spirit will have no reasonable alternative but to remove those resources and place them under new management. In a sense, this will be "just business," something that will have to happen for Spirit to continue on in the way that it must. For Spirit to sustain itself and continue to grow within your consciousness, it must be fed, must be given sufficient time and attention. Spirit is the tree that provides the fruit. If that tree is not watered and pruned and cared for properly, it will become sickly, fail to thrive, and stop producing fruit. This parable tells you that the tree, Spirit, will not, *cannot*, allow this to happen. If it is not taken care of it will find another caretaker, plain and simple. At this point the teacher makes a very interesting comment:

> *Have you never read in the Scriptures: "The stone the builders rejected has become the capstone; the Lord has done this, and it is marvelous in our eyes"?*

The question is, what does this "rejected" stone represent? Standard interpretations differ on this score but close examination reveals that, within the context of the parable, the stone that is rejected must have to do with the watchtower. For the only thing that has been built, the only building within the parable that would have a "cornerstone," is the watchtower.

The watchtower represents perception, elevated vision, the heightened powers of discrimination and intuition that have developed automatically as you, the student, have progressed in spiritual depth, while walking the path of learning outlined by the parables. And the capstone? Actually, three Greek terms are used to describe the type of stone the teacher is talking about in the story. This first is *eis*. Although often translated simply as "the," this is a great oversimiplification, for this little word can have many meanings. Actually, one of the common uses of *eis,* according to *Strong's Concordance,* is to indicate "abundance" in some sense. The second term used in the parable is *kephale,* which means "*head*—in the sense of the part that is most easily taken hold of." The third term used is the Greek *gonia,* which means "angle" *or* "corner."

Some orthodox translations group these terms together as "capstone" and others translate them as "cornerstone." In light of the above information, however, neither alone seems adequate. A true translation would incorporate the concepts of "abundance," "head," "most easily grasped," and being at a "corner." This is actually a very curious conjunction of concepts. To understand why, consider first what a cornerstone is for an actual builder.

When laying out any building, it is essential to start with a firm, fixed point, and a single accurate ninety-degree angle. A cornerstone is just that for a builder, it is the reference point from which all else proceeds. A cornerstone is the *first* stone laid and never something that is added later, much less put at the *top* of a building. Every single stone within the entire building that follows, even if it is a very large building such as a watchtower, "grows" from, and is oriented to, the cornerstone. A capstone, on the other hand, is the very *last* stone that is laid by a builder. It is at the highest point and is the apex, the culmination, the crowning achievement of the builder.

A stone that is the combination of a cornerstone and a capstone is therefore impossible, at least from a builder's standpoint, for there is no stone in a building that can be the first and lowest stone, *and* the last and highest stone. This is why the teacher tells us that this stone is "marvelous," something that only God could have done. "Marvelous" here is a code word for "mystery."

All of this is made yet more curious by the context in which these three terms appear. The metaphorical watchtower in the story represents an elevated vantage point of perception; that much seems fairly straightforward. This heightened perception or powerful intuitive ability is "built" as you progress along the path of the parables. And here, at the end of the whole sequence of parables, this intuitive power is one of your crowning achievements, one of the ultimate and most highly evolved of the blessings. This heightened perception is one of the fruits that comes with mastery of the parable sequence.

What, then, is the "stone the builders rejected"? To answer that we have to know first who the builder is. If we continue to work on the premise that the parables are all about *you,* then the builder is, of course, *you*—specifically the higher "you." The stone that you originally rejected is the stone that is now at the top. The stone at the top is the ability to perceive, it is the power to intuit at a very high level. Recall that the first of the three words to describe this special "stone" or building component is "abundant(ly)." The stone therefore represents not just perception, but a heightened and highly evolved *perception of abundance.* It symbolizes the ability to understand where your increase originates, it is the ability to perceive the Source of your overflowing prosperity, your spiritual and material blessings. And that is God, to be sure, but the beneficial circumstances that manifest in your life also represent the sum total of your thought forms as a cocreator with God.

This understanding was originally rejected by you, to one degree or another, before you achieved mastery of the mysteries. Before you began, a large part of you believed that circumstances in your life usually developed *outside* you, that things were mostly happening *to* you.

But as you progress in awareness and skill and persistence with positive thought forms and intentions, you increasingly see or "perceive" that you are not a victim of circumstance, and chance, and the influences of those more powerful. Now, the stone that you rejected is your crowning achievement.

There is one more interesting thing about the use of these three curious terms together. And that concerns the fact that the stone the teacher is talking about is a stone that is both a cornerstone—the stone from which the rest of the building grows—*and* at the *top*. Logically, this can only mean one thing, that the building *starts* at the top or the head and grows *downward*. It means that the building, the reality, the material circumstances you find yourself experiencing down here on the "ground," in hard cold reality, have grown *from* the head, from your thoughts, and not vice versa, as conventional common sense would have us believe.

Now that you have improved your circumstances and are in a place of comfort and security, you will have to continue to be acutely aware of the fact that your thoughts are generating your reality, including the material circumstances. When such an awareness has been activated you will realize, on a moment-by-moment basis, that you have no sane alternative but to be extremely careful what kinds of thoughts you continue to sow as a steward working the fertile garden you have been given to cultivate.

Activating Parable Lesson 28

1. Make a list of the blessings in your life. Now, write a brief paragraph next to each showing how you understand, how you *perceive,*

at a deep level, how these blessings are not, strictly speaking, yours, but rather things that are under your stewardship.

2. Now, meditate carefully on each of these blessings, seeing with ever deeper clarity who they really belong to and giving appropriate thanks for them.

3. Carry your new perception into your daily life, dwelling on your role as a steward, a caretaker of the precious blessings that your work with Spirit has provided to you.

4. Be on the lookout for any "messengers" who may appear in your life "asking" for the dues you know that you owe. Expect that there may be mail, people, or circumstances that will bring to your attention tithes, contributions, or gifts that you can make to help the "owner" of the spectacular resources that you have been entrusted to work.

The Ten Virgins

The Law of Perception II

MATTHEW 25:1–13

At that time the kingdom of heaven will be like ten virgins who took their lamps and went out to meet the bridegroom.

Five of them were foolish and five were wise.

The foolish ones took their lamps but did not take any oil with them.

The wise, however, took oil in jars along with their lamps.

The bridegroom was a long time in coming, and they all became drowsy and fell asleep.

At midnight the cry rang out: "Here's the bridegroom! Come out to meet him!"

Then all the virgins woke up and trimmed their lamps.

The foolish ones said to the wise, "Give us some of your oil; our lamps are going out."

"No," they replied, "there may not be enough for both us and you. Instead, go to those who sell oil and buy some for yourselves."

But while they were on their way to buy the oil, the bridegroom arrived. The virgins who were ready went in with him to the wedding banquet. And the door was shut.

Later the others also came. "Sir! Sir!" they said. "Open the door
for us!"

But he replied, "I tell you the truth, I don't know you."

Therefore keep watch, because you do not know the day or the
hour.

THIS PARABLE DISCUSSES the second part of the Law of Perception. It is a lesson designed to teach us about the way the five senses should be managed—so as to facilitate a light worker's efforts. This lesson takes the form of a story about five virgins, who all have *empty* lamps, and five other virgins who all have lamps that are *full* of oil. The five virgins represent the five senses, first in an undeveloped, undisciplined state and then in a well-developed, disciplined state.

In the first sentence, we are also notified of another character who will be instrumental in delivering the message, a "bridegroom." The bridegroom represents that which will engage and and stimulate the senses. The bridegroom represents sensory stimuli—light, sound, touch sensations, and biochemical conditions, phenomena in the external world that deliver information to our sensory organs, our nervous systems—and ultimately, to our deeper selves. But the bridegroom doesn't represent just any sensory data. The bridegroom is a symbol for very special sensory data, information that will be arriving that will help us find something we have been looking for, or striving to manifest. The bridegroom is information that we should be expecting, information that will take us to a new quantum level.

The senses, once impregnated with incoming sensory stimuli, produce powerful and convincing impulses that are then sent to the brain for interpretation. And the interpretation of such incoming impulses is called, of course, "perception." Perception, as you well know at this late state of your progress along the parable path, is not an absolute, something that makes us passive victims to energies external to our selves. Perception is the way we *learn* to put complex sensory impressions together to "create" what we refer to as "reality." Two different people, each with a different system of interpretation, may perceive the same thing in two entirely different, and equally valid, ways. Perception is therefore not an absolute, but rather malleable, something that can be changed and *shifted,* with practice. And, as A Course in Miracles states so strongly, a shift in perception is a very large part of a miracle. It is no wonder the teacher put this parable in one of the most auspicious of locations, second to last. Who would not be quick to agree that knowing how to shift one's current state of perception to that of a miracle worker's would be a skill of incalculable value?

THE FIVE FOOLISH VIRGINS are women who have never had sex. They represent the senses in a state of rest, waiting to receive incoming sensory data. At a deeper level, the five *foolish* senses are the senses of a person who has not yet received initiation into the mysteries. The senses of such a person—a person who doesn't have the knowledge and skill conferred by the previous lessons—often lead to unwise and unhelpful perceptions of reality, i.e., they can "fool" us into believing that something is "reality" when in fact it is not. They can fool us into believing that a situation is hopeless and unsolvable when, in fact, it can be miraculously transformed.

The other five virgins, who are described as "wise," represent the senses of a person who *has* been initiated into the previous twenty-eight mysteries and the profound preparatory exercises they require to fully understand. The senses of a person so armed with spiritual wisdom and expertise are far more likely to lead to beneficial interpretations of sensory data, *perceptions* of reality that are far more useful for a person who seeks to change the world for the better.

The lamps represent the ability to illuminate a situation with consciousness and knowledge—knowledge, of course, of the *mysteries*. Always remember that the teacher told us at the outset that the parable sequence is all about the "mysteries." The senses have to "carry" this knowledge in order for them to function properly, in order for them to work with the conscious mind properly, in order for them to produce *miraculous perceptions* of reality. Before initiation, the senses don't have any oil in their lamps, they have not received the requisite spiritual knowledge to form accurate perceptions and can still fool and be fooled, i.e., are "foolish." After initiation, a person is fully loaded with the right knowledge needed to get the senses under control, to be able to *shift them at will,* so as to perceive things accurately, the way a miracle worker would see things.

Before evolution, before mastery, the senses are incapable of helping us with our work. More likely, they are liable to confuse us and hinder our efforts. But after the mind and body have received the benefits of the parable lesson sequence, the senses are actually capable of *helping* us with our work. And would we not hope that this would be so? For like it or not, the senses persist as a massive feature of our being. We would hope to find from a spiritual teacher that the senses are not completely detrimental to accurate, miraculous perception and can actually be harnessed, put to work in some beneficial capacity.

The five foolish virgins represent initiates who have become aware that spiritual knowledge is a requirement for accurate perception. These virgins are described not as ignorant but as "foolish" because *they know better.* They know, just as well as the wise virgins, that they have to have oil in order to get their lamps to burn, i.e., they have to have the spiritual knowledge and experience that initiation into the mysteries confers. But the initiates so described here have not as yet had the foresight and initiative to work through the rest of the mystery initiations laid out in the parable lesson sequence and therefore haven't developed the spiritual knowledge they need in order to handle things properly.

At this point in the story, all the virgins are waiting for the bridegroom. As said, the bridegroom represents incoming sensory data, but not just *any* sensory data. When *this* data arrives, something big will happen, something miraculous. When this information arrives, there will be a wedding, representing the fulfillment of the dream, the solution to the problem, the correction of the perceived lack, the *miracle*. So much of a miracle is information—information on *where* to find the soul mate or the job, information on *how* to solve the problem, information on *which* medicine or doctor will cure the disease. It is an *inspiration* on how to make a work of creation. Miraculous information is all around us. But it is only when we can *perceive* with the *miraculous shift in perception* that we can become aware of the right information at a *conscious* level.

With its myriad sensory stimuli, the world is a bit like a newspaper, including its long pages of information on stocks and commodities. If we could perceive with miraculous perception, we could interpret and filter the massive columns of data so contained in any daily newspaper such that we would become *conscious* of the precise information that would easily make us billionaires in the space of a week or two.

The teacher seems to be telling us that at some point in the dream that is unfolding around you, data will arrive that is extremely important, data that can tell you exactly how to make the quantum leap to your fulfillment, your evolutionary synthesis. This parable tells us that if we have not primed ourselves with the right kinds of spiritual knowledge, the kind conveyed by the parable lesson sequence, we may not be able to perceive the data for what it is when it finally arrives. We may thus miss our big chance and find ourselves waiting vainly and impatiently once again.

THE TIMING IS CRITICAL at this point in the allegory. The critical information will likely come at "midnight"—which means that the information will arrive when the conscious mind is asleep and its guard is down. Midnight is also the very end of the day, a most appropriate time to cite in this, the second to last parable. In such a relaxed state, conscious awareness will not suffice for it is simply not present. Only the *subconscious reflexes* that a truly evolved self has developed through long training and practice of the parable lesson sequence will suffice to allow the accurate processing, the accurate *perception* of stimuli coming at such a totally unexpected and unpropitious ebb tide of the soul. Like a prizefighter whose brilliant reflexes operating far quicker than any possible thought allow him to react correctly to a totally unexpected rain of punches, it will be your deepest spiritual reflexes that will allow you to react correctly when your big chance is offered to you. And reflexes can't be developed overnight. Reflexes result from repetition and practice and persistence and diligence and faithful practice of the spiritual principles you have been working on.

Another critical point to be aware of regarding the timing of the story is that this parable is the second to last in the sequence. The preceding parable, the parable of the wicked husbandmen, also contains critical, final information that provides closure to the full sequence of parable lessons. That parable reminds us that as all the parable lessons are mastered and manifestation begins to occur on a regular basis, we have to stay acutely aware of the true nature of the manifestation process, that it is something we are doing for God, that we have been placed as stewards of his resources. The parable of the wicked husbandmen indicates that we are allowed, even expected, to produce rewarding circumstances for ourselves, but will be held accountable for the portion that belongs to the true owner of the garden. That parable reminds us that in order for us to continue to be entrusted with the manifestation process, we have to return resources to the source. If we do, we will ensure that the garden itself is maintained—something that is our responsibility.

In the parable of the ten virgins, we find the very last of the messages that we are to remember. As the story proceeds, the foolish virgins leave, hoping to obtain the oil of wisdom before the bridegroom arrives. But they have no such luck. The bridegroom, the critical information, arrives while they are gone. The wise virgins, on the other hand—the senses of a person who possesses deep spiritual wisdom—are able to catch the data. The data merges with the conscious mind and the person *knows* what is necessary to make the final leap to manifestation and fulfillment.

ACTIVATING PARABLE LESSON 29

1. *Contemplate your senses and their role in your life.* Realize what a powerful force they are. Realize what a deep impact they can make on your perception of reality. Realize that they can either serve you or hinder you. *Make a conscious decision* to master your senses so that they will work with your positive intentions and not against them.

2. *Keep watch,* because you do not know the day or the hour. *Pay attention and remain vigilant. Expect* that the information you need to make

your breakthrough will arrive in due course. Don't be caught with your guard down. According to the parable, there is no question as to *if* your critical information will arrive, only *when* it will arrive.

3. *Invite God into the process of perception.* Don't take this step for granted. Make a point of specifically *asking* God to help you apply your spiritual wisdom to the activity of your senses. Ask God to help you perceive reality accurately—with a miracle worker's eyes.

THE TALENTS

The Law of Intelligent Risk

MATTHEW 25:14–30

Again, the kingdom is like a man going on a journey, who called his servants and entrusted his property to them.

To one he gave five talents of money, to another two talents, and to another one talent, each according to his ability. Then he went on his journey.

The man who had received the five talents went at once and put his money to work and gained five more.

So also, the one with the two talents gained two more.

But the man who had received the one talent went off, dug a hole in the ground and hid his master's money.

After a long time the master of those servants returned and settled accounts with them.

The man who had received the five talents brought the other five. "Master," he said, "you entrusted me with five talents. See, I have gained five more."

His master replied, "Well done, good and faithful servant! You have been faithful with a few things; I will put you in charge of many things. Come and share your master's happiness!"

The man with the two talents also came. "Master," he said, "you entrusted me with two talents; see, I have gained two more."

His master replied, "Well done, good and faithful servant! You have been faithful with a few things; I will put you in charge of many things. Come and share your master's happiness!"

Then the man who had received the one talent came. "Master," he said, "I knew that you are a hard man, harvesting where you have not sown and gathering where you have not scattered seed.

So I was afraid and went out and hid your talent in the ground. See, here is what belongs to you."

His master replied, "You wicked, lazy servant! So you knew that I harvest where I have not sown and gather where I have not scattered seed?

Well then, you should have put my money on deposit with the bankers, so that when I returned I would have received it back with interest.

Take the talent from him and give it to the one who has the ten talents.

For everyone who has will be given more, and he will have an abundance. Whoever does not have, even what he has will be taken from him."

THE PARABLE OF THE TALENTS—along with a slightly different version found in Luke called the parable of the pounds—is one of the best known of all the parables. The meaning of both versions seems fairly clear: Use it or lose it. If you are given resources and abilities, you had better be sure that you use these gifts to the maximum, even if the gifts are modest. Regardless of the degree of your abilities, regardless of the amount of resources you are given to work with, you must make absolutely sure to try to increase that with which you have been entrusted.

For if you are responsible, resourceful, and willing to take some intelligent risks to maximize what you have, if you have been "faithful with a few things," God will put you in charge of many things and you will be given even better resources to work with. This is how you will advance in evolution, advance in the Kingdom, advance in the mysteries. Although this conventional level of interpretation is undoubtedly true, it is only partly correct. For there are two flaws in standard translations that obscure the full depth of the parable's message. Let's examine them.

The parable begins with a man who is preparing to go on a journey. He has an estate and will need caretakers to manage his assets while he is away. He calls three of his managers to him and gives each of them a number of talents. A talent, to be sure, can refer to a measure of money used in either ancient Greece or the Roman empire. But there is more to this word. Here's what *Strong's Exhuastive Concordance* has to say:

> *talanton,* a presumed derivative of the original form *tiao*—to *bear or carry;* a *balance,* or *weight.*

Is it possible the teacher meant that the three managers were given several burdens to bear, several responsibilities, perhaps several problems to solve? Possibly. To see if this could be so, we need to see how such an interpretation of the word *talanton* will affect the internal consistency of the metaphor as the remainder of the parable is accordingly deciphered. If it turns out that thinking of a talent as a "weight" or "responsibility" or "problem" fits logically and naturally into the rest of the parable, then we may reasonably assume that this is in fact the meaning the teacher truly intended.

The next statement will add to our knowledge and allow us to proceed with more certainty. It states that the three managers are given three different levels of responsibilities, problems with three degrees of difficulty, three burdens or responsibilities of three different weights. These problems are to be solved and the burdens carried "each *according to his ability.*" The word normally translated as "ability" is the Greek *dunamis.* *Strong's Concordance* has the following information about this word:

> (*dunamis*,) from *dunamai*, to be able or possible; *force*, specifically a *miraculous power,* (usually by implication *a miracle itself*), *ability, abundance, meaning, might* (-ily, -y, -y deed), (worker of) *miracle* (-s), power, strength, violence, mighty, (wonderful) work.

The notion of "miraculous power" is most interesting. It certainly seems reasonable to assume that a spiritual teacher, giving a spiritual lesson, might well use the more spiritual meaning of the word, which in this case is "miraculous powers"—not "abilities." The sentence would then read more like this:

> *To one man he gave a burden or weight of five, to another a burden of two, and to the last a burden of one—each according to his miracle-working powers.*

The manager who had strong, well-developed, and highly reliable powers is given extensive responsibilities and formidable problems that will require highly developed miracle-working abilities. The manager who has weak miracle-working abilities is given a minor burden, a minor problem to deal with.

The master then leaves and the managers, the miracle workers, begin their work. The miracle worker who is given five serious challenges to resolve, uses his powers and corrects all five. Then he takes on additional burdens, working additional miracles. The miracle worker who has the moderate miracle-working powers is given two problems, and uses his powers to resolve and correct each. He, too, then takes on additional problems and solves them as well. But the miracle worker who has few powers, perhaps the novice or initiate, perhaps you or me, is *afraid*. What is he afraid of? In Matthew 25:24–25, the third manager tells the master why he felt fear:

> *Then the man who had received the one talent came. "Master," he said, "I knew that you are a hard man, harvesting where you have not sown and gathering where you have not scattered seed.*
> *So I was afraid and went out and hid your talent in the ground."*

This is most perplexing. We are told here that the master is a "hard man" who reaps where he does not sow. It sounds on the surface as though the master is a harsh, unforgiving man who takes more than he gives, a man who may in fact be stealing or otherwise unethically taking money from other people. The servant is afraid because the man is so severe and because he feels that if he loses the one talent he has received he will be punished harshly.

Although this sounds plausible, this interpretation does not pass a more rigorous examination in which the internal consistency of the metaphor is carefully tested for accuracy. The problem is that if this master is such a bad person, why would it be a good thing for the managers, perhaps you, to *help* him out by squeezing even more money out of the townspeople via interest-bearing loans?

In addition, this level of interpretation completely rules out the idea that the master represents God, who bestows upon us varying degrees of resources and abilities. The teacher we have come to know would never describe God as a "hard" or "harsh" being. So we have to go back and look once again at the exact wording to see if we can get things to make more sense—without fudging anything or forcing anything to fit.

One of the key words that makes this statement so difficult to understand is the word "hard," from the Greek *skleros*. What does *Strong's Exhaustive Concordance* have to say about this word?

Skleros 4642, from the base of 4628: *skelos*,(to parch); through the idea of *leanness. Dry, i.e. hard or tough.* Harsh, severe, fierce, hard.

What would happen to our overall interpretation of the parable if we interpreted *skleros* as "tough" or "resilient," as opposed to "harsh"? If we took that fork in the road we are left with the idea that the teacher meant that the master in the story was able to withstand great adversity and harsh conditions and was very strong. Who do we know who is resilient and able to withstand great adversity?

We have every reason to believe the teacher was either an Essene or had very strong Essene influences. And the Essenes were people who lived in the harsh conditions of the desert, people with legendary discipline, people who fasted, people who worked hard each day in the difficult environment of the desert.

But what of the statement that tells us that the master of the parable is a being who reaps where he does not sow? How could anyone reap where they have not sown? For all humans operate within the laws of cause and effect. The causes we set into motion lead to the effects we experience. We cannot possibly have anything to harvest if we have not planted the right seeds and cultivated them in the right way. We cannot receive, at least not for very long, if we have not given. The law is clear on this point. The answer is that normal human beings cannot reap where they have not sown. Therefore, it clearly follows that the master represents a being who is able to operate above the laws of cause and effect. And that would be either God or a person such as the teacher, who is able to circumvent the known laws of time and space with miraculous powers and elements such as "grace," in order to generate increase.

Could the teacher be addressing the fact that you, the initiate, might well be feeling uncertainty or insecurity about your fledgling miracle-working powers, now, toward the end of the parable sequence as you are ready to "graduate" and begin to take your newly developed wisdom and creative powers out into the world? Could it be that as novices we may be unsure of ourselves and as yet unwilling to assume the mantle of power that is naturally ours—the power to manifest reality, entire universes, with our thought forms? Could it be that as we gradually awaken to the fact that we have been given the awesome power to create reality with our thought form, we are also becoming aware of the fact that we have such poor control over those very thought forms, try as we might, it is extremely difficult not to generate doubt and resentment and so reap the effects such negativity produces?

No reasonable novice, represented by the third manager, would fail to have uncertainty and insecurity about accepting and using such an awesome responsibility, the responsibility of creating entire worlds. The other two managers, the other two miracle workers, who are more experienced and more confident, have seen what their powers can do. They know that they can take some intelligent risks and still do very well. They are more secure and are not paralyzed by anxiety.

The master has entrusted all three servants, even the novice, with responsibilities and problems to solve. Why? Because we are his children. And as children created in his own image we have his same powers of creation and healing. God created us because he wants us to *help* him, *expects* us to help him create new worlds and guide them to successful, happy realities. So, he is very pleased that the two experienced managers with well-developed miracle-working powers have accepted their responsibilities, unafraid to take on the difficult problems entrusted to them, unafraid to take the responsibility for their thoughts and attitudes, unafraid to take the inevitable *risks* that are integral to the creation process.

This is very much like what a physician goes through while young and uncertain. Other professions have equally valid analogies. For a novice physician, it is unbelievably terrifying to be left alone in a hospital at night with no experienced older physicians present for backup. It is hard to explain what it feels like to know that any number of horrible situations, "weights," may spring up at anytime, perhaps even several at the same time, and that you will be responsible for knowing precisely what to do in every instance to assure that people, including small children, won't die.

The older residents have gone through this. They have learned that the education and the healing abilities their education has given them will indeed pull them through these circumstances. So they are able to move ahead and take intelligent risks, to make life-and-death decisions, even when they are not 100 percent sure of the outcome—without being immobilized by fear.

This parable lesson is telling you that you may likely have to work through a stage in which you will feel uncertainty and fear as you "graduate" from the parable sequence. As you learn the lessons in the parable sequence and practice their activation steps, you will steadily grow in spiritual power, spiritual fitness. You will be increasingly able to help God with the creation and adjustment of realities. You will develop stronger and more reliable miracle-working powers, and you will be expected to chip in and *use* them—to do your job as a cocreator. You can expect, as this process unfolds, to be given assignments, problems, the "weights" or "burdens" the parable speaks of.

And you are going to be monitored, the parable tells us. You will be expected to begin practicing using the powers growing surely within you. The last thing you will want to do, the parable warns, is to succumb to fear and insecurity to the point where you do nothing, like the third manager. Even though you will be frequently unsure of yourself, you will be expected to have courage and move forward anyway. Courage is simply the ability to act when you are afraid.

Do not worry. The parable clearly seems to indicate that the problems you will be given will be ones that have been selected especially because they are ones that are within your reach to solve. The burdens that must be managed will be assigned "each to [your] abilities." The point of that statement is that you can be sure when experiencing any problem, however terrifying or hopeless, that your existing spiritual powers, your miracle-working powers, *will* be sufficient for the task at hand. The point is that you are being directed to trust, take a bit of risk, take the leap of faith, and move forward.

If you do, you will succeed. And when your success is noted, you will be given more powers and more problems, more creations to work with. If you do *not* take the leap and act to solve the burdens placed before you, and instead hide yourself, your powers, and your head in the sand, you will lose your developing powers and will have to go back and repeat some course work. The idea is therefore true—that we are never given a problem by God that is too severe for us to handle, *provided we follow all the guidelines for living the teacher has delineated.*

Activating the Final Parable Lesson

1. Make a list, on paper, of all the different kinds of "weights"—challenges to overcome, problems to solve—with which you have been entrusted at this point in your progress. Be sure to include everything. Don't gloss over anything because it seems "unimportant" to you, or because you have accomplished so little. This is all a learning process and you can only learn, only advance, if you are honest with yourself. You will be writing a page or more on each of these entries, so write each problem on a separate sheet of your notebook.

2. Now, make a list of your abilities, your miracle-working powers. Use a separate page for each of these as well. Don't be unduly modest and don't leave out an ability that is only in its early stages of development. All your talents are important to Spirit, especially the ones you need to work on.

3. This is a most crucial step: Go back to the first list and carefully write out every possible way that you can think of that you can apply each of the abilities that you listed in the second list to each problem now, working with your abilities in their current state of development.

4. Now, go over your list of problems and projects and write out how you will use your abilities when they have grown much stronger. This is a very powerful act. Here, you will be implanting into your subconscious potent suggestions that will expand your concept of what you can do, will do, as your progress advances. Do not be

modest, or fearful, or insecure about this in any way, shape, or form. Instead, be lavish, generous, and bold. Be confident and show that you are ready to take intelligent risks to increase the resources that you have been entrusted to increase and improve.

5. Finally, meditate carefully on the whole matter. Imagine, as vividly as you can, that the master, God, is there in the room talking with you. Imagine what he would say about each of the problems you are working on. He may have different reactions to different problems, thinking that you have done a great job on some issues but need considerable work on others. Using the first person, write out what God is saying to you in your mind about the problems and your abilities.

About the Author

Todd Michael, D.O., has served as the medical director of an emergency room and level-three trauma center. He is a popular national speaker and workshop presenter. Dr. Michael is the author of *The Twelve Conditions of a Miracle* and the successful self-published work *The Evolution Angel*. He lives in Colorado.

His workshops and appearances can be scheduled through the website www.TwelveConditions.com, or by calling (303) 818-8859.